HEROIN AND POLITICIANS

Recent Titles in
Contributions in Political Science
Series Editor: Bernard K. Johnpoll

The Italian Communist Party: Yesterday, Today, and Tomorrow
Simon Serfaty and Lawrence Gray, editors

The Fiscal Congress: Legislative Control of the Budget
Lance T. Leloup

Iran, Saudi Arabia, and the Law of the Sea: Political Interaction and Legal Development in the Persian Gulf
Charles G. MacDonald

Improving Prosecution? The Inducement and Implementation of Innovations for Prosecution Management
David Leo Weimer

Creating the Entangling Alliance: The Origins of the North Atlantic Treaty Organization
Timothy P. Ireland

The State as Defendent: Governmental Accountability and the Redress of Individual Grievances
Leon Hurwitz

Ethnic Identities in a Transnational World
John F. Stack, Jr., editor

Reasoned Argument in Social Science: Linking Research to Policy
Eugene J. Meehan

The Right Opposition: The Lovestoneites and the International Communist Opposition of the 1930s
Robert J. Alexander

Quantification in the History of Political Thought: Toward a Qualitative Approach
Robert Schware

The Kent State Incident: Impact of Judicial Process on Public Attitudes
Thomas R. Hensley

Representation and Presidential Primaries: The Democratic Party in the Post-Reform Era
James I. Lengle

HEROIN AND POLITICIANS

The Failure of Public Policy to Control Addiction in America

David J. Bellis

CONTRIBUTIONS IN POLITICAL SCIENCE, NUMBER 58
GREENWOOD PRESS
WESTPORT, CONNECTICUT • LONDON, ENGLAND

Library of Congress Cataloging in Publication Data

Bellis, David J 1944-
Heroin and politicians.

(Contributions in political science ; no. 58
ISSN 0147-1066)
Bibliography: p.
Includes index.
1. Heroin. 2. Heroin habit—Treatment—United States. 3. Narcotic addicts—Rehabilitation—United States. I. Title. II. Series.
HV5822.H4B42 362.2'93'0973 80-21373
ISBN 0-313-22557-5 (lib.bdg.)

Library of Congress Catalog Card Number: 80-21373
ISBN: 0-313-22557-5
ISSN: 0147-1066

First published in 1981

Greenwood Press
A division of Congressional Information Service, Inc.
88 Post Road West, Westport, Connecticut 06881

Printed in the United States of America

10 9 8 7 6 5 4 3 2 1

To my parents and my wife Ann

Contents

Figure and Tables

Introduction

This study focuses on treatment and rehabilitation of heroin addicts.[1] Part I explores heroin addiction treatment from a decision-making perspective and asks: In terms of policy *formulation*, what factors accounted for the most recent expansion of heroin addiction treatment and rehabilitation capacity, and how were specific therapeutic alternatives formulated and subsequently chosen by federal officials?

The second part of the study concerns *impact* of government-sponsored treatment programs: Have the programs under current policy reformed addicts? In other words, what has been the broad *impact* of heroin addiction treatment policies and programs relative to their goals?

FEDERAL ADDICTION TREATMENT AND REHABILITATION EXPENDITURES

By 1974 federally sponsored substance-abuse treatment, rehabilitation and prevention/education programs, taken together, exceeded the combined federal investment in all other mental health programs.[2] Since 1969 the federal government has spent several *billion* dollars treating heroin addicts. While in 1971 there were only three hundred federally funded programs treating 16,000 addicts, by 1973 over 1,000 such centers were providing drug-free and methadone maintenance treatment to about 75,000 addict-clients. In 1977 100,000 addicts were enrolled in federally funded treatment projects, and an additional 170,000 nonfederally funded treatment "slots" were available nationwide. Between 1969 and 1974, under President Nixon, federal addiction treatment and rehabilitation budgets jumped from $28 million to over $300 million a year. What has this outlay accomplished?

CAN PUBLIC POLICY SOLVE PEOPLE PROBLEMS?

An extensive literature indicates the substantial failure of *public welfare programs, public housing projects, national food programs, public health efforts, Model Cities programs, federal manpower programs, prisoner rehabilitation efforts,* and *juvenile delinquency prevention.*[3] Despite an auspicious beginning, President Johnson's War on Poverty foundered on similar shoals.[4] The same ideology that fostered massive public welfare schemes, criminal rehabilitation programs, the War on Poverty and a host of other policy initiatives against social problems also fueled the more recent "war on heroin."

Failure to obliterate heroin addiction and a multitude of other social problems is often blamed on the values and interests of those who create and administer public policies and programs or, significantly, on the victims themselves. A clear picture is emerging: Resolving issues like poverty, crime and addiction, especially in isolation from one another and unmediated by economic, social and political factors, may be impossible.

"MOON SHOT" PUBLIC POLICYMAKING

Can we conquer drug abuse the same way we conquered the moon? America's tradition of "good old Yankee know-how" has led citizens and governments to believe there are "quick-fix" solutions to age-old people problems like crime and addiction, misbehavior, mental illness, overanxiety, underanxiety, unhappiness, nervousness, sadness and rage. Policymakers, their advisers and constituents presumably believe that if some terrible social problem exists, government need only pass the necessary laws, erect the agencies to implement them, pour in the money and manpower, and somehow out will pop the magic solution. This view of scientifically and technologically oriented policy solutions to social problems operates on a "moon-shot" metaphor or paradigm.[5] Government assaults on national problems like poverty and drug abuse have been presented as politically neutral "scientific cures" for disturbing social maladies. According to this vending-machine concept of public policymaking and social problem-solving, the desired outcomes are expected to emerge automatically. John Gardner, former secretary of the Department of Health, Education and Welfare, verbalized this concept: "Put a coin in the machine and out comes a piece of candy. If there is a social problem, pass a law and out comes a solution."[6]

But social problems are with us more than ever and have turned out to be more deeply rooted, irrational and unmanageable than the pragmatic, technical approaches have led many to believe. It is even argued that for some issues, like pollution of the biosphere, *there is no technologic fix*.[7]

DISEASE, DOOMSDAY WEAPONS AND SPACE FLIGHT

Many events have shaped our images of science and technology, but three stand out. First is a series of major medical advances for controlling dread diseases like poliomyelitis, tuberculosis, and some forms of cancer. The second was successful production of a nuclear fission bomb during World War II. The third was landing men on the moon in 1969. These historic enterprises involved dramatic, rapid advances in science, engineering and technological organizations.

This "moon-shot" experience dominates today's thought, both in popular discussion and to a surprising extent among professional and technological people. This experience reinforces a view of science as a heroic enterprise, conducted on a large scale, systematically managed by large and dynamic organizations, and resulting in miraculous "breakthrough" technology with readily applicable "social spin-offs." The implication is that every obstacle can be eliminated and every human or environmental problem solved without any fundamental reordering of society itself if we devote sufficient effort to finding the appropriate technological or policy "cure."

The "moon-shot" paradigm has significantly affected our thinking about domestic problems and how to deal with them through government policy. One effect is on our expectations: If we can go to the moon, why can't we solve the problems we face here on earth? Claude Pepper, former chairman of the House Select Committe on Crime, asked his colleagues this question when he exhorted them to solve the heroin addiction problem:

> It is my belief that the scientific and technical genius of America has not been fully enlisted in the fight against heroin addiction . . . for surely, a nation which can send men to the moon, sustain them on the moon, and then bring them safely home, can find the means to effectively control the heroin epidemic, and find those means now.[8]

President Nixon added that it was not a question of " . . . whether we conquer heroin addiction," but "how soon."[9]

Pepper, Nixon and others encompassed a belief that there are technological and scientific shortcuts to controlling complex personal and social problems like drug addiction. But is doing away with heroin addiction comparable to landing men on the moon or developing newer, more sophisticated weapons systems? Are drug abuse and other social maladies targets waiting in isolation for crash government programs to wipe them out?

EXPLAINING THE "MOON-SHOT" PARADIGM

Among humans, security may be *the* prime political symbol, and mass security comes largely from symbolic reassurances emanating from scientists and government officials—sources on whom people depend as authoritative and competent to cope with grave threats like war, pestilence or rampant drug addiction.[10] In survey after survey the American people have equated the "heroin problem" with crime and the state of the economy as sources of extreme worry. Governments have been moved to heavy-handed action because policymakers believe that the public imposes a high priority on coping with threats posed by problems like widespread heroin abuse. Government response to heroin has been to push the panic button periodically.

However, rehabilitation and rational solutions to social problems occur mainly in political rhetoric, not in fact.[11] There are few instances in domestic public policymaking where the social spin-off from the moon-shot approach has approximated the promise. Nevertheless, the rhetoric evoked salves our combined conscience and permits us to live with ourselves and our problems.

So the breakthrough mentality and "moon-shot" paradigm drag on and continue to shape policy research, policymaking and government programs, if not overtly, at the level of underlying images and aspirations. Why? Because there are painfully few metaphors or politicians to replace the "moon-shot" approach to public policymaking and social problem-solving. It also is difficult to admit that there may be no technological shortcuts for intractable problems like war, poverty, pollution and the wandering normlessness of modern society, of which heroin addiction is an example.

NOTES

1. In this book, *treatment* is defined as a regimen, with or without medication, to alter the course of disease toward health. Therapy is a synonym for treatment. *Reform* or *rehabilitation* of addicts, as used here, is the restoration to useful activity of people who suffer physical and/or emotional disability associated with illegal heroin use. Rehabilitation usually includes addiction treatment. *Addiction* is *physical dependence* on a drug. Its scientific formulation must include the development of *tolerance* and *dependence*. Examples of widely used addictive drugs are narcotics, sedative barbiturates, hypnotics, tranquilizers and alcohol.

2. *Substance abuse* is the use of any drug (legal or illegal) for a medical or recreational purpose when alternatives are available, practical or warranted, or when drug abuse endangers either the user or others with whom he may interact. (The possessive article "his" will be used throughout this book instead of the more cumbersome "his/her" construction. Even though today more than 30 percent of heroin addicts are females, editorial ease requires the more chauvinistic grammatical construction.)

3. On the basic failure of public welfare as a "cure" for poverty, see Gilbert Y. Steiner, *Social Insecurity* (Chicago: Rand McNally, 1966); Thomas Gladwin, *Poverty U.S.A.* (Boston: Little, Brown and Co., 1967);

Gilbert Y. Steiner, *The State of Welfare* (Washington, D.C.: The Brookings Institution, 1971); Frances Fox Piven and Richard A. Cloward, *Regulating the Poor: The Functions of Public Welfare* (New York: Vintage Books, 1971); Dorothy Buckton James, *Poverty, Politics and Change* (Englewood Cliffs, N.J.: Prentice-Hall, 1972), especially chapter 2; and Richard A. Cloward and Frances Fox Piven, "The Acquiescence of Social Work," *Society* 14 (January/February 1977): 55-63. On the general failure of public housing to live up to the claims of the Fair Housing Act of 1946, see J. Jacobs, *The Death and Life of Great American Cities* (New York: Random House, 1965); R. L. Hurley, *Poverty and Mental Retardation: A* William Morrow Publishers, 1965); Joseph Lyford, *The Airtight Cage* (New York: Harper and Row, 1966); Alvin L. Schorr, *Slums and Social Insecurity* (Washington, D.C.: U.S. Department of Health, Education and Welfare, U.S. Government Printing Office, 1966); Lawrence M. Friedman, *Government and Slum Housing* (Chicago: Rand McNally, 1968); L. Freedman, *Public Housing* (New York: Holt, Rinehart and Winston, 1969); and Eugene J. Meehan, *The Quality of Federal Policymaking: Programmed Failure in Public Housing* (Columbia, Mo.: University of Missouri Press, 1979). National food programs also have come under their fair share of academic criticism. See T. Moore, *The Slaves We Rent* (New York: Random House, 1965); R. L. Hurley, *Poverty and Mental Retardation: A Causal Relationship* (New York: Random House, 1969); and Nick Kotz, *Let Them Eat Promises: The Politics of Hunger in the United States* (Garden City, N.Y.: Anchor Books, 1971). Federal public health efforts are criticized in Hurley, *Poverty and Mental Retardation*; E. Spencer, "Medicaid Lessons and Warnings," *Social Policy* 1 (January/February 1971): 47-51; Barbara Ehrenreich and John Ehrenreich, eds., *The American Health Empire: Power, Profits and Politics* (New York: Vintage Books, 1971); Robert R. Alford, "The Political Economy of Health Care: Dynamics Without Change," *Politics and Society* 2 (Winter, 1972): 127-64; Robert Stevens and Rosemary Stevens, *Welfare Medicine in America: A Case Study of Medicaid* (New York: Free Press, 1974); and Robert R. Alford, *Health Care Politics: Ideological and Interest Group Barriers to Reform* (Chicago: University of Chicago Press 1974). Model Cities programs, an element of Lyndon Johnson's War on Poverty, have been evaluated in Daniel P. Moynihan, *Maximum Feasible Misunderstanding* (New York: Free Press, 1969); Dale Rogers Marshall, *The Politics of Participation in Poverty: A Case Study of the Economic and Youth Opportunities Agency of Greater Los Angeles* (Berkely, Calif.: University of California Pess, 1971); and Bennett Harrison, *Urban Economic*

Development: Suburbanization, Minority Opportunity, and the Condition of the Central City (Washington, D.C.: The Urban Institute, 1974). Federal manpower programs are critiqued in Roger H. Davidson, *The Politics of Comprehensive Manpower Legislation* (Baltimore; Md.: Johns Hopkins University Press, 1972). There is a broad literature on the failure of prisons to rehabilitate prisoners. Some of the better works are Leslie T. Wilkins, *Evaluation of Penal Measures* (New York: Random House, 1969); Erik Olin Wright, *The Politics of Punishment: A Critical Analysis of Prisons in America* (New York: Harper Colophon Books, 1973); and D. J. Rothman, "Prisons: The Failure Model," *The Nation* (December 21, 1974), pp. 656-59. For the failure of juvenile delinquency prevention policies and projects to reform youthful offenders, see W. Pink and M. White, eds., *Delinquency Prevention: A Conference on Issues and Directions* (Portland, Ore.: Portland State University, 1973); and M. Dixon and W. Wright, *Juvenile Delinquency Prevention Programs: An Evaluation of Policy Related Research on the Effectiveness of Prevention Programs* (Nashville, Tenn.: Peabody College for Teachers, 1975).

4. On the failure of the War on Poverty to achieve its goals, see John C. Donovan, *The Politics of Poverty* (New York: Pegasus Books, 1967); Saul Alinsky, "The War on Poverty—Political Pornography," in *Poverty: Power and Politics*, ed. Chaim Waxman (New York: Grosset and Dunlap, 1968); James Ridgeway, "The More Glorious War," in *Poverty: Power and Politics* ed. Chaim Waxman (New York: Grosset and Dunlap, Inc., 1968); Daniel P. Moynihan, *Maximum Feasible Misunderstanding*; and Sar Levitan, *The Great Society's Poor Law* (Baltimore, Md.: Johns Hopkins University Press, 1969).

5. For an early statement of the "moon-shot" metaphor as applied to the eradication of heroin addiction in America, see David J. Bellis, "In Quest of a Technological Fix For an Old Problem: Preliminary Notes on the Cost-Effectiveness of Heroin Addiction Control Strategies," unpublished paper, Department of Political Science, University of Southern California, 1972. For other statements on quick-fix policy solutions, see R. Nelson, "Intellectualizing About the Moon-Ghetto Metaphor: A Study of the Current Malaise of Rational Analysis of Social Problems," *Policy Sciences* 5 (December 1974): 1101-14; and Richard A. Rettig and John G. Wirt, "On Escaping the 'Moon Shot' Metaphor," *Policy Studies Journal* 5 (Winter 1976): 168-70.

6. John W. Gardner, *No Easy Victories* (New York: Harper and Row, 1968), p. 28.

7. See biologist Garret Hardin's, "The Tragedy of the Commons," *Science* 162 (December 13, 1968): 1243-48.

8. U.S. Congress, House Select Committee on Crime, *Narcotics Research, Rehabilitation, and Treatment*, 92d Cong., 1st sess., Pt. 1, p. 341.

9. U.S. President, "Omnibus Drug Control Legislative Message by the President," June 17, 1971, p. 1.

10. See Murray Edelman, "Language, Myths and Rhetoric," *Society* 12 (July/August 1975): 15–21.

11. Murray Edelman, *The Symbolic Uses of Politics* (Urbana, Ill.: University of Illinois Press, 1967), pp. 172-87.

PART I

FORMULATING HEROIN-CONTROL POLICY

1

The Criminalization of Heroin

The use of mind-altering drugs and drug-induced behavior is a common thread in the social fabric of humanity. For thousands of years people have taken drugs to alter mood, relax, feel better, feel different, escape and avoid pain. This has eventuated in an increasing demand for a variety of psychoactive substances. Of all the drugs, heroin may have received the most attention.

ANCIENT HISTORY

Records show that narcotics have been used for at least 8,000 years. Over the centuries admiration for the pain-relieving effects of opiates has been tempered by increased awareness of their addictiveness.

Opium (Greek: *opion,* poppy juice) is in the milky exudate obtained by incising the unripe seed pod of the poppy *papaver somniferum*. Sumerians in what is now southern Iraq around 7000 B.C. told of its power to produce a sense of delight or satisfaction. Opium was among the most common drugs of the Assyrians and the ancient Egyptians. In Europe opium poppies were found in Hungary around 1200 B.C., and traces of their cultivation have been uncovered near ancient lake dwellings in Switzerland.

Pictorial representations of the poppy are frequently found in classical Greek culture where opium was widely used in magic, religion, medicine, and as an intoxicant. In Rome opium was considered a cure-all for various afflictions. Galen (121-201 A.D.), Rome's famous Greek physician, prescribed it for headaches, vertigo, deafness, epilepsy, apoplexy, dimness of sight, asthma, coughs, jaundice, stones, fever, leprosy, women's diseases and depression, among other illnesses. He warned, however, not to give the powerful drug to children and that frequent use leads to poisoning of the human flesh.

Around 600 A.D. Arab traders introduced opium into China, and so began a long process by which its distribution was monopolized and chronic use came to be regarded as deviant and therefore of legitimate concern to authoritative decisionmakers. Opium use became so widespread in China around 1400 that, according to legend, the last Mongol emperor asked for divine help to stem its spread. The heavenly assistance came in the form of a "red rain" (probably similar to the red tobacco virus), which destroyed the evil opium crop.

MODERN HISTORY

The writer Garcia da Orta described opiate addiction in India around 1560. Travel reports from Asia and other parts of the world were popular reading during the seventeenth and eighteenth centuries, and they frequently mentioned "the opium habit."

The symptoms of opium addiction were clarified only in the course of time. While medical statements on opium's habit-forming effects were still vague in the early 1700s, by 1800 there existed a more precise description of addiction stressing *tolerance* and physical *dependence*. The term addiction is not easily defined, but in all cases it manifests itself in the twin phenomena of tolerance and physical dependence. *Tolerance* refers to the situation wherein after repeated administration of a drug higher doses are required to elicit effects previously produced by smaller doses. Tolerance also can develop with nonaddicting drugs. Physical dependence is characterized by withdrawal symptoms upon discontinuing chronic use of addictive drugs. For the extreme alcoholic withdrawal symptoms include the tremulousness, convulsions and visual hallucinations of "delirium tremens." For the severe opiate addict there is extreme anxiety, insomnia, craving for narcotics, sweating, increased respiratory rate, fever, chills, goose flesh (hence "cold turkey"), dilated pupils, cramping, explosive diarrhea and vomiting, and almost unbearable pains.[1]

AWARENESS BY THE MASS PUBLIC

With more books, newspapers, journals and reviews came more public awareness of opium addiction and its effects. Samuel Taylor Coleridge (1772-1834), hooked on opium as a teenager, published poetry written under its influence. In 1822 Thomas DeQuincey, an opium addict at nineteen, introduced the theme of opiate addiction into belletristic literature through his *Confessions of an English Opium-Eater*. William Blair, another teenage addict and an American admirer of De Quincey's book, wrote his own version in 1835, *Confessions of an Opium Eater in America*. Artistic works like Hector Berlioz's *Symphonie Fantastique* (1830) depicting opium dreams, perhaps in an autobiographic fashion, contributed to increasing popular awareness of the effects of opium and addiction.

THE CIVIL WAR, MORPHINE AND SOLDIERS' DISEASE

Advance in drug technology led to increase experimentation with narcotics and subsequent abuse. In 1803 a young German pharmacist, Friedrich Sertürner, isolated an opium alkaloid he called morphine after Morpheus, the Greek god of dreams, and by the mid-nineteenth century use of pure morphine rather than crude opium preparations had spread widely. The addictiveness of morphine was recognized only after the drug had become an established feature of clinical medicine. Codeine, another opiate alkaloid, was discovered in 1832 and became widely used for relief of pain, cough and diarrhea.

The first hypodermic injections of morphine were given in America in 1856. Medical journals enthusiastically endorsed its therapeutic value and, reminiscent of Galen, suggested it as a remedy for an endless variety of physical ailments. During the Civil War intravenous injection of morphine spread rapidly and addiction became so pronounced that an American narcotics "problem" was spoken of for the first time.[2] Soldiers were given morphine to deaden pain from battlefield injuries and illnesses. After the war, ex-soldier addicts continued to use morphine and often "turned on" friends and relatives. Newspapers began to feature the evils of "soldiers' disease."

NARCOTIC-BASED PATENT MEDICINES

By 1870 pharmaceutical manufacturing firms included huge doses of morphine in numerous proprietary medicines sold over the counter without prescription as household remedies. Sears Roebuck and Company advertised narcotic-injecting paraphernalia. No state or federal laws regulated the sale and distribution of medicinal narcotic drugs, and pharmacists openly sold them upon customer request. Before 1900 drug manufacturers very effectively prevented federal action to require even the disclosure of opium derivatives in these commercial preparations, although anti-morphine laws spread in various states in the 1890s. Loopholes in such laws, however, permitted the uncontrollable sale of patent medicines containing narcotics.[3]

HEROIN: THE WONDER DRUG

In 1895 it was estimated that 2 to 4 percent of the American population were morphine addicts, hooked mainly on patent medicines.[4] By way of comparison, today only a tiny fraction of 1 percent of the American population is addicted to heroin. In 1874 the English chemist C. R. Wright developed a semi-synthetic derivative of morphine, diacetylmorphine, for the first time. In 1897 Professor Heinrich Dreser, Head of the Pharmacological Institute of the "Farbenfabriken vorm. Friedr. Bayer & Co., Elberfeld," began pharmaceutical testing of the substance. He immediately coined the new drug "heroin" because it performed so heroically in controlling pain—weight for weight it was three times more potent than morphine. Originally, heroin was hailed as a nonaddictive analgesic and as a wonder cure for morphine addiction, until it was discovered to be even more addictive than morphine.

By 1900 heroin was on the scene to stay, sold over the counter as a patent remedy for many different conditions. Subsequently it would become the most influential single factor in hardening public opinion against drug addiction.[5]

WHITE MIDDLE-CLASS ADDICTS

A startling aspect of narcotics addiction at the turn of the century was not so much its extent as the sociodemographic distribution of the known addict population. Addiction seemed most prevalent

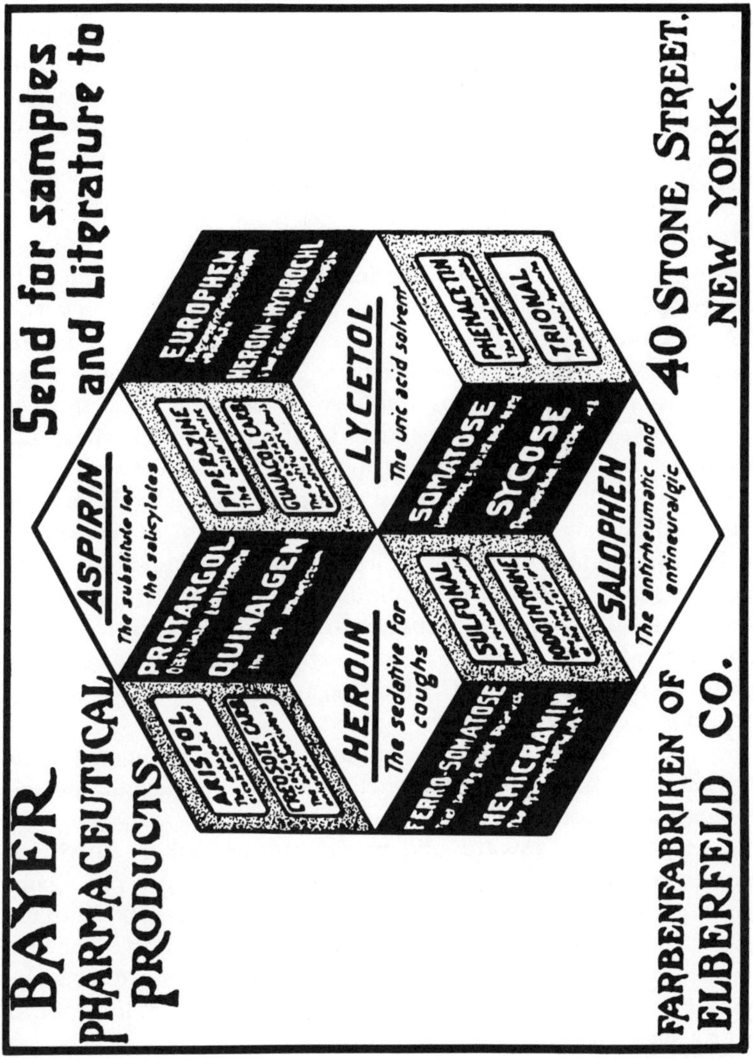

Figure 1.1 Bayer Heroin Advertisement, *circa* 1900. Available Over-the-Counter, No Prescription Required. (Used by permission of Bayer AG., West Germany.)

among middle- and upper-class white women.[6] In 1903 a survey by the American Pharmaceutical Association of selected communities in the United States and Canada found that "the sale of opium derivatives to those of higher incomes exceeded the amount sold to lower income persons."[7] Perhaps because of the growing temperance movement, many of the better-off in American society, especially women, turned to morphine and heroin preparations as a substitute for alcohol. Their "problem," however, was regarded more "physiological" than criminal.

THE CRIMINALIZATION OF NARCOTICS ADDICTION

Prior to 1900 narcotics addiction was accepted by American society as behavior which, although in conflict with its norms, was still tolerable. Narcotic drugs could be obtained legally and inexpensively, and with many respectable members of society using them, addiction simply was not seen as criminal. The modern addict, forced by anti-narcotic laws to burglarize, rob, cheat and deal in heroin to support his expensive habit had not yet appeared.

Around 1900, however, a moral juxtaposition was in the making which ultimately redefined narcotics addiction as criminally deviant, intolerable behavior subject to governmental control and negative sanction. Aware of continually increasing alcoholism and heroin use, society gradually began to lower its level of tolerance. The new punitive spirit was aptly expressed by the specifically American term "dope fiend" which began to appear in newspapers around the turn of the century.[8]

Several explanations may account for the development of the new punitive attitude toward addicts and addiction. Addiction and deviance of all sorts were associated with the "evils" of urbanism.[9] The new attitude toward addicts was influenced by increased opium smoking in American cities.[10] As more city types—gamblers, prostitutes and underworld characters—began smoking opium, the public came to associate its use with deviance. The new trend toward popular indignation gained momentum during the rapidly growing "Prohibition Movement," and soon lower-class addicts were distinguished from those of higher class.[11] Whereas in 1900 the addict population was distributed fairly evenly over the social classes (with the higher classes having slightly more), by 1920 medical journals were speaking of the "overwhelming" majority coming from the "unrespectable" parts of society. An apparent reversal of attitude took place between 1900 and 1920 in the demographic and social class characterization of addicts. The sex distribution of the addict population reversed itself, too, and by 1920 most addicts were men.[12]

Musto suggested that the most passionate support for criminalization of narcotics was associated with fear of the drug's effect on specific minority groups in American society.[13] Heroin, especially, was feared because it seemed to undermine essential social restrictions which kept these groups under control. Thus, the use of narcotics, particularly heroin, came to be associated with groups that were already feared and despised by the white, Anglo-Saxon majority. Addicts became easier to hate.

With isolationism rampant in the early 1900s, it became easy to blame foreign nations for the American narcotics problem. This projection of blame on foreign nations for domestic evils harmonized with the ascription of drug abuse to ethnic minorites huddled in large American cities. Both the external cause and the internal locus could then be dismissed as un-American.

THE HARRISON ANTI-NARCOTIC ACT

Some of the most important actions of government in the narcotics field involve the passage of laws—laws to punish and laws to rehabilitate, laws to restrict narcotic drugs and laws to make them available, laws to treat the symptoms and, much less often, laws to remove the presumed causes of addiction. The first major piece of federal narcotics control legislation was the Harrison Anti-Narcotic Act, unanimously passed by Congress on December 17, 1914. It marked the point at which *all* narcotic addicts came to be defined by society as criminal deviants, even though many of them had been respectable citizens.

The Harrison Act concluded a generation of concern and agitation against drug abuse. In 1914 the ideal of temperance hit an all-time high in American life. Influential groups agitated to prohibit both alcohol and drugs. Also at a high point were the concomitant reformist aims of facing reality and of individual commitment to rectifying social ills. The Age of Liberalism had arrived and marched under the banner of the Progressive Movement: scientific principles applied to the art of governing. The heroin scare, a new commitment to fight the international drug traffic and mounting attacks on patent medicines dramatized demands for a uniform national narcotic-control policy.

Possibly the change in society's view of narcotics addiction was partially the result of the major change in public policy. Reciprocally, attitudinal change led to passage of the Harrison Act. This legislation laid the legal foundation for the punitive approach to the narcotics problem, realized mainly through an unusually rigorous and repressive implementation aimed at discovering and then suppressing the illicit distribution of narcotics. Aggressive enforcement of the act took place with great public fanfare through much-publicized seizures, large-scale raids on physicians and pharmacists, the opening and subsequent closing of the famous narcotic-dispensing clinics, and sensational trials and Supreme Court decisions.

Enforcing the Harrison Act

The Harrison Act had three main provisions. First, anyone engaged in the production or distribution of narcotics had to register with the federal government. This requirement was designed to give officials a precise knowledge of legal traffic in narcotics. Second, all parties buying or selling narcotic drugs had to pay a tax. This put enforcement programs in the U.S. Treasury Department's Bureau of Internal Revenue. The third major provision of the Harrison Act was its subtle "sleeper": the provision that unregistered persons could purchase narcotic drugs only upon the prescription of a physician. *All nonprescription narcotics became illegal.*

Could doctors dispense narcotics to addicts to maintain their habits? The Harrison Act, in vague language, stipulated that physicians could prescribe narcotics to addicts only for "legitimate" medical purposes. Is prescribing a narcotic for an addict a "legitimate" medical purpose?

Supreme court decisions cut off legal supplies. When physicians became the only legal source of narcotics, thousands of law-abiding and criminal addicts appeared on doctors' doorsteps, and physicians began prescribing morphine and heroin for them. It is estimated that by 1915, a year after the Harrison Act went into effect, there were 215,000 morphine addicts in the United States.[14]

The question of the legality of such prescriptions under the meaning of the Harrison Act came before the U.S. Supreme Court in 1919 in the case of *Webb* v. *United States*. The case involved the conviction of a physician who wrote 4,000 morphine prescriptions for addict-patients. The Supreme Court ruled that a prescription of narcotics for an addict "not in the course of professional treatment in the attempted cure of the habit . . . but being issued for the purpose of providing the user with morphine sufficient to keep him comfortable . . ." was henceforth illegal.[15]

After *Webb*, thousands of doctors were arrested, prosecuted, fined, imprisoned and held up as examples to other physicians who would attempt to supply addicts with narcotics. Addicts suddenly found themselves cut off from all legal sources of supply and turned to illicit suppliers who immediately sprang up to service the demand. Many addicts became criminals to finance their expensive habit. The Harrison Act and its interpretation by the Supreme Court provided the final condition and context for a moral and legal redefinition of what had previously been regarded as a physiological problem. The development of the black market in illicit narcotics and crime was nurtured. The country could now connect *all* addicts with their newfound underworld associates and could begin to talk about a different class of people, who were not only consorting with criminals to get dope but were criminal "fiends" themselves.

The unintended consequence of enforcing the Harrison Act was to push the price of illicit narcotics even higher, resulting in more instead of fewer money crimes.[16] In general, narcotic law enforcement programs in and of themselves are criminogenic—they cause as much crime as they ameliorate.[17]

Some have argued that the symptoms so often noted in heroin addicts are not so much related to heroin use per se but to the drug's illegality and subsequent lifestyle forced on the user through criminalization. My experience with over 15,000 street heroin addicts indicates their "diseased" state is related to difficulties in obtaining heroin, not to taking it. In fact, there is little or no valid evidence that sterile, unadulterated, properly administered heroin is any more dangerous than tobacco or alcohol. Some evidence suggests that pharmaceutically pure heroin is *less* toxic than, say, alcohol or tobacco. Winick found absolutely no evidence that sustained heroin or morphine use produces severe toxic effects or that either results in damage of any kind to the central nervous system.[18]

One is reminded of William Halsted, founder and chairman of the Department of Surgery at Johns Hopkins University School of Medicine. Famous and revered as the inventor of rubber surgical gloves, the use of silk sutures, the radical operation for breast cancer, a prototype operation for inguinal hernia and numerous other important surgical contributions, Halsted was a heavy morphine addict well into his eighties.[19]

THE NARCOTIC CLINICS: SHADES OF METHADONE MAINTENANCE

In 1919 some physicians and Treasury Department officials recognized the anomalous situation *Webb* created for addicts. Temporarily cities throughout the country were permitted to set up legal narcotics-dispensing clinics, which numbered forty-four in only sixteen months. They were located in major cities like New York, Atlanta, New Orleans, Shreveport, Memphis, Cleveland, Kansas City, San Diego and Los Angeles. Abruptly closed down by government order in 1922 under heavy pressure from the Bureau of Internal Revenue and an outraged public, these clinics are still a focal point in the heated debate over what constitutes a "rational" addiction control policy.

The rationale for dispensing narcotics to addicts on an outpatient basis rested, as it still does, upon three simple observations. The first is that permanent abstinence is difficult for most morphine or heroin addicts. Second, experience validated the conclusion that the maintenance of a state of addiction is not necessarily lethal—physiologically or psychologically—if the narcotics are properly administered and the dosage regulated. Third, apparent after the Harrison Act between 1914 and 1919, the worst aspects of narcotic addiction appeared to be attributable to the very illegality of opiates. With the huge black market in narcotics flourishing, government officials properly reasoned that if drugs were readily available at the clinics, addicts theoretically would have no cause to deal in the black market, the illicit supply network would dry up, and addicts no longer would have to commit crimes to meet exhorbitant narcotics costs. The New Orleans clinic lasted four years and reported highly successful results in treating morphine addicts. M. W. Swords, the physician in charge, pointed out that his patients were able to live relatively normal lives as a result of the dispensary and that "narcotics peddlers in the city [of New Orleans] were forced to move away . . . as there was no profit possible."[20]

Shreveport, Louisiana, police were quite pleased with the clinic there. The chief of police said:

> The Narcotics Clinic . . . is a model that should be copied over the entire United States. I wish to say that from a police standpoint, the City of Shreveport is greatly benefited by its being here. It has practically eliminated the bootlegger who deals in narcotics, and in this way alone has reduced the number of possible future dope users. The authorities in charge of the Police Department in Shreveport would regard it as a calamity should this Clinic be removed.[21]

Nevertheless, abuses in the New York City Narcotic Clinic and the attendant adverse newspaper sensationalism brought about an atmosphere of near panic in the general public. The Treasury Department almost immediately set about discrediting the clinics. One of its 1920 reports asserted:

> Prominent physicians and scientists who have made a study of drug addiction are practically unanimous in the opinion that such clinics accomplish *no good* [emphasis added] and that the cure of narcotic addiction is an impossibility unless accompanied by institutional treatment.[22]

In the heyday of yellow journalism, New York papers sent out their best muckraking reporters, who portrayed the clinics as sinful places where addict-criminals came to satisfy their morbid pleasures by pursuing the "thrills of narcotics." An editorial in the *San Francisco Examiner* said that the proposal to reopen the San Francisco clinic ". . . must go into the ash can along with the man who suggested it."[23] A banner headline in *The Seattle Post-Intelligencer* warned, the "STATE SHOULD NOT TAKE OVER SELLING OF DOPE."[24]

Closing the Clinics

Bending to governmental and media pressure, physicians in charge of the clinics were goaded by public opinion to publish second thoughts. S. Dana Hubbard, chief of New York City's Narcotic Clinic, with a number of distinguished colleagues, concluded that:

> The public narcotic clinic [is] . . . not desirable. We have given the clinic careful and thorough as well as lengthy trial, and we honestly believe it is unwise to maintain it any longer. . . . Ambulatory treatment is farcical and useless. . . . Physicians should not be permitted, under the guise of treatment, to prescribe narcotics for such indulgence. . . . Treatment of the narcotic addict by . . . dispensing [narcotics] . . . is wrong. The giving of a narcotic drug into the possession of an addict for self-administration should be forbidden. . . . The only hope is cutting off the supply of drugs as completely as possible. Therefore, no public clinics.[25]

On March 22, 1920, the New York City clinic was closed.

By 1923, after four years of trial, all forty-four clinics had been closed. Addicts once again turned to illegal activities to obtain their now-illicit drugs.

ALCOHOL PROHIBITION

In 1919 soon after the Harrison Act, the Volstead Act outlawed the use of alcoholic beverages, as though in one gigantic burst of morality two of mankind's oldest foibles could be expunged by legislative fiat. Suppression of illicit alcohol and narcotics traffic became the primary concern of law enforcement agencies and reformers. Careers were made, and the seeds of bureaucratic empires were sown. Billy Sunday, the noted evangelist and leading crusader against "Demon Rum," greeted the onset of alcohol prohibition with high hopes: "The reign of tears is over. The slums will soon be only a memory. We will turn our prisons into factories and our jails into storehouses and corncribs. Men will walk upright now, women will smile and the children will laugh. Hell will be forever for rent."[26]

Though it began as an idealistic gesture, Prohibition ended as a sordid fiasco. To many Americans, drinking was the preeminent vice of immigrants and corrupt city life. Nationwide prohibition itself was a product of the moral idealism of the Progressive Era and of the stresses of World War I. Criminalizing alcoholic beverages had two immediate effects. For many, liquor took on a glamor it might not otherwise have had, and illegal drinking became an exciting adventure. Putting outside the pale of the law a personal habit that millions of Americans would not give up also opened a new field of illegal enterprise to gangsters and bootleggers like Al Capone and Sam Giancana, who erected vice empires on the sale of illegal beer and liquor, which they transferred to narcotics after Prohibition was repealed in 1933.

Harry J. Anslinger joined the Treasury Department's Bureau of Prohibition in 1926 and in 1930 was promoted to assistant commissioner of prohibition. Anslinger never really believed that Prohibition could work, but he did his job zealously. In 1930, with the repeal of Prohibition in the wind, he was asked to preside over the new Federal Bureau of Narcotics (FBN), which provided a refuge for thousands of Prohibition agents who otherwise would be shortly unemployed. Anslinger swiftly laid the groundwork for an entirely new approach to narcotics enforcement—a hysterical campaign of anti-dope propaganda within the United States.[27]

The Moral Foundations of Prohibition

The moral foundations of prohibition policy were firmly rooted in the belief that it is morally bad to be dependent on or to be enslaved by drugs or alcohol; it is *good* to fight any form of dependency or weakness. It is masculine, and thus admirable, not to be drug-dependent. It is a sign of weakness, it is effete, contemptible and shameful to be dependent. Very simply, narcotics addiction was now a full-blown symbol of dependence that could arouse the same scorn as other forms of so-called passive-dependent behavior such as homosexuality, effeminacy in men, or cowardice.

NOTES

1. For a good summary of drug withdrawal syndromes, see Glenn Hodding, Michael Jann, and Irving Ackerman, "Drug Withdrawal Syndromes: A Literature Review," *Western Journal of Medicine* 133 (November 1980): 383-391.

2. Charles E. Terry and Mildred Pellens, *The Opium Problem* (1928; reprint ed., Montclair, N.J.: Patterson Smith, 1970), p. 28.

3. David F. Musto, *The American Disease: Origins of Narcotic Control* (New Haven, Conn.: Yale University Press, 1973), pp. 3–5.

4. Marie E. Nyswander, *The Drug Addict as Patient* (New York: Grune and Stratton, 1956), pp. 1-13.

5. H. Wayne Morgan, ed., *Yesterday's Addicts: American Society and Drug Abuse, 1865-1920* (Norman, Okla.: University of Oklahoma Press, 1974), p. 28.

6. Terry and Pellens, *The Opium Problem*, pp. 470-71.

7. This 1903 survey is reported in ibid., p. 468.

8. *The Oxford Universal Dictionary on Historical Principles. Supplement* (Oxford, England: Clarendon Press, 1933), chapter 3.

9. Charles N. Glaab and A. Theodore Brown, *A History of Urban America* (New York: The Macmillan Co., 1967), chapter 3.

10. Alfred R. Lindesmith, *Addiction and Opiates* (Chicago: Aldine Publishing Co., 1968), p. 212.

11. G. D. Swaine, "Regarding the Luminal Treatment of Morphine Addiction," *American Journal of Clinical Medicine* 25 (August 1918): 611; see also Terry and Pellens, *The Opium Problem*, p. 499.

12. J. McIver and G. E. Price, "Drug Addiction," *Journal of the American Medical Association* 66 (February 12, 1916): 477-91.

13. Musto, *The American Disease*, p. 245.

14. L. Kolb and A. G. DuMez, "The Prevalence and Trend of Drug Addiction in the United States and Factors Influencing It," *Public Health Reports* 39 (January 1924): 1179-204.

15. Quoted in Alfred R. Lindesmith, *The Addict and the Law* (Bloomington, Ind.: Indiana University Press, 1965), p. 6.

16. The criminogenic effect of the Harrison Act has been analyzed by, among others, Pearce Bailey, "The Heroin Habit," *The New Republic* (April 22, 1916), pp. 314-16; J. C. Densten, "Drug Addiction and the Harrison Anti-Narcotic Act," *New York Medical Journal* 105 (April 21, 1917): 747-48; and, more recently, by economist Thomas C. Schelling, "Economics and Criminal Enterprise," *The Public Interest* 7 (Spring 1967): 61-78.

17. Sanford Kadish, "The Crisis of Overcriminalization," *Annals of the American Academy of Political and Social Science* 37 (November 1967): 158-70.

18. Charles Winick, "Narcotics Addiction and Its Treatment," *Law and Contemporary Problems* 22 (Winter 1957): 9-33.

19. William Stewart Halsted's morphine addiction, which came to light only in 1969, is highlighted in Edward M. Brecher and *Consumer Reports*

Editors, *Licit and Illicit Drugs* (Boston: Little, Brown and Company, 1972), p. 34; Thomas Szasz, *Ceremonial Chemistry: The Ritual Persecution of Drugs, Addicts, and Pushers* (Garden City, N. Y.: Anchor/Doubleday, 1974), pp. 83-84; and, most recently, see the book review by Peter O. Olch of Owen and Sarah Wangensteen's *The Rise of Surgery from Empiric Craft to Scientific Discipline* appearing in *Bulletin of the History of Medicine* 54 (Spring 1980): 145.

20. Quoted in Guy P. Seaberg, "The Drug Abuse Problem and Some Proposals," *Journal of Criminal Law, Criminology and Police Science* 58 (September 1967): 366.

21. Quoted in Nathan Straus, III, ed., *Addicts and Drug Abusers: Current Approaches to the Problem* (New York: Twayne Publishers, 1971), pp. 20-21.

22. *Annual Report of the Commissioner of Internal Revenue for the Fiscal Year 1920* (Washington, D.C.: U.S. Government Printing Office, 1921), pp. 33-34.

23. "No To Re-Opening Narcotics Clinic," *San Francisco Examiner*, (December 17, 1938), p. C-1.

24. "State Should Not Take Over Selling Dope," *Seattle Post-Intelligencer*, (February 17, 1938), p. 22.

25. New York City Health Department, *The New York City Narcotic Clinic* (New York: Bureau of Public Health Education, Health Department, 1920), p. 30.

26. Billy Sunday quoted in "Narcotics Prohibition," *Newsweek* (May 1, 1972), p. 104.

27. See Harry J. Anslinger and William F. Tomkins, *The Traffic in Narcotics* (New York: Funk and Wagnalls, 1953).

2

The Nixon War on Heroin

> Got a problem—political, personal, local, national, global or interplanetary? Need rain? Feel anxious or afraid? Worried about pot-smokers, alcoholics . . . and dope addicts? Don't delay another minute—call or write: The Grand Shaman, 1600 Pennsylvania Avenue, Washington, D.C. Rain dances, rituals, razzle-dazzle incantations, witchcraft, magic of all kinds. Evil spirits slain. Plagues banished. Demons exorcised. Warts cured. Commissions appointed. Promises made. Maledictions pronounced. Laws passed. Agencies created. Names Changed. Attention diverted. Mumbo jumbo spoken.
>
> Amitai Etzioni, 1972

One twentieth-century president after another has found it politically advantageous to exploit, or at least cater to, the American public's near hysteria over heroin. During the Nixon presidency there appeared to be great political potential in battling heroin, as there had been for fighting drugs and alcohol under previous administrations.[1] Public battles against drugs and drug addicts serve to quiet public fears regarding crime and intoxication. Recent presidential politics has led to an emphasis on quick, dramatic enactment of programs and symbolic actions in the short run in the pursuit of reelection and personal fame.

What social, epidemiologic and political factors transformed heroin addiction into a hightly salient political controversy in the late 1960s and early 1970s? The Nixon administration launched its much-vaunted "war on heroin" in 1969. What treatment policies and programs were implemented under this offensive? Did they serve political functions? Nixon hoped that street crime could be reduced by altering demand for heroin through treating addicts. If such therapies lowered crime, they would be a signal of Nixon's all-out commitment to law and order, thereby ensuring his re-election in the Watergate-marred 1972 contest.

GENESIS OF THE RECENT WAR ON HEROIN

Between 1965 and 1970 the estimated number of active heroin addicts in the United States grew from about 68,000[2] to some 500,000.[3] Extremely high and rapidly spreading incidence and prevalence were taken as indicators of "epidemic" heroin abuse, which supposedly grew to peak rates in American cities between 1969 and 1972.[4] Medically, an "epidemic" is a disease attacking many people in a region at the same time, widely diffused and spreading rapidly.

The phrases "heroin epidemic" and even "pandemic" were used repeatedly to describe the rapid spread of heroin use after 1965. This rhetoric escalated into an invocation of a "doomsday of infection" and to a fanatical quest for freedom from heroin. In 1971 heroin addiction ranked third in polls, behind only Vietnam and the economy, as the most serious problem facing the United States.[5]

NIXON'S TEN-POINT PLAN TO WIPE OUT HEROIN

Nixon gave nascent stages of the so-called "heroin epidemic" a fairly high priority as a campaign issue in 1968 but couched it mainly in a "law-and-order" framework. In an Anaheim, California, campaign speech he called heroin addiction America's "Public Enemy Number One."[6] Once elected, he immediately outlined a new ten-point drug law enforcement and addiction treatment strategy aimed at wiping out heroin abuse.

His plan included the following:

1. New federal drug control legislation, reclassifying some substances;
2. Uniform state drug control legislation;

3. International cooperation to stop heroin distribution;
4. Suppression of drug smuggling into the United States;
5. Suppression of domestic heroin distribution;
6. More local law enforcement aid to crack down on narcotic sellers;
7. New drug abuse education programs;
8. More addiction treatment programs;
9. More research in drug abuse prevention;
10. Training in drug abuse treatment, rehabilitation and prevention.[7]

His "treatment" rhetoric belied the fact that most federal funds went to the criminal justice system—police, courts and corrections—as the main program for controlling heroin abuse.

Operation Intercept

To kick off his law enforcement "war" on heroin, Nixon launched "Operation Intercept" in 1969, requiring close searches of all vehicles and persons crossing legal ports of entry between Mexico and the United States. The plan was to publicize Nixon's commitment to fighting heroin. G. Gordon Liddy, who masterminded the Watergate break-in, helped put together Operation Intercept and other federal narcotic law enforcement efforts.[8] Egil "Bud" Krogh, a close narcotic policy adviser to President Nixon, said the border operation fizzled out, ultimately evolving into a less-abrasive "Operation Cooperation." Said Krogh:

> Operation Intercept was developed through the spring and early summer of 1969. It was . . . somewhat embarrassing. . . . [It] resulted in tying up traffic, and seizure of marijuana. In terms of heroin, nothing really was accomplished.[9]

Joel Fort, a criminologist, told Congress that Operation Intercept was ". . . the latest in a series of carefully designed smokescreens to make the public believe that something effective and important is being done about the drug problem."[10]

Stressing the spillover effects of Operation Intercept, David Smith, another criminologist, told a Senate subcommittee that the government's crash program to dry up the supply of heroin at San Ysidro and other ports of entry was only reducing the supply of Mexican marijuana. The whole program was backfiring by driving California teenagers to more dangerous drugs:

> . . . the use of dangerous drugs by adolescents increased dramatically following the implementation of Operation Intercept and the subsequent shortage of marijuana at their level. The youthful experimenters seemed to prefer marijuana, but in its absence, willingly accepted any substitute.[11]

Gooberman, a sociologist, also studied the unintended consequences of Operation Intercept and concluded that more heroin users were created by the program than cured by it.[12] In a like vein, the unintended consequence of heavy police crackdowns sponsored by the Nixon administration on heroin suppliers in Washington, D.C., was an outbreak there of intravenous amphetamine abuse.

CRIME, ADDICTION, AND VIETNAM

The Nixon administration promulgated the opinion that heroin addiction was: (1) responsible for the rise in crime, (2) radiating outward from the central cities, and (3) of "epidemic" proportions in Vietnam.

THE RISE IN CRIME

Crime during the Nixon administration seemed to be rising faster than before, and the president pledged to meet this problem directly. Empirical evidence collected in the 1960s suggested that criminal behavior in many cases precedes addiction,[13] but Nixon was convinced that addiction was ". . . a major contributor to crime" and that he could significantly reduce crime rates by rehabilitating addicts.[14] Since heroin abuse seemed to be exacerbating an already explosive urban crime situation, addiction control moved quickly to the top of his policy-making agenda.

Nowhere was the rise in crime as dramatic as in Washington, D.C., itself dubbed America's "crime capital." Between 1966 and 1969 rates of both addiction and crime in that city appeared to peak simultaneously. Much of this crime was attributed by medical researchers, the police and the media to heroin addiction.[15]

One explanation given for the heroin "epidemic" among young Washington, D.C., blacks was pathologic, and went something like this: Thousands of economically obsolete rural poor were redistributed to cities like New York, Detroit and Washington, D.C., following World War II. The majority of these newcomers, especially blacks, were not absorbed into the urban environment. Automation had wiped out thousands of lower-skill jobs, and the post-Korean War years were marked by periodic recession and unemployment. As the structure of these poor families eroded, teenagers and young adults coming of age in the 1960s were hit hardest because they were partly detached from the family system but not fully absorbed into the occupational structure. The litany of urban disorders in the wake of these declining occupational and family controls included rising rates of gang delinquency, an alarming increase in juvenile crime and, finally, rapidly spreading heroin addiction.[16]

Nationwide, reported crime was up 16 percent in 1967, 19 percent in 1968, and 11 percent in 1969. In 1971, 52 percent of all criminal cases in the Los Angeles County Superior Court system were drug-related. Forty-seven percent of all adult felony trials in that year in Los Angeles County were for drug law violations.[17]

New York City's system for the administration of criminal justice nearly collapsed under the weight of drug-related offenses. Estimates were that over 50 percent of all inmates in New York City's jails were heroin addicts.[18]

Addict-Committed Burglary

The number one property crime in the United States is residential and commercial burglary. The assumption is that most burglars are addicts. Sgt. Larry Gallu of the Phoenix Police Department, for example, said, "Somewhere between 65% and 80% of all burglaries here and across the country are committed by heroin addicts."[19] Lt. Donald Betkey of the Los Angeles County Sheriff's Office says ". . . about four out of five burglary cases we close involve hypes. . . ."[20] A detective sergeant on the Los Angeles Police Department flatly concluded that "most burglars are hypes."[21] Testimony like this from across the nation led Nixon to conclude that heroin addiction and crime, particularly property crimes, were inexorably linked in a causal fashion.

THE RADIATION OF ADDICTION FROM CENTRAL CITIES

A second factor behind the Nixon administration's war on heroin was the belief that heroin use was radiating from inner-city areas into the veins of white, suburban middle- and upper-class youth, much like an "infectious disease."[22] Nixon declared, "Not very long ago . . . narcotic addiction was a class problem. . . . now the problem is universal."[23] No longer was heroin addiction apparently confined to more disadvantaged elements of society where people sought escape from poverty[24] or the opportunity to "be somebody" in an environment in which advancement through legitimate channels was closed.[25] The Nixon administration was aware that the parents of new, better-off heroin users tended to vote more frequently than ghetto and *barrio* parents. John Ehrlichman stated that Nixon exploited white middle- and upper-class voters' fears about their children turning to heroin: "Narcotics repression is a sexy political issue. Parents are worried about their kids using heroin, and parents are voters. This is why the Nixon White House became involved [in fighting heroin]."[26]

Does Addiction Spread Like a Disease?

The Nixon administration, medical reports, and the media gave the public the impression that heroin addiction was an infectious, communicable disease permeating all of society. A developing "doomsday of infection" was depicted. The sources of the supposed "infection" were presumed to be the "legions of pushers," and the solution was an "epidemiologic approach."[27] But is heroin addiction an "infectious" process? Do novice users "catch" the habit in the same manner as a communicable disease?

The spread of heroin is not comparable to the spread of disease. In epidemiologic theory the host is infected by a pathogenic agent like a bacterium, virus or fungus. Communicable diseases are spread directly from person to person or indirectly, through such things as contaminated kitchen utensils or food. Addiction extends from person to person, but there the analogy to communicable disease ends.

Victims get communicable diseases inadvertently. Polio or tuberculosis infects the victim without his knowledge and without his *willing consent* to the infection and its painful consequences.

Heroin addiction does not conform to this process. First, users do not inject or "infect" unknowing, unwilling victims. New heroin users are not unwilling pawns in the path of some virulent contagion. As to first heroin use by novices, heroin transmission typically occurs in a climate of friendship and relaxation, among peers. Addicts usually see themselves as sharing with the novice a controllable, pleasurable substance. Moreover, users typically "turn on" a novice because the experimenter *asks for* the heroin.[28] Thus, the communicable disease model of spreading heroin abuse employed by medical researchers and policymakers is not analogous to the transmission process of heroin addiction.

THE HEROIN "EPIDEMIC" IN VIETNAM

A third precipitating factor behind the Nixon administration's efforts against heroin was another "heroin epidemic" reported among American forces stationed in Southeast Asia.[29] After an influx of potent heroin into Vietnam, an estimated 20 percent of the U.S. enlisted troops were addicted at one time or another during their tour of duty.[30] Some commentators have questioned this high incidence figure,[31] but the fact remains that many soldiers were using heroin.

U.S. Complicity Along the Southeast Asian Opium Trail

Narcotics traffic is deeply woven into the social, economic and political fabric of Southeast Asia. Many people there depend upon this industry for livelihoods. United States government personnel were heavily involved in the narcotics traffic in Indochina during the Vietnam War.[32] Opium and heroin were moving about Southeast Asia on U.S.-supported Royal Lao Air Force Planes and on Air America, Inc., the CIA's clandestine airline. From Kuomintang bandit gangs in northern Thailand, to Lao generals, to the South Vietnamese governing elites, there appeared to be one clear and consistent pattern: United States involvement all along the Southeast Asian opium trail. By turning away from obvious official corruption, American authorities used opium profits to reward Asian elites for their support of American goals in Southeast Asia.

Nixon's Worries about Returning Addicts

President Nixon was haunted by the specter of "hundreds of

thousands" of G.I.-addicts returning from the war in Vietnam, many of them armed, trained in guerrilla warfare, and stalking big city streets in search of an angry fix. When he took office, there were only sixteen federally funded addiction treatment programs nationwide. He wanted to make sure there were more treatment programs, so that none of these addicts could claim they were still using dope and committing crimes because no therapy was available.

Significantly, the great majority of Vietnam addicts remained abstinent when they returned to the United States.[33] The situation, therefore, was not as severe as portrayed by the Nixon administration. Nevertheless, it fueled public fears and helped set the Nixon administration in action to mount an expanded addiction treatment effort at home.

THE FEDS IN ACTION

Three major factors, then—rising crime, the "epidemic" spread of addiction across class and status boundaries, and narcotics use in Vietnam by United States troops—precipitated the subsequent massive expansion of federal addiction treatment and rehabilitation capacity. These developments led Nixon to proclaim heroin addiction a ". . . national emergency," and he pledged to ". . . take every step necessary to deal with this emergency."[34]

TREATMENT AND REHABILITATION: A NEW EMPHASIS

Nixon's overall thesis was that heroin addiction and attendant crimes could be reduced through a two-pronged "war" on heroin: (1) expanded law enforcement activities on international, national and subnational levels to curtail *supply* of the drug, and (2) a massive treatment and rehabilitation effort to reduce heroin *demand*. The model employed was based on the economics of supply and demand, but Nixon placed a new, well-publicized emphasis on the drug demand side of the equation, since narcotics law enforcement alone had never provided the easy solution to the heroin problem it seemed to promise. Public policies and criminal justice system efforts to reduce supplies of narcotics have been more symbolic than effective.[35]

COMBINED STRATEGY

Nixon made it plain that dealing with addiction solely through surveillance, arrest, jail, courts, prison, civil commitments, fines, probation and parole was insufficient to solve the heroin addiction problem. He ordered that narcotic law enforcement programs henceforth be coupled with

> . . . *a rational approach to the reclamation of the [heroin] user himself.* The laws of supply and demand function in the illegal drug business as in any other . . . we must deal with demand. *We must rehabilitate the users* if we are to eliminate drug abuse and all the anti-social activities that flow from drug abuse [emphasis added].[36]

The Demand Side of the Equation

The policy choice to increase treatment capacity dramatically after 1969 was based on the theory that demand for heroin is what economists call "price inelastic": An addict in withdrawal will pay almost any price for the drug.[37] Nixon and his staff, along with relevant congressional committees therefore began focusing on the one irreplaceable factor in the heroin equation: the addicts themselves, who must have heroin to live and who live to use heroin. By reducing drug demand with methadone maintenance or other treatment, it was assumed that addiction and street crime would miraculously evaporate. Said the president:

> . . . as long as there is demand [for heroin] there will be those willing to take the risks of meeting that demand. So we must act to destroy the market for drugs, and this means the prevention of new addicts and the rehabilitation of those who are addicted. Our programs . . . must be judged by the number of human beings who are brought out of the hell of addiction and by the number of human beings who are dissuaded from entering that hell.[38]

Heroin does have algebraic properties: The more you shoot, the less you have. And the less you have, the more you need. The addict thus becomes a person in total need of dope. This algebra of need makes heroin the ideal product, the model merchandise. No sales talk is necessary. Users will assault, rob, steal, cheat, then crawl through the sewer and beg to buy. Could this kind of compulsive craving be controlled through addiction treatment?

NIXON MOVES CONTROL OVER TREATMENT STRATEGY TO WHITE HOUSE

When Nixon took office, the federal government's heroin control activities were a hodgepodge of divided, uncoordinated responsibilities. Myriad federal treatment and law enforcement programs were scattered over 7 cabinet-level departments and 114 federal agencies.[39] The National Institute of Mental Health (NIMH) had to let a $100,000 grant to find out which programs its own Division of Narcotic Addiction and Drug Abuse was funding.

Mayor John Lindsay of New York summarized the state of the federal heroin control apparatus when Nixon took office:

> Today the Federal effort, such as it is, is hopelessly fragmented. No fewer than four separate agencies fund [addiction treatment] programs in my own city. . . . Lacking coordination at the Federal level, there is an appalling waste of time and energy. . . . We must have a single Federal agency and top-level officials to direct a national anti-addiction strategy.[40]

Mayor Moon Landrieu of New Orleans called for concentrating federal treatment efforts into ". . . a compact, manageable unit which can accurately measure its successes and failures."[41]

The president and Congress, impelled by a lobby of metropolitan mayors, pledged to reorganize this "nonsystem" of overlapping duplication and bureaucratic wrangling. In proposing his drug abuse reorganization plan, Nixon lamented,

> [The federal government] promises much but it does not deliver what it promises. [Power is] exceedingly fragmented and broadly scattered throughout the federal establishment. . . . It is extremely difficult for either the Congress or the President to see their intentions carried out when lines of responsibility are as tangled and ambiguous as they are. . . ."[42]

THE 1972 DRUG ABUSE OFFICE AND TREATMENT ACT

To give him more direct control over the heroin battle, Nixon asked Congress for a Special Action Office for Drug Abuse Prevention (SAODAP) to be located in the Executive Office of the President.

Egil "Bud" Krogh was a key figure in the Nixon battle to control heroin abuse from the White House. Krogh, who worked for John Ehrlichman, is sometimes called the chief architect of Nixon's addiction treatment strategy. Best known as one of the "plumbers" who served time in jail for authorizing the burglary of a psychiatrist's office, Krogh played a key part in formulating White House addiction treatment policy, particularly methadone maintenance. By 1973, largely on the basis of his White House narcotics duties, Krogh became the youngest undersecretary ever appointed to the U.S. Department of Commerce.

Krogh said that SAODAP originated from Nixon's 1969 decision that crime in Washington, D.C., had to be stopped to symbolize the president's commitment to law and order. Krogh recalls how the Special Action Office was named:

> This idea came up one evening in my office. We said, "You know, we ought to think about something that is going to be taking action [against heroin]." Somebody said, "Yea, but it ought to be a special action—there are lots of action programs. Why don't we call it a special action office?"[43]

Nixon thus offered the legislative package establishing SAODAP and its successor, the new National Institute on Drug Abuse (NIDA) to highlight the addiction treatment issue dramatically and to coordinate and control all federal drug treatment efforts from the White House itself. Nixon promised the new law would ". . . root out the cancerous growth of narcotic addiction in America."[44] Later he would consolidate all federal drug law enforcement activities in a new Drug Enforcement Administration (DEA).

NIXON NAMES JAFFE TO HEAD SAODAP

Nixon immediately named Jerome Jaffe as director of SAODAP, and the press dutifully dubbed him the president's "Drug Czar." Jaffe, a psychiatrist, headed the Illinois State Drug Abuse Program and had trained at the U.S. Public Health Service narcotics hospital in Lexington, Kentucky. Based on his record, he was a mover. When Jaffe arrived in Illinois from the Bronx in 1966, there was not a single state-supported addiction treatment bed in Illinois. His first year there he got 300 such "beds"; by 1968 there were 1,800.

From the beginning, the emphasis was on heroin. Nixon immediately ordered Jaffe to ". . . concentrate federal resources on the heroin problem." Heroin addiction, Nixon told Jaffe, ". . . is the most socially destructive form of addiction . . . and it must command priority."[45] Jaffe ardently supported methadone maintenance which, he said, "In many instances for many people . . . permits them to function as law abiding, productive citizens. . . . If there is a medication that permits a man to function as a law-abiding citizen, it is appropriate that the medicine [methadone] be given to him."[46]

NIXON STRATEGY FOR THE 1972 ELECTION: THREE GOALS

Looking forward to the 1972 presidential campaign, Nixon strategists provided three major heroin-related goals:

1. To be in a position to say that the Nixon administration had mounted the most massive drug law enforcement and treatment effort in the nation's history. Statistical results would first come from the District of Columbia where the administration had direct control over the "comprehensiveness of the drug fight" and over the number of police who could be thrown into the battle.
2. To have developed "certain highly visible efforts in the area of narcotics distribution," such as drug raids, border blockades (of which Operation Intercept was an example) and other international agreements to demonstrate clearly in the public mind "the totality of the administration's commitment" to solving the heroin problem.
3. To have successfully shifted the burden of responsibility for controlling crime and addiction to state and local governments.[47]

DEMOCRATIC HOPEFULS ON THE ATTACK

Criticism of Nixon's crime and drug control efforts was mounting among Democratic hopefuls testing the water for the 1972 presidential nomination, especially Hubert Humphrey and Eugene McCarthy.[48] Nixon was "upset" by these challenges to his heroin control efforts and inertia in federal narcotic law enforcement and treatment agencies. He threatened to "knock heads together" if federal officials failed to cooperate in his heroin control efforts. Nixon said that if "petty bureaucrats" attempted to stand in the way of his war on heroin, ". . . then heads will roll."[49]

He felt particularly vulnerable regarding the crime picture in Washington, D.C. If he could not halt the increase in crime there, would he be able to do it anywhere? Krogh recalled:

> During the period from January to December, 1969, crime [in D.C.] continued to climb dramatically . . . and during November hit an all-time high. . . . When the President learned the news he became extremely upset and concerned. He . . . told [Ehrlichman] this [crime] must stop . . . and that every immediate measure had to be undertaken to reduce the crime rate by those in the District government, or else he would get a new team.[50]

Krogh said it was the president's concern for crime in Washington, D.C., ". . . that led to the development of a national drug control program."[51]

ODALE AND LEAA

In his 1972 State of the Union address Nixon previewed what would become the Drug Enforcement Administration: "I will soon initiate a major new program to drive drug traffickers and pushers off the streets of America . . . to assist state and local agencies in detecting, arresting, and convicting those who would profit from the misery of others."[52] With this, the president created a new Office of Drug Abuse Law Enforcement (ODALE) which sent law enforcement "strike forces" into thirty-three cities across the nation. He said the program would be ". . . built around a nationwide network of investigative and prosecutive units, utilizing special grand juries. . . ."[53] Using "heroin hotlines" and informant tips, the teams made numerous arrests of drug users and sellers, mostly small fries. Since most users are sellers (and vice versa), federal strategy struck directly at heroin addicts rather than untouchable, faceless, "higher ups" in the heroin empire. But ODALE served its purpose: It was the quintessence of Nixon's "get-tough" law enforcement approach against heroin. Utilizing the "no-knock" provisions of the 1968 Omnibus Crime Control and

Safe Streets Act (which allowed police officers to enter a suspect's premises unannounced), agents made midnight door-busting raids on the homes of suspected heroin dealers, sometimes terrifying and killing innocent people.[54] Perhaps for this reason ODALE had a short life and was merged with the Justice Department's Bureau of Narcotics and Dangerous Drugs (BNDD) and the Office of National Narcotics Intelligence in 1973 to form a new Drug Enforcement Administration. National and international narcotic enforcement efforts at this writing are primarily centered in DEA.

LAW ENFORCEMENT ASSISTANCE ADMINISTRATION

One way of demonstrating the administration's concern—and perhaps of making an impact on crime by the 1972 election—was to channel additional federal money to local police departments. This was part of the Nixon administration's goal to turn over more drug control responsibilities to local governments; if failure resulted, it could be blamed on them. The instrument for accomplishing this purpose was the Law Enforcement Assistance Administration (LEAA), an appendage of the Justice Department set up in 1968 by the Johnson administration to aid local law enforcement agencies in the wake of urban uprisings by blacks and massive anti-war protests.

Under Nixon, LEAA had almost no direction or goals, it failed to provide real leadership to the state and local agencies it funded, and it was in effect "a giant subsidy program."[55] The agency began spending most of its money on equipment, as if that would significantly reduce heroin addiction and street crime. Part of the problem was that state agencies receiving LEAA funds succumbed to public law-and-order pressures by funding state and local projects which were readily visible: riot control equipment, new guns, armored vehicles, helicopters and dope-sniffing dogs that cost up to $10,000 each to train. LEAA's programs did little to diminish the supplies of heroin available on the streets of large American cities.

ENTER METHADONE MAINTENANCE: THE FORLORN HOPE

While these widely publicized law enforcement programs might be expected to produce favorable "visibility" for the president,

Krogh personally did not believe they would have much of an effect on crime statistics. Heavy law enforcement crackdowns on heroin supply, he reasoned, would inevitably drive up the price of heroin, while lowering its quality. The result, he concluded, would be *more* rather than less crime.

Basing his judgement on positive reports on methadone maintenance emanating from New York City, he came to the conclusion that it provided a quick fix for the heroin problem. He said: "You had to provide an alternative to the heroin addicts whose price for the substance had increased; otherwise, it could lead to an increase in crime, because of the higher cost of obtaining [heroin]."[56]

Quite simply, as America has taken great pains to keep heroin from addicts, its price has been escalating. The same society then declares addicts "dangerous" because they engage in crime to secure the heroin that the law has priced beyond their ability to afford. Egil Krogh and a number of others in the White House were convinced that the only solution to this problem was legal maintenance with methadone.

NOTES

1. On the symbolic nature of political battles against demon drugs, see Joseph R. Gusfield, *Symbolic Crusade: Status Politics and the American Temperance Movement* (Urbana, Ill.: University of Illinois Press, 1963); also Gusfield's "The (F) Utility of Knowledge?: The Relation of Social Science to Public Policy Toward Drugs," *Annals of the American Academy of Political and Social Science* 417 (January 1975): 1-15; see also David F. Musto, *The American Disease: Origins of Narcotic Control* (New Haven, Conn.: Yale University Press, 1973).

2. L. G. Richards and E. E. Carroll, "Illicit Drug Use and Addiction in the United States," *Public Health Reports* 85 (December 1970): 1035-41. This figure is undoubtedly low.

3. David E. Smith and David J. Bentel, *Drug Abuse Information Project: Fourth Annual Report to the Legislature* (Sacramento, Calif.: Drug Abuse Information Project, 1970), p. 5.

4. An "epidemic" was claimed by many heroin researchers, including Robert L. DuPont, "Profile of a Heroin-Addiction Epidemic," *New England Journal of Medicine* 285 (August 1971): 320-24; Robert L. Dupont and Richard Katon, "Physicians and the Heroin Addiction Epidemic,"

Modern Medicine (June 28, 1971), pp. 128-39; Harry Atkins, "The Epidemiology of Heroin," *The Sciences* (April 1972), pp. 6-9; Robert L. DuPont, "Coming to Grips With an Urban Heroin Addiction Epidemic," *Journal of the American Medical Association* 223 (January 1, 1973): 46-48; Barry S. Brown et al., "Impact of a Large-Scale Narcotics Treatment Program: A Six Month Experience," *International Journal of the Addictions* 8 (Winter 1973): 49-57; Robert L. DuPont and Mark H. Greene, "Patterns of Heroin Addiction in the District of Columbia," in *Fifth National Conference on Methadone Treatment: Proceedings, 1973,* ed. National Association for the Prevention of Addiction to Narcotics (New York: National Association for the Prevention of Addiction to Narcotics, 1973), pp. 786-93; William I. Barton, "Narcotics-Related Deaths Decrease in 1972 from the Number of Narcotics-Related Deaths in 1971," *International Journal of Addictions* 9 (Winter 1974): 513-29; Robert L. Dupont, "Overview of Drug Abuse," in *Developments in the Field of Drug Abuse: Proceedings of the National Drug Abuse Conference—1974,* ed. Edward C. Senay, Vernon Shorty and Harold Alksne (Cambridge, Mass.: Schenkman Publishing Co., 1974), pp. 26-31; and Leon G. Hunt, *Recent Spread of Heroin Use in the United States: Unanswered Questions* (Washington, D.C.: The Drug Abuse Council, Inc., 1974).

5. "Vietnam Leads U.S. Worries," *Los Angeles Times* (June 18, 1971), pt. I, p. 28.

6. Nixon quoted in "Nixon Calls Heroin Addiction Public Enemy #1," *Long Beach Independent Press-Telegram* (October 16, 1968), p. A-1.

7. "Nixon Outlines Plan to Control Drug Abuse," *Long Beach Independent Press-Telegram,* (April 3, 1969), p. A-6.

8. For Liddy's drug abuse control exploits, see Pam Lloyd, "G. Gordon Liddy's Killer Narc Squad," *High Times* (August/September 1975), pp. 44-45.

9. Edward Jay Epstein, "The Krogh File—The Politics of 'Law and Order,' " *The Public Interest* 39 (Spring 1975): 114.

10. Fort is quoted in U.S. Senate, Committee on Labor and Public Welfare, *Alcoholism and Narcotics,* 91st Cong., 1st sess., Pt. 1, 1969-1970, p. 12.

11. Smith is quoted in "Operation Intercept: Cause or Cure?" *Los Angeles Times* (December 12, 1971), pt. I, p. 2

12. Lawrence A. Gooberman, *Operation Intercept: The Multiple Consequences of Public Policy* (New York: Pergamon Press, 1974).

13. For a review of the literature on the relationship between crime and addiction, see Stephanie W. Greenberg and Freda Adler, "Crime and Addiction: An Empirical Analysis of the Literature, 1920-1973," *Contemporary Drug Problems* 3 (Summer 1974): 221-70.

14. U.S. President, "Omnibus Drug Control Legislative Message by The President," Press Release, June 17, 1971, p. 1.

15. DuPont, "Profile of a Heroin-Addiction Epidemic," pp. 320-24.

16. This pathologic explanation of the etiology of heroin addiction is expressed by Daniel P. Moynihan, *Maximum Feasible Misunderstanding* (New York: Free Press, 1969); and by Frances Fox Piven and Richard A. Cloward, *Regulating the Poor: The Functions of Public Welfare* (New York: Vintage Books, 1971), pp. 337-38.

17. Los Angeles County, Grand Jury Report, *Report of the Narcotics and Dangerous Drug Committee*, November 29, 1971, p. 6.

18. See Vincent P. Dole, "Detoxification of Sick Addicts in Prison," *Journal of the American Medical Association* 220 (April 17, 1972): 366-69; also see "Most NY City Prisoners Addicts," *Los Angeles Times* (January 11, 1972), pt. II, p. 1.

19. "Serious Crime Up Nationwide," *Long Beach Independent Press-Telegram*, (April 21, 1971), p. A-24.

20. "Increase in Nation's Serious Crime Rate Slows," *Los Angeles Times* (December 9, 1976), pt. XI, p. 1.

21. "L.A. Burglaries Jump," *Los Angeles Times* (August 31, 1971), pt. II, p. 4.

22. A dire warning of the infectious heroin "epidemic" is given in Charles W. Sheppard, David E. Smith and George R. Gay, "The Changing Face of Heroin Addiction in the Haight-Ashbury," *International Journal of the Addictions* 7 (Spring 1972): 109-22; also, for analogous interpretations of heroin addiction as an "infectious disease," see Hunt, *Recent Spread of Heroin Use*; and D. Dwayne Simpson, Bill Curtis and Mark C. Butler, "Description of Drug Users in Treatment: 1971-1972 DARP Admissions," *American Journal of Drug and Alcohol Abuse* 2 (January 1975): 15-28.

23. U.S. President, "Omnibus Drug Control Message," p. 2.

24. For the theory that poverty causes heroin addiction, see Kenneth Clark, *Dark Ghetto: Dilemmas of Social Power* (New York: Harper and Row, 1965); and Jordan Scher, "Patterns and Profiles of Addiction and Drug Abuse," *Archives of General Psychiatry* 15 (November 1966): 1220-26.

25. For functional theories of addiction see Isadore Chein et al., *The Road to H: Narcotics, Delinquency, and Social Policy* (New York: Basic Books, Inc., 1964), pp. 380-81; and Edward A. Preble and John J. Casey, Jr., "Taking Care of Business — The Heroin User's Life on the Street," *International Journal of the Addictions* 4 (March 1969): 1-24.

26. Stated by Ehrlichman in a KNBC-TV Newsfilm, July 27, 1976.

27. Editorial, "The Drug Abuse Pandemic," *Journal of the American Medical Association* 214 (December 28, 1970): 2327.

28. Barry S. Brown, Mark H. Greene and N. J. Turner, "The Spread of Addiction—The Role of the 'Average Addict,' " *American Journal of Drug and Alcohol Abuse* 3 (October 1976): 527.

29. George F. Soloman, "Psychiatric Casualties of the Vietnam Conflict with Particular Reference to the Problems of Heroin Addiction," *Modern Medicine* (September 20, 1971), pp. 199-215.

30. M. Duncan Stanton, "Drugs, Vietnam, and the Vietnam Veteran: An Overview," *American Journal of Drug and Alcohol Abuse* 3 (October 1976): 557-70.

31. Thomas S. Szasz claimed that the high incidence figures in Vietnam were deliberately inflated to justify the Defense Department's countermeasures, and suggested that the claimed "epidemic" there represented a "pharmacologic Gulf of Tonkin." See his "Scapegoating 'Military Addicts': The Helping Hand Strikes Again," *Transaction* 9 (June 1972): 4-6.

32. For devastating accounts of U.S. complicity in Southeast Asian opium and heroin smuggling, see Alfred W. McCoy, with Cathleen B. Read and Leonard P. Adams, III, *The Politics of Heroin in Southeast Asia* (New York: Harper and Row, 1972); and Committee of Concerned Asian Scholars, *The Opium Trail: Heroin and Imperialism* (Boston, Mass.: New England Free Press, 1972).

33. Stanton, "Drugs and the Vietnam Veteran," pp. 565-68.

34. U.S. President, "Omnibus Drug Control Message," p. 1.

35. There is a large literature on the failure of the criminal law and its enforcement to reduce substantially the amount of illegal narcotics available to addicts. Among the best works are J. C. Densten, "Drug Addiction and the Harrison Anti-Narcotic Act," *New York Medical Journal* 105 (April 21, 1917): 747-48; Edwin H. Sutherland and Donald R. Cressey, *Principles of Criminology*, 6th ed. (Philadelphia: J. B. Lippincott Co., 1960); Edwin M. Schur, *Crimes Without Victims* (Englewood Cliffs, N.J.: Prentice-Hall, 1965); Herbert Packer, *The Limits of the Criminal Sanction* (Stanford, Calif.: Stanford University Press, 1968); Leo F. Hollister, "Criminal Laws and the Control of Drugs of Abuse: An Historical View of the Law (or, It's the Lawyer's Fault)," *Journal of Clinical Pharmacology* 9 (November/December 1969): 345-48; Troy Duster, *The Legislation of Morality: Law, Drugs, and Moral Judgement* (New York: Free Press, 1970); Rufus King, *The Drug Hang-Up: America's Fifty-Year Folly* (New York: W. W. Norton, 1972); Monroe E. Trout, "Drug Abuse: National and International Control," *Journal of Legal Medicine* 17 (March/April 1973): 56-60; Anthony Cagliostro et al., "Law & Order and Drugs—One Year Later," *Contemporary Drug Problems* 3 (Winter 1974): 547-67; Alan Chartock, "Narcotics Addiction: The Politics of Frustration," *Proceedings: The American Academy of Political Science* 31 (May 1974):

239-49; Norman Zinberg and Richard C. Jacobson, "The Social Basis of Drug Abuse Prevention," in *Developments in the Field of Drug Abuse*, ed. Senay, Shorty, and Alksne, pp. 3-13; and Richard Brotman and Frederick Suffet, "The Concept of Prevention and Its Limitations," *Annals of the American Academy of Political and Social Science*, 417 (January 1975): 53-65.

36. U.S. President, "Omnibus Drug Control Message," p. 1.

37. For the best economic statement on the price inelasticity of heroin demand, see James V. Koch and Stanley E. Grupp, "The Economics of Drug Control Policies," *International Journal of the Addictions* 6 (December 1971): 571-84.

38. U.S. President, "Omnibus Drug Control Message," p. 1.

39. Jerome H. Jaffe, "Responses to Drug-Abuse Problems," in *Contemporary Problems of Drug Abuse*, ed. Peter A. Levin (Acton, Mass.: Publishing Sciences Group, 1974), p. 16.

40. U.S. Senate, Committee on Labor and Public Welfare, *Alcoholism and Narcotics*, p. 18.

41. Ibid., p. 79.

42. "President Hits Drug Control Bureaucracy," *Los Angeles Times* (August 22, 1972), pt. I, p. 26.

43. Krogh is quoted in "Early Days Recalled by White House Plumber," *The Journal (May 1, 1975), p. 1.*

44. U.S. President, "Omnibus Drug Control Message," p. 1.

45. Jaffe quoted Nixon's order in his article, "As Far as Heroin is Concerned, The Worst Is Over," *Psychology Today* (August 1973), p. 75.

46. Jaffe's testimony appears in U.S. Senate, Committee on Labor and Public Welfare, *Drug Abuse Prevention, Treatment and Rehabilitation, 1971: Hearings on S. 2217*, 92nd Cong., 1st sess., 1971, pp. 333-34.

47. Nixon's goals are recorded in Epstein, "The Krogh File," 107.

48. On the 1972 presidential campaign hustings Hubert Humphrey said that "Drug Addiction is almost epidemic." "Epidemic Drug Addiction Seen," *Long Beach Independent Press-Telegram* (January 26, 1972), p. A-7; and Eugene McCarthy, also a presidential hopeful, took aim at Nixon's drug control record noting that the Vietnam War was not the most difficult problem facing the country. The most serious problem, he said, ". . . is the internal one of poverty with its related problems of . . . crime [and] drug use." "McCarthy Spells Out the Issues," *Long Beach Independent Press-Telegram*(September 17, 1971), p. A-4.

49. Nixon quoted in "Heads Will Roll If Drug War Fails—Nixon," *Los Angeles Times* (March 22, 1972), pt. I, p. 11.

50. Epstein, "The Krogh File," p. 107.

51. Ibid.

52. "1972 State of the Union Address, Richard Nixon" *Congressional Quarterly* (January 22, 1972), p. 126.

53. Ibid.

54. Joe Eszterhas, *Nark!* (San Francisco: Straight Arrow Books, 1974), p. 151.

55. Les L. Gaspay, "Pork Barrel for Police," *The Progressive* (March 1972), pp. 211-14.

56. Epstein, "The Krogh File," p. 115.

3

The Physiology of Methadone Maintenance

> Remember not the events of the past, the things of long ago consider not; see, I am doing something new! Now it springs forth, do you not perceive it?
>
> Is. 43: 18-19

Since hope recently centered on the ability of methadone hydrochloride to control heroin abuse in America, this chapter defines methadone maintenance treatment. What is methadone maintenance and what are its exact pharmacologic and behavioral effects? Is it different from addiction to other narcotics?

METHADONE MAINTENANCE DEFINED

Methadone (adolphine, dolophine, adanon, amidone, physeptone, althose, miadon, butalgin, diadone, polimadone) is a synthetic substitute for heroin. The drug was originally synthesized by the German firm I. G. Farben in 1941 and appropriately named "Adolphine." Since morphine was unavailable in Germany during World War II for relieving pain in battlefield injuries, methadone was developed as a synthetic substitute on orders from Hitler.

Methadone maintenance is the dispensing, for over twenty-one days, of methadone to treat dependence on heroin or other narcotics. Methadone maintenance should not be confused with use of methadone in detoxification treatment of heroin addiction; the goals and methods of the two therapies differ radically. Using methadone in detoxification from heroin is a short-term procedure whose goal is abstinence. Although methadone maintenance embodies abstinence as its ultimate goal, some individuals have been on maintenance since the 1950s.

The rhetorical obfuscation with methadone maintenance was to classify continued narcotic addiction as "success" rather than "failure." Rehabilitation thenceforth would mean more than simple abstinence, the historical goal of addiction treatment. The crucial modification was now to view continued addiction to narcotics, always considered failure before, as an indicator of "success" in maintenance therapy. Through this unbelievable mumbo-jumbo methadone maintenance gained many adherents. A patient could be "normal" and still hooked.

In the early 1970s the United States government, under the aegis of the Nixon administration, sponsored large-scale methadone maintenance for the treatment of heroin addiction. By 1971, some 9,000 addicts nationwide were receiving methadone.[1] In 1972 there were 25,000 in such programs. At the end of 1973, as federal grants poured into local governments and nonprofit corporations licensed to dispense methadone under strict regulatory policies, there were 73,000 clients. In 1976 Dole and Nyswander indicated that about 85,000 of the nations's estimated 500,000 to 600,000 street heroin addicts were being maintained on methadone in more than 500 outpatient programs around the country.[2] Methadone maintenance programs now exist in Canada, Mexico, Puerto Rico, Great Britain (where they have largely replaced the system of heroin maintenance), West Germany, Sweden, Thailand, Hong Kong—in fact, in most nations of the world.

In the United States methadone is a Class II controlled substance, unavailable for maintenance except in government-licensed and inspected clinics. Private physicians are forbidden to prescribe the drug for maintenance purposes, but it may be prescribed to relieve pain in terminal cancer patients. This attests to the drug's analgesic properties. When ingested by an addict, the drug has the same effects as heroin, though its duration of effect is much longer (twenty-four hours compared to six hours for heroin). By 1970 many clinicians agreed that methadone maintenance was ". . . the preferred treatment for long-established heroin addiction."[3]

The crux of the problem with abstinence-type treatment is that, although many addicts have been "clean" many times, both on their own and while in custody, "craving" for heroin persists. This craving has been defined variously.[4] Spoken of in terms of desire, "yen" or "yin," or conditioning, this compulsion almost invariably leads to continued heroin use, addiction and, to varying degrees, crime to support the habit. The most important pharmacologic effect of a sufficient methadone dose is to suppress this intense craving for heroin.[5]

THE DOLE/NYSWANDER RESEARCH PROJECT

Beginning in the mid-1960s Vincent Dole and Marie Nyswander published increasingly glowing scientific reports on the effectiveness of methadone maintenance. The close relationship between Dole and Nyswander (who subsequently married) began in 1963 when Dole, a researcher and prominent Rockefeller Institute for Medical Research biochemist, had a number of conversations with Nyswander, a psychiatrist, who like him had concluded that heroin addiction caused some kind of "metabolic changes" in body chemistry that made abstinence impossible.

THE METABOLIC THEORY

Dole and Nyswander suggested a physiological conception of heroin addiction in place of the older concepts that addiction was symptomatic of an underlying psychological disorder or attributable to environmental factors like poverty. In their view addiction leads to a "metabolic deficiency"[6] that contributes to the high relapse rate associated with traditional treatment. They presented their addiction theory as a kind of flow chart, tracing a possible sequence of involvement with, and addiction to, heroin. The Theory suggested that "curiosity" and "availability of the drug" led to "experimental drug use" which, in turn, led either to a "normal"—no addiction—state or through the intermediary condition of a "neurological susceptibility" to an "altered response to narcotics," and finally to "addiction." Any attempt to leave the condition of "addiction" through "detoxification" leads to "recurrent symptoms of abstinence" and subsequently back to addiction. What they mean is that addicts like dope.

Dole and Nyswander were aware of this well-known heroin cycle and teamed up for research. Five individuals were experimentally addicted to injected morphine to make "enzymatic tests." They found, however, that they could not continue the tests because their subjects were always "on the nod" from the morphine injections. so they decided to detoxify them using gradually decreasing dosages of methadone over a fifteen-day period. This technique of withdrawal treatment of heroin addiction had been developed by Nyswander and others at Lexington in the early 1950s. During the detoxification regimen they found that the subjects were no longer "nodding-out," that they were alert and that the enzymatic tests could be completed. While performing these tests Dole and Nyswander found they could "stabilize" their subjects on methadone for a prolonged period of time at a fixed dosage, which varied between 120 mg and 180 mg per day. Weight-for-weight this represents about three grains of morphine a day, or an "average" heroin habit.

THE DOLE-NYSWANDER CONCLUSIONS

This work, performed in 1963, seemed to confirm the following:

1. In sufficient doses methadone produces physiological cross-tolerance to other opiates. Methadone-tolerant addicts are not susceptible to the effects of equal amounts of parenterally injected heroin;
2. Methadone is orally effective for about twenty-four hours (and newer forms for seventy-two hours), compared with four to six hours for heroin. A clinic system for dispensing was therefore a logistic possibility;
3. Methadone maintenance showed some potential for reducing criminal behavior among experimental addict-patients, leading to "social rehabilitation," usually defined as discontinued heroin use, decreased criminal activity and holding a job of some kind;
4. Methadone seemed to have a fairly low diversion potential due to its longer duration of effect (clients do not have to be given "take-home" doses) and the government-regulated clinic system for its distribution (addicts are tested at the clinic to make sure they are taking methadone and not using other drugs);

5. Methadone maintenance, compared to other drug-free treatment modalities, appeared to be a cost-effective form of therapy. Yearly cost per client in methadone maintenance is about $1,500, compared to $6,000 a year in residential treatment, $3,000 for a year in aftercare counseling, $1,500 for each inpatient detoxification attempt, and more than $20,000 a year to keep an addict in prison.

Nyswander describes "typical" behavior of their early addict-patients receiving from 110 mg to 180 mg of methadone a day:

> Striking alterations in behavior and appearance were taking place in the . . . patients. We sent them off to school, outside the hospital grounds. . . . [None] copped heroin on the outside. . . . they turned from slugabeds into dynamos of activity. . . . We found that methadone blocked out all other narcotics. They couldn't feel the effect of another narcotic when they were on methadone. Accordingly, there was no craving for heroin. We found out that methadone could be given only once per day. . . . As for tolerance, there was no escalation problem. The dosage remained stable. . . . Methadone had no deleterious effects anywhere.[7]

FAVORABLE RESULTS SPUR PROGRAM EXPANSION

In 1964 the Dole/Nyswander program had only twenty-two addict-patients enrolled. By 1965, with a grant from New York City, they expanded their outpatient maintenance project at the Morris J. Bernstein Institute of the Beth Israel Medical Center. It included an inpatient "induction center" and an outpatient maintenance clinic. By spring 1967 there were three methadone clinics in New York: Bernstein, Harlem Hospital, and Van Etten Hospital in the Bronx. About 350 outpatients were enrolled in them, with long waiting lists developing.

Initial reports[8] suggested that these early programs retained well over 90 percent of all addicts admitted to them, a dramatic reversal from the results of drug-free treatment modalities. Noting these impressive short-term results for the high-dose experimental program, in late 1967 New York City allocated enough money to treat 2,000 addicts with methadone. Other cities and states expressed increasing interest in the New York experiment. Nyswander called for rapid and massive program expansion outside the umbrella of a "research protocol" (which requires that dispensing agencies run elaborate research programs according to specified protocols) making the drug available to clinics which would function strictly as treatment programs.

HEROIN "BLOCKADE"

Dole was an aggressive public fighter determined to alleviate suffering among addicts. To get support for methadone maintenance, he deliberately turned to the popular media, giving interviews in *The New Yorker*. There were books written about him, and he made himself very accessible to journalists, making some nontechnical statements which attracted public attention to his and Nyswander's work.

One such statement was that methadone creates a physiologic "blockade" against the effects of heroin.[9] Nyswander also referred to "the methadone blockage procedure for treatment of heroin addiction. . . ."[10] This blockade supposedly extinguishes the desire to use heroin and makes addicts receptive to "rehabilitation." Others also commented on the drug's "blockade" abilities. Harvey Gollance, then associate director of Beth Israel Medical Center, noted: ". . . The methadone blockade against opiates frees the addict from his hunger so that he becomes receptive to rehabilitation."[11]

No Blockade

Methadone, however, *does not* physiologically block the effects of heroin or any other opiate. Dole, Nyswander and Gollance, among others, used the term "blockade" incorrectly. W. J. Russell Taylor, director of the Clinical Pharmacology and Toxicology Center at Philadelphia General Hospital, stated:

> Methadone has no blockade effect; it doesn't exist; pharmacologically it's not a truth. When you're talking to medical people and you put the word "blockade" beside the name of a drug, it should be used to mean an actual pharmacologic blockade.[12]

Methadone does produce what is called *cross-tolerance*. Methadone-tolerant addicts are not susceptible to the effects of *equal amounts* of other opiates. The methadone addict, however, can always use enough heroin to break through this cross-tolerance and achieve a greater "high." Larger dosages of heroin always bring on narcotic euphoria in the methadone addict, particularly if his methadone dosage is low (under 50 mg a day). Methadone itself produces a "high." Later, Dole said he should have used the correct term, cross-tolerance, rather than blockade, but that political persuasion was more important than scientific precision when he claimed in a scientific paper that methadone blocks the effects of heroin or other narcotics.

Dole's medical colleagues spotted this error and labeled his misrepresentation of methadone's blockage capabilities "sloppy reporting of medical research."[13] Jaffe himself wrote: "Pharmacologists are amazed by [Dole's use of] the term "blockade" because it is not the classical way to use it. It's actually cross-tolerance—induced reduction of effect."[14]

Narcotic antagonists do physiologically and pharmacologically block the effects of narcotics. These drugs, like cyclazocine, naltrexone and nalaxone, are unpopular with addicts, however, since they block the pleasurable effects that heroin users seek. The hope that antagonists would somehow become a workable "vaccine" against heroin addiction (their use was recommended in the early 1970s for grade school children in Harlem) vanished with the question: What addict would *want* an antagonist? Antagonists are therefore not widely used today in addiction treatment, except in emergency medical treatment of narcotic overdose.

PHARMACOLOGIC EFFECTS OF METHADONE MAINTENANCE

Smith and Bentel said that "Patients on regular doses of oral methadone are *virtually unimpaired* in physical and mental functioning [emphasis added]."[15] Kreek noted that ". . . after oral ingestion of methadone, no euphoria or narcotic effect is experienced. . . ."[16] Nyswander said methadone ". . . has no deleterious effects anywhere."[17]

A survey of the medical literature, however, indicates that these statements are incorrect. A growing body if evidence supports the conclusion that there *are* physiological side effects associated with methadone addiction, just as there are with addiction to heroin.[18] In fact, there are more pharmacological *similarities* than differences between methadone and heroin addiction.

SIDE EFFECTS OF METHADONE MAINTENANCE

Do toxic side effects accompany methadone maintenance? There is disagreement in the scientific literature on this point. Dole and Nyswander said, "Patients have shown no major ill effects from the use of methadone."[19] In one paper Kreek flatly stated that methadone maintenance is ". . . medically safe, with minimal side effects and with no toxicity."[20] But in another research paper she observed that:

> . . . side effects of methadone maintenance treatment . . . [include] euphoria or "high," drowsiness, somnolence, "nodding," constipation, excessive sweating, and insomnia . . . interference in sexual functioning and menstrual irregularities. [Other side effects include] edema, transient joint pains and swelling, upper gastrointestinal symptoms including pain, nausea, and vomiting, and bradycardia and hypotension. Transient skin rashes have [also] been reported.[21]

Are these *minimal* side effects?

My experience with over 2,000 methadone-maintained addicts indicates there *are* methadone side effects, and they closely resemble what Yaffe and others described in a clinical study of addict-patients in the St. Louis Methadone Program:

> Constipation was reported by 57% of all patients surveyed; excessive sweating, 47%; loss of interest in sex, 26%; nausea, 25%; sleepiness and drowsiness, 23%; insomnia, 23%; being jittery and tense, 23%; loss of appetite, 19%; headache, 12%; body aches and pains, 11%; and chills, 10%. Average severity ratings were all at or above the midpoint on a seven-point scale.[22]

Salmon and Schrier noted similar side effects including ". . . constipation, weight gain, decreased sexual desire and potency, dry mouth, persistent thirst, drowsiness, nasal catarrh and nervousness."[23] Cuskey, in a study of clients on methadone, reported that ". . . about 15% of addict patients developed minor side effects."[24]

Martin noted ". . . persistent physiological and metabolic changes associated with chronic methadone administration."[25]

Whether early "no side effect" reports were part of a snow job—an attempt to build broader support for maintenance therapy—or whether their conclusions were based on insufficient clinical experience with the drug, hard facts stand out: Methadone is not a simple "medicine," devoid of side effects. In sufficient doses it is a powerful narcotic whose effects are qualitatively and quantitatively similar to morphine and heroin, although oral administration delays onset of symptoms.

MIND-ALTERING EFFECTS OF METHADONE

Does methadone maintenance interfere with the client's ability to live what the average person would call a "normal" life? Is mental functioning of methadone addicts impaired to any degree? Dole reported that among methadone clients ". . . the cognitive and other emotional and intellectual faculties of the mind are normal."[26] Cushman testified in court that he had seen thousands of methadone maintenance clients, they were basically "indistinguishable" from "comparable non-drug people," and there is "no difference between a normal subject and the methadone-maintained patient after he has been stabilized on methadone."[27] Lowinson concluded that there ". . . is no way of distinguishing a person on methadone from a person who is not on methadone," and that a methadone addict ". . . is in no way changed, and is no different after he has taken his medication."[28] One doubts, however, whether these highly trained physicians have ever been on methadone maintenance.

I have found personally and other addicts have told me that the drug *does* change one's mood or sensations, just like any narcotic. It does produce a "high." The most prominent effects of methadone involve central nervous system depression. The principal pharmacological actions of methadone, like other opiates, are *analgesia* and *sedation*. In the tolerant addict, of course, these effects are less pronounced, but methadone does produce the long-lasting, slow-developing narcotic effect that is identified by addicts as a feeling of repose, suffusing warmth and relaxation. When administered parentally, methadone produces this effect immediately; taken orally, the onset is slower but basically the same.

"The behavior of the methadone addict," observes Jaffe, "is strikingly similar to that of the heroin addict."[29] William Burroughs, heir to the adding machine fortune and an old-time addict whose judgement on such matters is well informed, said ". . . methadone is completely satisfying to the addict, an excellent pain killer at least as addicting as morphine."[30]

Comparisons of Methadone and Morphine

Vogel and his colleagues reported that the "high" that methadone produces is" . . . equal to that of morphine, so that its habituation liability is high."[31] Julian Villarreal stated, "With regard to analgesic activity, methadone and morphine are practically equivalent in potency and duration."[32] Isbell described the behavior of hospitalized methadone addicts:

> The behavior of the men addicted to methadone was similar to the behavior seen during morphine addiction. The patients ceased all productive activity, neglected their persons and their quarters, and spent most of the time in bed in a semi-somnolent state which they regarded as very pleasurable. During addiction to methadone, patients continually required increased dosage.[33]

The early studies by Vogel and associates and Isbell, however, differed from Dole and Nyswander's later outpatient program. Isbell and Vogel and associates administered increasing doses of methadone over a very brief period to hospitalized subjects maintained under circumstances that might have caused them to become "stoned" more readily. This contrasts with the gradual dosage increase in Dole and Nyswander's outpatient program, in which the subjects were much more active than those in the Vogel and colleagues or Isbell studies.

Nevertheless, the Vogel/Isbell and the Dole/Nyswander groups disagree over whether or not:

1. Methadone maintenance creates the same escalation problem as heroin—addicts need more and more of the dιug to overcome tolerance (Vogel/Isabell yes; Dole/Nyswander no)
2. Methadone produces euphoria or "high" (Vogel/Isabell yes; Dole/Nyswander no)

3. Methadone produces side effects (Vogel/Isabell and many others yes; Dole/Nyswander no)

Who is correct? After exhaustive comparisons of the two drugs in an experimental setting, Isbell could only conclude that methadone addiction was *more debilitating* than morphine addiction:

> The degree of somnolence and lack of activity was greater [with methadone] than that seen during morphine addiction. The men complained about this, and said that while addicted to methadone, they could do little but stay in bed. . . . The patients stated . . . that when they were receiving morphine at least they thought they were ambitious, but when they were taking methadone they know that they were lazy.[34]

With these contradictory reports, based on personal experience with heroin, morphine and methadone (oral and injected), my conclusion is that methadone *does* get patients "loaded," although the degree of central nervous system depression and narcotic euphoria produced by methadone (and by other narcotics) is dependent on dosage and tolerance. Thus, there are many similarities between methadone and heroin addiction (given two pharmaceutically pure preparations administered in equivalent dosages at regular intervals). The main difference, it appears, is that methadone is legal and heroin is not.

METHADONE ABSTINENCE SYNDROME

What are the acute physiological and psychological effects of the methadone abstinence syndrome? Is it similar to heroin withdrawal? Personal experience with methadone withdrawal indicates it is qualitatively similar to heroin withdrawal and quantitatively more severe, although onset of symptoms is slower. Symptoms are the same as those experienced during heroin withdrawal: lightheadedness, dizziness, sedation, nausea, vomiting and sweating. Other reactions commonly include euphoria, dysphoria, weakness, headache, insomnia, agitation, disorientation and visual disturbances. Lipkowitz and his colleagues commented on experimental methadone withdrawal:

> Without the controls present in a prison setting such as the one in which these observations were made, there is little doubt that each of these men

[withdrawing from methadone addiction] would have made immediate attempts to acquire narcotics illicitly. Symptoms are severe: sweating, restlessness, lacrimation, muscle cramps, lightheadedness, dizziness, drowsiness, mental clouding, puruitis, nausea and vomiting.[35]

Severity of Methadone Withdrawal

Most addicts insist methadone abstinence syndrome is *more* severe than heroin withdrawal. The course of withdrawal from methadone, they contend, is more prolonged and painful because street heroin that addicts obtain is a low-dose (1 to 5 percent), adulterated substance used at irregular intervals. Clinic-supplied methadone, on the other hand, is a fairly high-dose pharmaceutical preparation ingested like clockwork at regular intervals. The result is that clinic methadone addicts literally are more "hooked" or "strung out" than street heroin addicts. Their withdrawal symptoms are consequently more severe.

OVERALL EFFECTS OF METHADONE MAINTENANCE

Methadone not only reduces heroin hunger. It affects respiration, digestion and sexual behavior. Like any opiate, it affects social and psychological behavior; it slows and reduces perception and responsiveness, reduces somatic and visceral sensations, and narrows the range of human experience.

Methadone affects not only the person taking it but everyone in close contact with him: children, spouse, parents and friends. Maintenance places those who share the social life of the addict in a relationship with an individual who uses a potent narcotic. The addict's family and associates thus live with the limitations in responsiveness, alertness and potential for feeling that the drug imposes on the methadone client.

NOTES

1. Marie E. Nyswander, "Methadone Therapy for Heroin Addiction: Where Are We Going?" *Drug Therapy* 12 (January 1971): 281.

2. Vincent P. Dole and Marie E. Nyswander, "Methadone Maintenance Treatment: A Ten-Year Perspective," *Journal of the American Medical Association* 235 (May 10, 1976): 2117.

3. Avram Goldstein made this statement, with Barry Brown, Jr., in their paper, "Urine Testing Schedules in Methadone Maintenance Treatment of Heroin Addiction," *Journal of the American Medical Association* 210 (October 12, 1970): 311.

4. The tendency for addicts to crave heroin and relapse after withdrawal is addressed in Perry M. Lichtenstein, "Narcotic Addiction," *New York Medical Journal* 100 (November 14, 1914): 962-66; Marie E. Nyswander, *The Drug Addict as Patient* (New York: Grune and Stratton, 1956); Isadore Chein et al., *The Road to H: Narcotics, Delinquency, and Social Policy* (New York: Basic Books, 1964); two books by Alfred R. Lindesmith, *The Addict and the Law* (Bloomington, Ind.: Indiana University Press, 1965), and *Addiction and Opiates* (Chicago: Aldine Publishing Co., 1968); Edward M. Brecher and Consumer Reports Editors, *Licit and Illicit Drugs* (Boston: Little, Brown and Co., 1972); and, finally, T. S. MacDonough, "The Validity of Self-Recording Reports Made by Drug and Alcohol Abusers in a Residential Setting," *International Journal of the Addictions* 11 (June 1976): 447-66.

5. See Robert L. DuPont, "Coming to Grips With an Urban Heroin Addiction Epidemic," *Journal of the American Medical Association* 223 (January 1, 1973): 46-48.

6. Dole and Nyswander laid out this "metabolic" theory in their paper, "Heroin Addiction: A Metabolic Disease," *Archives of Internal Medicine* 120 (July 1967): 19-24.

7. Nyswander is quoted in Nat Hentoff's biography of her entitled *A Doctor Among the Addicts* (New York: Grove Press, 1968), pp. 114-15.

8. Glowing retention data are reported in a series of papers by Vincent P. Dole and Marie E. Nyswander, including "A Medical Treatment for Diacetylmorphine ('Heroin') Addiction," *Journal of the American Medical Association* 193 (August 23, 1965): 646-50; "Rehabilitation of Heroin Addicts After Blockade with Methadone," *New York State Journal of Medicine 66* (April 1966): 2011–17; "Heroin Addiction: A Metabolic Disease," 19-24; and "Successful Treatment of 750 Criminal Drug Addicts," *Journal of the American Medical Association* 206 (December 16, 1968): 2711.

9. Dole and Nyswander, "Rehabilitation of Heroin Addicts After Blockade with Methadone," 2011-12.

10. Quoted in Hentoff, *Doctor Among the Addicts*, p. 123.

11. Harvey Gollance, "Methadone Maintenance Treatment Program," *Maryland State Medical Journal* 19 (November 1970): 74.

12. Taylor is quoted in "Methadone Maintenance: How Much, For Whom, for How Long?" *Medical World News* (March 17, 1972), p. 55.

13. Avram Goldstein blasts Dole's use of the term "blockade" in his paper, "Methadone Blockade," *Journal of the American Medical Association* 219 (March 6, 1972): 1276-77.

14. "Methadone Maintenance: How Much, for How Long?" p. 55.

15. David E. Smith and David J. Bentel, *Drug Abuse Information Project: Fourth Annual Report to the Legislature* (Sacramento, Calif: Drug Abuse Information Project, 1970), p. 40.

16. Mary Jeanne Kreek, "Physiological Implications of Methadone Treatment," in *Fifth National Conference on Methadone Treatment: Proceedings, 1973*, ed. National Association for the Prevention of Addiction to Narcotics (New York: National Association for the Prevention of Addiction to Narcotics, 1973), p. 827.

17. Nyswander, "Methadone Therapy for Heroin Addiction," p. 23.

18. On the toxic side effects of methadone maintenance, see Sidney Salmon and Robert W. Schrier, "Medical Staff Conference: Medical Complications of Heroin Addiction," *California Medicine* 115 (November 1971): 42-50; Walter R. Cuskey, "Methadone Use in the Outpatient Treatment of Narcotic Addicts," *Bulletin on Narcotics* 23 (July-September 1971): 23-30; and G. Jon Yaffe, Richard W. Strelinger and S. Parwatikar, "Physical Symptom Complaints of Patients on Methadone Maintenance," in *Fifth National Conference*, ed. National Association for the Prevention of Addiction to Narcotics, pp. 507-14.

19. Dole and Nyswander, "A Medical Treatment for Addiction," p. 646.

20. Mary Jeanne Kreek, "Medical Safety and Side Effects of Methadone in Tolerant Individuals," *Journal of the American Medical Association* 223 (February 5, 1973): 668.

21. Kreek, "Physiological Implications of Methadone Treatment," pp. 827-28.

22. Yaffe et al., "Physical Symptom Complaints of Patients on Methadone," p. 510.

23. Salmon and Schrier, "Medical Complications of Addiction," p. 47.

24. Cuskey, "Methadone Use in Outpatient Treatment," p. 507.

25. William D. Martin, "Commentary on the Second National Conference on Methadone Treatment," *International Journal of the Addictions* 5 (September 1970): 548.

26. Dole is quoted in Thomas P. Griesa, "Carl Beazer v. New York City Transit Authority," *Contemporary Drug Problems* 4 (Fall 1975): 361.

27. Cushman's testimony is quoted in ibid., p. 362.

28. Lowinson quoted in ibid.

29. Jerome H. Jaffe, "Narcotic Analgesics," in *The Pharmacologic Basis of Therapeutics*, 3rd ed., ed. L. S. Goodman and A. Gilman (New York: The Macmillan Co., 1965), p. 247.

30. William S. Burroughs, *Naked Lunch* (New York: Grove Press, 1959), p. 241.

31. Victor H. Vogel, Harris Isbell and K. W. Chapman, "The Present Status of Narcotics Addiction," *Journal of the American Medical Association* 138 (December 4, 1948): 1019.

32. Julian E. Villarreal, "Recent Advances in the Pharmacology of Morphine-Like Drugs," in *Drug Dependence*, ed. Robert T. Harris, William M. McIsaac and Charles R. Schuster, Jr. (Austin, Texas: University of Texas Press, 1970), p. 89.

33. Harris Isbell, "Methods and Results of Studying Experimental Human Addiction to the Newer Analgesics," *Annals of the New York Academy of Sciences* 51 (October 1, 1948): 112.

34. Harris Isbell, "Liability of Addiction of 6-dimethyl-amino-4-4-diphenyl-3-heptanone (Methadone, 'Amidone,' or '10920') in Man: Experimental Addiction to Methadone," *Archives of Internal Medicine* 82 (October 1948): 362.

35. Marvin Lipkowitz, Daniel Schastz and Robert Lazarus, "Abrupt Withdrawal of Maintenance Methadone," *Journal of the American Medical Association* 217 (September 27, 1971): 1861.

4

The Politics of Methadone Maintenance

How, for the first time since the famous morphine maintenance clinics of the 1920s, did legal narcotic maintenance reemerge on a large scale in the United States? In addition to crime, addiction and Vietnam, what factors accounted for this turnabout?

SUPPORT BY OFFICIAL SPOKESMEN

Support by medicine's research community was critical for implementing methadone maintenance on a large scale. New York physicians took an early lead in promoting methadone maintenance in the 1950s. It was estimated that there were more addicts in New York than any other city in the world. This may have given New York physicians a special familiarity with the multiple dimensions of the heroin problem. Many doctors dealt daily with narcotic-related overdose and other medical complications caused by unsterile paraphernalia and adulterated heroin, maladies like talc granulomatosis, subacute bacterial endocarditis, hepatitis and microangiopathic hemolytic anemia.[1]

In 1954 the New York State Medical Association, which had called for closing the New York City Narcotics Clinic in the early 1920s, recommended that methadone clinics be established under auspices of the Federal Bureau of Narcotics of the U.S. Department of Justice. Under the New York Medical Association's scheme, methadone would be supplied to addicts at low cost under a rigid, federally controlled dispensing system. In 1962 the New York

County Medical Society decreed that doctors working in methadone clinics were definitely practicing "ethical" medicine.[2] For the first time in nearly sixty years organized medicine was speaking out in support of legal narcotic maintenance. This turnabout was significant because it gave medical/scientific legitimacy to government methadone maintenance policy, thus easing public acceptance of it.

THE CONCEPT OF DRUG ADDICT AS PATIENT

In her 1956 book, *The Drug Addict as Patient*, Nyswander said that the only way physicians could ever hope to get addicts to come to them rather than to pushers for help was to offer them dope. Nyswander hammered home two themes in her book: (1) There were no significant differences between the personalities of heroin addicts and nonaddicts; the differences were "metabolic"; and (2) the punitive, criminal approach to addiction had failed and was wrong.

Nyswander's was the first book of its kind since the criminalization of heroin following the Harrison Act. The book was part of her campaign to dissolve addict stereotypes common among medical professionals and laymen. She said addicts were not fiends and dangerous people, but passive individuals who cannot tolerate pain. Why else would they self-medicate with a powerful painkiller like heroin? Her book, she wrote ". . . helped pave the way. If only in terms of its title. The idea was gotten across that drug addicts can be a patient rather than a 'fiend' or an outcast. The book helped hospital people feel easier—some of them anyway— about assuming responsibility in the treatment of addicts."[3]

Nyswander's book was part of a larger and laudable attempt to transform addiction from a moral or criminal problem into a medical/scientific one, amenable to therapy. The contemporary policy approach to the "heroin problem" is dominated by the *criminal* and *medical* models. The criminal model assumes that supplies of the drug can be reduced through the criminal law and its enforcement by the judicial system. The medical model, on the other hand, argues that addicts rather than requiring punishment are *sick*, either physically, psychologically or socially and therefore require treatment, which if successful will "rehabilitate" them and reduce overall demand for heroin. The basic theme of the medical model and its sociological formulation is the "addict as victim."

The transition from the criminal model of heroin addiction to the medical/scientific one espoused by Nyswander paralleled similar redefinitions of alcoholism,[4] insanity,[5] and juvenile delinquency.[6] Liberals like Nyswander offered the medical interpretation of addiction to policymakers as a step forward into an Age of Reason.

SUPPORT BY THE LEGAL ESTABLISHMENT

Many attorneys and judges wholeheartedly joined the demand for government sponsored methadone maintenance clinics. The American Bar Association recommended ". . . an experimental clinic for the outpatient [methadone] treatment of drug addicts. [The ABA/AMA Joint Committee] should consider supplying the addict with sufficient drugs for his needs, so that he does not have to patronize the illicit peddler."[7]

In June 1964 the Advisory Council of Judges of the National Council on Crime and Delinquency endorsed the medical model of addiction when it labeled the addict:

> . . . a *sick* person, physically and psychologically, and as such entitled to qualified medical attention just as are other *sick* people. As a *sick* person, the addict should receive whatever medical care he may need, as an outpatient of a clinic or private physicians or, when necessary, in a hospital.[8]

The kind of "qualified medical attention" the judges alluded to was methadone maintenance. Their reference to addicts as "sick" people was a reiteration of the classic medical position stated by the U.S. Supreme Court in *Linder* v. *United States* (1925) that addicts were diseased and proper subjects for medical treatment. Thus, the legal profession, familiar with narcotics cases, added its imprimateur to the medical model of addiction and massive methadone maintenance as proper therapy.

By 1965 the National Council of Churches prayed that the federal government would give doctors "full power to determine the appropriate treatment of addicts."[9] Methadone maintenance was even becoming the forlorn hope of organized religion.

PROMOTION BY THE LIBERAL PRESS AND SOCIAL SCIENTISTS

The liberal image of the heroin user in the 1950s and 1960s was one of "addict as victim."[10] In this view, only by providing narcotics to this "victimized" minority, either free or at cost, could crime and addiction be contained.

SOCIAL SCIENTIFIC SUPPORT IN LIBERAL OPINION JOURNALS

In response to the criminal model of addiction, liberal newspapers like *The New York Times* and journals of opinion such as *The Nation* and *The New Republic* turned toward the idea of large-scale methadone maintenance in the 1950s and 1960s.

Alfred Lindesmith

Alfred Lindesmith was an especially articulate social scientist backing methadone maintenance. His continuing series over an eight-year period in *The Nation* on the epidemiology and public policy of heroin prompted discussion about the comparative costs and benefits of methadone maintenance. In a 1956 article in *The Nation* he argued that ". . . the black market and the criminal tieups with drugs should be undermined by legal clinical dispensation of narcotics."[11]

Always taking the medical model as his springboard, Lindesmith termed addiction an "illness," labeling addicts "sick." To him, heroin addiction was a "medical problem," a "disease" characterized by the tendency to relapse to heroin use after withdrawal. His reading of the problem was similar to Dole/Nyswander's "metabolic theory." The orthodox insistence on abstinence from heroin as a treatment goal, he said, was not only unobtainable but also unnecessary with methadone in the chemotherapeutic armamentarium.

The Nation, which carried Lindesmith's series, noted in 1970 that:

> Most important is [methadone's] capacity to block the effect of heroin and other opiates. . . . if the addict takes a shot of heroin [while on methadone,] he feels nothing. And unlike heroin, methadone does not give the

user a "high." An addict on methadone can function normally. He is as alert as anyone who is drug-free. He can hold a job, support his family, in every way live a normal life.[12]

The New York Times

The New York Times, a respected early supporter of methadone maintenance, called society's prevailing approach to addiction in the 1950s and 1960s "barbaric"[13] and "uncivilized."[14] In editorials, the *Times* conveyed the medical impression that addicts were "sick," not criminal, and that the appropriate forms of social intervention should be "medical" rather than "punitive." Their editorials carried titles like "Drugs a Medical Problem"[15] and, borrowing from Nyswander, "Drug Addicts as Patients."[16] The paper cried out for immediate distribution of methadone to addicts, under strict medical-governmental controls: "The best hope for smashing the illicit traffic in narcotics lies in the dispensing of [methadone] under medical controls—particularly . . . in needy sections of the city."[17]

The More Conservative Press

Even the not-so-liberal press supported methadone maintenance. In California, the *Long Beach Independent Press-Telegram*, not known for radical stands on social issues, jousted with the local police department over the pros and cons of methadone therapy and editorialized "The Case for Methadone":

> Certainly, treating heroin addiction purely as a police problem has been ineffective in this century. The U.S. is the only western nation that does not use maintenance techniques for addicts. Methadone offers this city and society as a whole a chance to hit the narcotic peddlers where it hurts—by taking away their customers.[18]

Similarily, an article in *Look* depicted methadone as a "Cinderella drug" that induces "miracle change" in heroin addicts, explaining that "a teaspoon of [the] medicine taken daily in a cup of juice is changing former dope addicts into decent law-abiding men."[19]

Misrepresentations of the Facts

Even the more sophisticated newspapers, opinion journals, legal and social science advocates, let alone magazines like *Look* and *The Reader's Digest*, failed to examine carefully the basic pharmacology and toxicology of methadone maintenance. Nor did they know the effects of an impersonal clinic system for dispensing or whether heroin addiction is really a disease amenable to a public policy/chemotherapeutic solution. Most written pieces left the average reader with the false impression that methadone was some kind of magic bullet the government could use to solve the heroin problem, a benign medicine like penicillin, not a synthetic heroin substitute as powerful and addicting as the street drug it was supposed to replace. Both mass circulation journals and opinion leaders in America led millions of people throughout the United States and the world to believe that the menace of heroin addiction was now comparable to that posed by poliomyelitis after vaccination with the scrupulously tested Salk vaccine.

THE ROLE OF THE WHITE HOUSE DOMESTIC COUNCIL

Thus, many physicians, legal experts, social scientists and the news media supported Nixon's choice to offer maintenance as the final solution to the heroin problem. Inside the White House itself, where the official decision to support maintenance would have to be made, Nixon's new Domestic Council and its Drug Abuse Task Force took the lead in promoting methadone. The Domestic Council also touted maintenance therapy to executive branch agencies, Congress and the media.

John Ehrlichman created the Domestic Council as the base for his personal fiefdom and as a counter to the former Bureau of the Budget (now the Office of Management and Budget), which he regarded as a nest of bureaucrats who would do anything in their considerable power to sabotage the aims of the Nixon presidency. Under Ehrlichman, the Domestic Council staff supervised the workings and often dictated the policies of the principal domestic federal departments.[20]

Mass methadone maintenance, as opposed to principal reliance on drug-free therapy, was supported in a 1970 Domestic Council Summary Option Paper. It described the optimum policy choice available to Nixon:

> Mayor Lindsay has recently announced a $4.4 million methadone [maintenance] program in NYC. . . . If methadone does prove to be successful in New York on a large scale, Lindsay can claim credit for taking a bold step while the [Nixon] Administration remained cautiously skeptical. . . .
>
> In 1972 citizens will be looking at crime statistics across the nation in order to see whether expectations raised in 1968 have been met. *The federal government has only one economical and effective technique for reducing crime in the streets—methadone maintenance.*[21] [Emphasis added]

Based on the advice of experts and support in the media, the Nixon administration addiction treatment strategy evolved into principal reliance on maintenance as the most efficacious treatment weapon against heroin addiction *and* street crime. In June 1970 after a whirlwind tour of local methadone treatment programs in New York City and Chicago, SAODAP Assistant Jeffrey Donfeld composed a sixteen-page memorandum for President Nixon with the catchy title, "Different Strokes for Different Folks." In it Donfeld, Krogh's man at SAODAP, argued that treating heroin addicts was a *"virgin yet fertile area for . . . political gain."*[22] (Emphasis added)

MOUNTING CRITICISM

Ten years before Nixon assumed the presidency, Ploscowe warned that there would be ". . . violent opposition to plans for legalizing the distribution of narcotics to confirmed addicts."[23] Donfeld recognized this and cautioned that the "political price" of methadone maintenance would be escalated by blacks claiming the government ". . . was trying to addict them. If it were middle-America that were hooked on heroin the government would sponsor group therapy, not narcotic maintenance."[24] According to the Domestic Council, however, crime reduction was more important than the ". . . inevitable outcry from some people . . . that the Administration is subjugating the black addict to the white man's opiate. . . ."[25]

The Charges Against Methadone

Criticism of implementing massive methadone maintenance centered along two lines. First, disproportionate numbers of methadone maintenance clients were young, black and poor.[26] A number of blacks and Hispanics charged that this treatment was just one more weapon of the white power structure used to pacify potentially rebellious minorities in inner-city areas. Critics were quick to point out that growth in federal support for methadone maintenance coincided with the ghetto urban uprisings of the late 1960s, accounting for the "pacification" charge.

The second criticism of maintenance policy was that substituting methadone for heroin was no better than an alcoholic switching from scotch to bourbon—one was as bad as the other; legal addiction may be no better than illegal addiction.[27] This moral argument ("simple substitution") was important to politicians, the clergy, the public and some physicians, particularly doctors with a vested interest in government-funded, drug-free treatment clinics. The Nixon administration would have to answer the criticism that morally, methadone maintenance was as indefensible as heroin addiction[28] and that methadone maintenance clients were no more than ". . . basket cases walking around in an emotional fog without will."[29]

These issues—the pacification charge and the moral argument—had to be neutralized before Congress would fund an expanded methadone maintenance treatment capacity. One way neutralization was achieved was through the Nixon administration's reliance on "multi-modality" rhetoric stressing the availability of drug-free treatment alternatives, in addition to narcotic maintenance.

Criticism of methadone maintenance by some black citizens was especially vehement. Charges began flying that methadone was no more than a chemical tool of the white "power structure" designed to control a large pool of unemployed, potentially rebellious, disadvantaged blacks and latinos. It was true that in large eastern and middle western cities—New York, Washington, D.C., Detroit, Chicago, Philadelphia and St. Louis—most addicts identified by criminal justice system and treatment agencies were black. DuPont and Katon estimated in 1971 that of 17,000 presumed addicts in

Washington, D.C., 91 percent were black.[30] Dupont concluded: ". . . opiate addiction is concentrated in the lower social classes. In Washington, D.C., only about 4 percent of our patients [on methadone maintenance] are white, which means that there is an underrepresentation of whites in our patient group."[31]

Harvey Gollance, speaking for the Beth Israel Medical Center's Methadone Maintenance Program in New York City, which treated thousands of addict-patients on methadone, said in 1971 that the clientele of his program was 50 percent black, 25 percent Puerto Rican, and only 25 percent white.[32] Prior to 1977 the race/ethnic distribution for all clients admitted to both the Beth Israel program and New York City's Methadone Maintenance Treatment Program was 40 percent black, 25 percent Hispanic, 34 percent white and 1 percent Chinese.[33]

Bertram Brown, former director of NIMH, reported that "patients being treated [on methadone maintenance] in community centers [all across the nation] are over ⅔ black or chicano."[34] In St. Louis in 1976 where 41 percent of the city's 600,000 population was black, the methadone maintenance program was 85 percent black.[35]

In California, "The patients in community [maintenance] treatment centers are over ⅔ Black or chicano."[36] The same holds true in Arizona, Texas, New Mexico and Colorado.[37] I surveyed admissions to a large methadone maintenance program in southern California and found chicanos disproportionately represented. While in 1970 Hispanics constituted less than 15 percent of San Bernardino County's population, 75 percent of the methadone maintenance clients enrolled in the county's Ontario facility in 1975 were Hispanic.[38]

At the 1971 Annual Conference on Methadone Maintenance Treatment, an incensed splinter group separated itself from the promaintenance majority and charged that:

1. The white "power structure" encourages methadone maintenance because it affects mainly those who have the most to gain from "revolution," weakening their will to resist "illegitimate authority";

2. Methadone maintenance programs expose clients to constant surveillance. Since methadone is highly addictive, addicts on the programs remain under "life-long government supervision";
3. The "ruling class" gains more from methadone maintenance than the addict-patient. In this view, a methadone client need not steal, so the establishment's property is safe. Property values replace the human value of restoring addicts to "dignified participation in society." Methadone maintenance is no more than a political response to the demand that addicts be taken off the streets and out of the public's pockets, purses and dresser drawers.[39]

The implication of this argument was that elites in power have much to gain from methadone maintenance. Just as relief giving turned out to be the most expeditious way to deal with political pressures created by dislocated poor,[40] methadone giving was equated with the same technique. Methadone, it was argued, would make depressed groups oblivious to the miserable realities of their existence. James Baldwin always maintained that what kept Harlem quiet for so many years was a "combination of Jesus and junk." Kenneth Clark found that "many ghetto dwellers become heroin addicts because they see few alternatives. Living under conditions of great emotional, spiritual, and/or economic deprivation, these individuals view reality as being extremely painful."[41]

Without delving into the multiple etiological factors behind heroin addiction, the implication is that if Washington and Wall Street could not rely on heroin or methadone to cool things down, they would have many more angry people on their hands.

CONGRESSIONAL EXCHANGES ON RACIAL OPPRESSION THROUGH METHADONE

Congress was particularly sensitive to the racial oppression issue. Then–Senator Harold Hughes (D–Iowa) worried about black criticism of federally sponsored methadone maintenance programs:

> We get a lot of criticism from blacks about methadone. I had several witnesses testify from Harlem that they felt [maintenance] was a part of a

conspiracy to simply get more blacks on methadone and get a new narcotic introduced into the black community. . . . There is a feeling in the community that [maintenance] is actually a conspiracy to destroy the black man and the Spanish Americans involved.[42]

Arnold Boyce, a black physician in Harlem, was one of the critics:

Methadone is another addictive drug, and if we . . . implement the program . . . all I can see is that we are leading to genocide of poor and innocent people, particularly genocide of people who live in communities like Harlem.[43]

I studied over 10,000 pages of congressional hearing testimony and noted the following exchanges between Congressman Rangel (a black), Senator Hughes (a recovered alcoholic), and Vincent P. Dole and Jerome Jaffe, two government-backed scientific proponents of large-scale methadone maintenance:[44]

Mr. Rangel: I am wondering, Dr. Jaffe, if a different economic group were afflicted by a similar type of disease, whether or not we would be talking about making methadone so available as a possible cure to disease or whether or not there would be a concentration of research rather than just expansion of methadone programs . . . the best thing American research has come up with yet has been methadone; is that your professional opinion?

Dr. Jaffe: Well, for large-scale operation, yes.[45]

Mr. Rangel: Don't you believe it would be different if we were dealing with a more affluent group? We find many distinguished doctors proudly saying that we have community people in charge of community programs to dispense methadone to community victims. I suggest . . . that this would not be the case if the victims were more affluent. . . . I suggest that America would do what it has always done in fighting disease, and that is to mobilize the scientific resources to treat it as a national problem, and to come up with some viable answers.

Sen. Hughes: Dr. Dole, in your opinion, how valid is the concern expressed by Congressman Rangel that methadone maintenance is an effort by medicine and by doctors to make our black population drug addicts on methadone rather than truly fighting the heroin problem?

Dr. Dole: It is totally wrong. Probably the people who would speak most vigorously to the wrongness of that statement are the black addicts themselves. For many black addicts in Harlem this treatment has been the one opportunity they have to become self-respecting, decent citizens.[46]

Defending methadone maintenance against minority group criticism, Dole continued:

> Militant members of some minority groups view methadone [maintenance] as simply another means by which our predominantly white society can keep minority groups from getting completely free. In reality, methadone [maintenance] is probably one of the most useful tools by which minority group members who are presently "hooked" on heroin will ever get free. The reality of the situation is this: the great majority of heroin addicts, both white and minority group, would never get away from heroin without something like methadone [maintenance]. Rather than being viewed as just another means of keeping minority members down, methadone maintenance should probably be seen as a good way to allow them to move up and away from heroin, the thing that is presently keeping them down.[47]

Some black treatment professionals defend methadone maintenance. Beny J. Prim, a physician, said he *could* use methadone as a "political tool" but does not. "There are many devious ways one could use it [methadone maintenance]. It is quite possible. But I don't think it is being done. And I don't think our government is involved in any conspiracy of that nature."[48] Prim said that as a black man, his own decision to support maintenance treatment of addicts had caused him personal torment. He underwent, he says, "a great deal of mild crucifixion" and was labeled, among other things, a "handkerchief-head black and a nigger" for supporting methadone maintenance. Charles J. Burks, a Pittsburgh black physician, said that "methadone maintenance is by far the most practical [therapy] for the needs of our [black] community."[49]

Other minority physicians, however, continued to articulate their criticisms before Congress. Efrem Ramirez, former commissioner of New York City's huge Addiction Services Agency, testified that from a doctor's standpoint giving methadone is:

> . . . like saying, "we don't care what happens to you; just don't steal from me." That's why this goddamned thing [maintenance] is so popular. Because it strikes a chord. . . . It is a simple solution, people think, to a complex problem; very attractive. Well, the problem is much deeper than that.[50]

Daniel Casriel, another physician and director of a drug-free residential treatment program in New York City, told Congress that methadone maintenance was medical malpractice:

> While it is true that methadone [maintenance] will prevent stealing, it doesn't cure [the addict's] personality. No chemical does . . . to maintain a person with a symptom, by a change of the drug heroin to methadone, is to me malpractice.[51]

Senator Hughes then asked Casriel if he thought there was any place at all for methadone maintenance in the federal government's rapidly expanding addiction treatment armamentarium. Casriel replied:

> [Methadone maintenance] is a temporary expediency and I think if we put our money and our investment in methadone as the answer, we will create more and more problems. I am utterly and completely opposed to the . . . use of methadone [maintenance] as a treatment for drug addiction. I feel we are opening a Pandora's box.[52]

DOLE ON THE SUBSTITUTION ARGUMENT

In the midst of this critical hearing testimony, the Nixon administration played its trump card: the testimony of Vincent Dole at the hearings. Many times Dole had faced the argument that giving methadone to addicts was just like an alcoholic substituting bourbon for scotch. Dole posed the rhetorical question himself: "Since methadone is itself a narcotic, isn't the methadone approach merely shifting the patient's addiction from one drug to another?"[53]

Dole, an articulate and experienced spokesman for methadone maintenance, outlined to listening congressmen the dramatic differences, as he saw them, between heroin and methadone addiction, and shifted narcotic maintenance from a moral to a medical/scientific context:

> The differences between the two drugs is like the difference between night and day. Heroin is a drug which must be taken intravenously, demands increasing doses to produce the same effect, has serious side effects, and interferes markedly with the patient's ability to function normally. Methadone is a drug which can be taken orally, does not require continually increasing doses for the same effect, has no serious side effects and does not interfere with the patient's ability to live a normal life. Therefore, to equate methadone with heroin use is rather unfair; one is a dangerous, euphoria-producing, illegal injectable drug; the other is a medication given under a physician's direction.[54]

Dole's comments might have been criticized on several points. First, the most serious effects of heroin use may not be caused by heroin itself, but rather by the criminalization of heroin. Dole himself admitted, for example, that "Cigarette smoking is unquestionably more damaging to the human body than heroin."[55] Second, chronic methadone administration *does* result in toxic side effects and *does* affect one's ability to live a "normal life." Further, methadone *does* induce euphoria, even in tolerant addicts. While addicted to heroin, for example, I used methadone both orally and by injection and found it produced the same pleasant somnolence as heroin. None of the congressmen to whom he was speaking, however, had either the knowledge or temerity to engage Dole or other scientists in debate over the comparative benefits of methadone over heroin addiction.

Just as a whole set of new terms and compact little lies were used to blunt the impact of the Vietnam War on the American conscience ("routine, limited duration, reinforced protective reaction air strike," "anti-personnel device," and so on), so methadone became simply "medication" and dope fiends "patients" in a similar euphemization process. This helped catapult maintenance therapy into the forefront as the most rational approach to rampant heroin addiction. To ease public and political acceptance of methadone maintenance, medical experts emphasized that regular, oral doses of methadone would place the addict in the socially acceptable position of a "patient" taking a "prescribed medication" under a "physician's prescription." No longer would he be in the surreptitous role of an outcast "dope fiend shooting junk." Said Dole, "We have to convert the addict to a patient, with all that implies."[56] Dole was sincere and a real humanist. Recently he wrote, "The most important item not mentioned in my curriculum vitae is my great debt to Marie Nyswander, my close professional associate and my wife. She taught me how to see addicts as patients and not simply as problems."[57]

Slowly, Congress and the media were moved toward accepting the arguments of the scientific community and the Nixon administration for the dispensing of methadone to heroin addicts on a large scale at taxpayers' expense.

THE IMPACT OF SCIENTIFIC KNOWLEDGE: WHERE POLITICS AND EVALUATION RESEARCH MEET

To whom, then, did federal policymakers turn for advice on the methadone maintenance issue? What was the extent of the scientific contribution to the policy formulation process? Blum maintained that when it comes to narcotic control policy, the sources legislators consider most reliable and trustworthy are physicians. Doctors—especially the ever-hovering representatives of organized medicine—more than anyone else most often receive a respectful hearing.[58] Physicians are held in high esteem by the public and command greater access to decisionmakers. As a consequence, physicians are more likely than others to receive attention from decisionmakers who seek advice on addiction treatment strategies. My research on the formulation of addiction treatment policy during the Nixon era confirms Blum's results: It was (and remains) physicians, biochemists, pharmacologists and, to a less extent, academic social scientists who were heeded most frequently by federal decisionmakers considering treatment policy choices. Their viewpoints have thus become important weapons in the power struggles both within and between addiction treatment policies and programs.

Research Utilization

If scientific research results agree with their predetermined ideological preferences, policymakers use them; if not, they note only the research that does fit their preconceptions. Carol Weiss says that:

> The most common use of research in government decision making is probably as support and ammunition for a predetermined position. The advocates of a position latch on to research conclusions that legitimate their case and strengthen their bargaining power.[59]

This is exactly the situation with research on the effectiveness of various addiction treatment strategies: Reports by scientists that demonstrate "success" are cited and used repeatedly by decision-makers to legitimate their predetermined positions, while studies showing program "failure" are neglected or ignored. Thus, pro-methadone physicians and scientists replaced the seers of old with ostensibly objective medical/scientific readings of the signs, however flawed they were. Represented in 10,000 pages of legislative hearing testimony on addiction control strategies, for example, were multiple studies inserted in the record to show how "successful" methadone maintenance was, but not one report critical of this therapy or questioning its efficacy.

"Mixed Modality" Rhetoric

To counter criticism that the federal government was relying principally on methadone maintenance to curb demand for heroin, Donfeld, who had no background in addiction treatment or experience with addicts (his main claim to fame was being an ex-UCLA student body president), skillfully recommended clothing methadone maintenance in "multi-modality" rhetoric to avoid further criticism from anti-methadone forces:

> There are a number of sound reasons for describing any new drug rehabilitation initiative . . . in terms of a multi-modality approach rather than a methadone maintenance approach. . . . Implicit in the multi-modality approach is the notion that we are still searching for effective techniques to rehabilitate. . . .[60]

Countering Criticism from within the Federal Establishment

Donfeld and the Domestic Council also had to undermine or discredit whatever reservations executive branch agencies themselves had about a massive federally sponsored methadone maintenance scheme.

Donfeld cast doubt on the objectivity of NIMH, for example, which argued that by dispensing methadone, government is sanctioning one addiction over another to reduce the burden on society of heroin addiction. Bertram Brown, then director of NIMH, told Congress that ". . . the exact degree of safety and efficacy of methadone maintenance treatment is unknown at this time.[61] Donfeld and others suspected NIMH of being oriented in favor of psychotherapy. If NIMH endorsed chemotherapy with methadone, it would be an admission that psychiatry had failed to deal successfully with addicts.

Similarly, the Food and Drug Administration (FDA), which objected to maintenance because researchers there felt that the long-term physiological effects of maintenance were not known, was attacked by Donfeld for its bureaucratic inertia: "FDA bureaucrats . . . are arrogant egocentrics, incensed at anyone who questions their research [which was inconclusive regarding long-term effects of chronic methadone use]."[62]

Finally, Donfeld challenged the argument of the old BNDD that methadone would inevitably be diverted out of the clinics and into the streets for illicit use:

> Even if heroin addicts were to obtain supplies of methadone [illegally], society is not hurt in a direct way because methadone will help sustain an addict until he can get his next heroin fix. The addict will have less compulsion to commit crimes to obtain money to buy that fix.[63]

Convincing President Nixon

Donfeld, Egil "Bud" Krogh and the Domestic Council made sure that the message the president got was that ". . . methadone maintenance programs . . . significantly reduce arrest and crime rates with large economic benefits as a consequence.[64] Ironically although Nixon ultimately lent his wholehearted support to methadone maintenance and surrounded himself with promaintenance narcotic policy advisors, staffers had some difficulty convincing him that maintenance should be the lead modality in his therapeutic war on heroin. Krogh recalls that:

> With the President as well as Mr. Mitchell [at Justice] and Mr. Richardson [at HEW] there was a basic hostility to developing a [maintenance] program. The President in fact expressed himself that methadone was, if anything, more dangerous than heroin itself. . . . There was at first quite a strong feeling that the government should not be funding drug addiction. . . . It took some time to persuade both Mr. Mitchell and John Ehrlichman . . . that it was better to have a person on methadone maintenance . . . than to have him on the streets using heroin. . . . I think there was a feeling that it was moving too fast and more time was necessary to study the effectiveness of [methadone maintenance]. Nevertheless, *we became persuaded based upon expert opinions of Dr. Jaffe and others, that it was a doable program,* that it could be on line within a year, and that some very direct results could be presented to the President in time for the 1972 election.[65] [Emphasis added].

So Nixon, unsure at first, was ultimately convinced that methadone maintenance was the optimum policy strategy in terms of addiction treatment, and that it could be deftly incorporated into a "multi-modality" lexicon. In this way he could avoid charges that the federal government had given up on a "cure" and was simply preparing to hand out free dope to addicts at taxpayers' expense.

WINNING THE WAR ON HEROIN

There was great to-do and publicity in 1972, just in time for the election, as "the tide of heroin addiction" apparently "began to turn."[66] The Turkish opium ban, arranged by Nixon in 1971, seemed to have had some effect, mainly on the East Coast where a few heroin shortages developed in early 1973. Massive seizures of heroin, publicized as the "shutting down of the French Connection," etched on the public consciousness the image of an unmerciful law-and-order administration. A motion picture was released entitled "Panic in Needle Park."

Nixon proclaimed that the "corner has been turned." On March 21, 1972, he declared that ". . . we are having some success in the war on heroin."[67] In 1973 DuPont and Greene noted that ". . . the epidemic is ending."[68] Jaffe said in April 1973 that ". . . as far as heroin is concerned, the worst is over."[69]

DIP IN CRIME

Coincident with the apparent reduction in heroin abuse, crime rates decreased somewhat. In 1971, for instance, "serious" crime rose only 6 percent above 1970, while serious crime had risen 10 percent in 1970 over 1969. In 1972 there was a 4 percent *decrease* in serious crime nationwide, ". . . the first such decline in 17 years."[70]

Although crime statistics such as these are notoriously slippery, inaccurate and self-serving, most experts attributed the apparent decrease in 1972 to two factors: (1) better drug law enforcement, and (2) expanded methadone maintenance and drug-free addiction treatment programs. In February 1970 the D.C. government established the Narcotics Treatment Administration (NTA). Robert L. DuPont, a Harvard psychiatrist not yet forty who served as director of NTA from 1970 to 1973, was appointed to head the program. In June 1973 President Nixon appointed him director of the SAODAP to replace Jaffe. DuPont held that post until the SAODAP was terminated on June 30, 1975. He was director of NIDA from 1973 to 1979.

In 1970 DuPont immediately launched a drive aimed at getting all of the capital's estimated 17,000 heroin addicts into treatment, mainly methadone maintenance. A year later, "major crimes" reported by the Washington, D.C. police dropped 17 percent, due largely to a big decline in property crimes, offenses often associated with addiction.[71] Washington, D.C. police later were heavily criticized for "manufacturing" this drastic decline in the crime rate through artifice, such as reporting burglaries and grand thefts (always "major crimes" and felonies) as petty thefts ("minor crimes" and misdemeanors). Whether the decreases were real or manufactured,[72] it appears that the massive methadone maintenance effort in the nation's capital helped the president to hold up Washington, D.C., the most overpoliced, overmethadoned city in America, as a model of Nixon-style crime fighting.

AMERICA MAY NOW REST EASY

Spring 1972 saw a celebration in the White House Rose Garden to commemorate the reduction of "major" crimes in Washington, D.C., by one-half from the peak in November 1969 to the new low in March 1972.[73] In October 1972 then Attorney General Richard Kleindienst told the seventy-fourth annual conference of the League of California Cities that: "The crime wave which shocked us in the 1960s is now under control and America once again is becoming a safe and lawful society."[74] Kleindienst did not fail to mention that with success like this being achieved by the Nixon administration, "George McGovern's election as President would be a disaster for the country."[75]

Thus, in 1973 it seemed that science and technology had come to grips with another age-old dilemma—chronic opiate abuse. It appeared, on the surface at least, that the rapid expansion of addiction treatment services, especially methadone maintenance, was having a major impact on the incidence and prevalence of heroin addiction, and that the apparent reduction in street crime was associated with altering heroin demand by treating addicts.

NOTES

1. The worst effects of heroin addiction are directly attributable to adulterants in the illegal drug. On the medical complications of polluted dope and unsterile paraphernalia, see Lloyd H. Smith and Charles E. Becker, "Medical Complications of Heroin Addiction," *Western Journal of Medicine* 115 (November 1971): 42-50; Roger J. Lewis, "Infections in Heroin Addicts," *Journal of the American Medical Association* 223 (February 26, 1973): 1036-37; Abraham White, "Medical Disorders in Drug Addicts: 200 Consecutive Admissions," *Journal of the American Medical Association* 223 (March 26, 1973): 1469-71; Robert H. Mosler, "Heroin Addiction: Medical Complications," *Journal of the American Medical Association* 230 (November 4, 1974): 728-31; Paul B. Szanto, "Morphologic Findings in the Narcotic Addict," *International Surgery* 60 (June-July 1975): 331-34; George R. Gay and J. Gary Trantham, "Medical-Surgical Complications of Drug Abuse: Detection and Management," *International Surgery* 60 (June-July 1975): 327-31; and Albert Yellin, "Ruptured Mycotic Aneurysm," *Archives of Surgery* 112 (August 1977): 981-86.

2. Quoted in Nat Hentoff, *A Doctor Among the Addicts* (New York: Grove Press 1968), p. 40.

3. Quoted in ibid., p. 94.

4. Steven S. Manos describes the transition from a criminal justice model of public intoxication to a civil model in his paper "Anatomy of a Revolution: Law, Change, and the Public Inebriate," *Journal of Drug Issues* 5 (Summer 1975): 207-19.

5. Michel Foucault, *Madness and Civilization: A History of Insanity in the Age of Reason*, trans. Richard Howard (New York: Vintage Books, 1965).

6. Sheldon Glueck and Eleanor Glueck, *Unraveling Juvenile Delinquency* (Cambridge, Mass.: Harvard University Press, 1950); Richard A. Cloward and Lloyd E. Ohlin, *Delinquency and Opportunity* (Glencoe, Ill.: Free Press, 1960); Travis Hirschi, *Causes of Delinquency* (Berkeley, Calif.: University of California Press, 1969); Travis Hirschi and David Rudisill, "The Great American Search: Causes of Crime 1876-1976," *Annals of the American Academy of Political and Social Science* 423 (January 1976): 14-22; and Anthony M. Platt, *The Child Savers: The Invention of Delinquency* (Chicago: University of Chicago Press, 1969).

7. Morris Ploscowe, "Some Basic Problems in Drug Addiction and Suggestions for Research," in *Drug Addiction: Crime or Disease? Interim and Final Reports of the Joint Committee of the American Bar Association and the American Medical Association on Narcotic Drugs*, ed. Advisory Committee to the Federal Bureau of Narcotics (Bloomington, Ind.: Indiana University Press, 1961), pp. 99, 105.

8. The Advisory Council of Judges is quoted in Hentoff, *A Doctor Among the Addicts*, p. 45.

9. Quoted in ibid., p. 45.

10. For a classic statement of the addict-as-victim labeling process, see Edwin M. Schur, *Crimes Without Victims* (Englewood Cliffs, N.J.: Prentice-Hall, 1965).

11. Alfred R. Lindesmith, "Traffic in Dope," *The Nation* (April 21, 1956), p. 337.

12. Richard O'Mara, "Methadone Maintenance," *The Nation* (September 21, 1970), p. 242.

13. "Society's Response to Heroin Barbaric," *New York Times* (March 28, 1962), p. 38.

14. "Our Uncivilized Drug Laws," *New York Times*, (July 7, 1964), p. 34.

15. "Drugs a Medical Problem," *New York Times*, (April 12, 1963), p. 63.

16. "Drug Addicts as Patients," *New York Times*, (March 24, 1964), p. 34.

17. "Methadone Maintenance," *New York Times*, (February 27, 1965), p. 36.

18. "The Case for Methadone Maintenance," *Long Beach Independent Press-Telegram* (December 1, 1971), p. B-2.

19. "Methadone Maintenance for Heroin Addicts," *Look*, (November 30, 1965), p. 23.

20. For an excellent account of the formation and role of the Domestic Council under Nixon, see John J. Kessel, *The Domestic Presidency: Decision-Making in the White House* (North Scituate, Mass.: Duxbury Press, 1975); and John Osborne, "Carter in Transit," *The New Republic* (December 11, 1976), p. 13.

21. This option paper is quoted in Edward Jay Epstein, "The Krogh File—The Politics of 'Law and Order,' " *The Public Interest* 39 (Spring 1975): 115.

22. Donfeld quoted in Ibid., p. 116.

23. Ploscowe, "Basic Problems in Drug Addiction," p. 100.

24. Quoted in Epstein, "The Krogh File," p. 116.

25. Quoted in ibid., p. 115.

26. A number of investigators have noted disproportionate representation of minorities on methadone maintenance caseloads, including Michael Zwerin, *The Silent Sound of Needles* (Englewood Cliffs, N.J.: Prentice-Hall, 1969; Florence Heyman, "Methadone Maintenance as Law and Order," *Society* 9 (June 1972): 15-25; John N. Chappel, "Methadone and Chemotherapy in Drug Addiction: Genocidal or Lifesaving?" *Journal of the American Medical Association* 228 (May 6, 1974): 725-28; David J. Bellis, *Methadone Treatment Program Evaluation* (Ontario, Calif.: West End Drug Abuse Control Coordinating Council, Inc., 1975); and Edward Jay Epstein, "Methadone: The Forlorn Hope," *The Public Interest* 36 (Summer 1974): 3-24.

27. Many have raised the moral and chemical argument that methadone addiction is no improvement over heroin addiction. See, for example, Joel Fort, "Addiction Fact and Fiction," *Saturday Review of Literature* (September 18, 1962), pp. 30-31; David P. Ausubel, "The Dole-Nyswander 'Treatment,' " (Unpublished paper, Department of Health Science and Safety Studies, California State University, Los Angeles); Louis Yablonsky, "Stoned on Methadone," *The New Republic* (August 13, 1966), pp. 14-16; Max Proctor, "The Habit," *International Journal of Addictions* 6 (March, 1971): 15-18; Henry L. Lennard, Leon J. Epstein and Mitchell S. Rosenthal, "The Methadone Illusion," *Science* 176 (May 26, 1972): 881; James F. Maddux and Charles L. Bowden, "Critique of Success with Methadone Maintenance," *American Journal of Psychiatry* 129 (October

1972): 440-46; and Joel Fort and Jerome H. Jaffe, "Methadone Maintenance: Con and Pro," *Medical World News* (April 13, 1973), pp. 69-71.

28. Ausubel, "The Dole-Nyswander 'Treatment,' " p. 3.

29. Yablonsky, "Stoned on Methadone," p. 14.

30. Robert L. DuPont and Richard Katon, "Physicians and the Heroin Addiction Epidemic," *Modern Medicine* (June 28, 1971), p. 123.

31. DuPont's analysis is contained in congressional hearing testimony, U.S. Congress, House Select Committee on Crime, *Narcotics Reasearch, Rehabilitation, and Treatment*, 92d Cong., 1st sess., 1971, Pt. 1, p. 157.

32. Gollance's congressional hearing testimony is contained in ibid., p. 243.

33. Paul Cushman, Jr., et al., "Methadone Maintenance Treatment of Narcotic Addiction: A Unit of Medical Care Based on Over 50,000 Patient Treatment Year," *American Journal of Drug and Alcohol Abuse* 3 (April 1976): 224.

34. U.S. Congress, House Select Committee on Crime, *Narcotics Research*, p. 243.

35. James A. Halikas, Harriet S. Darvish and John D. Rimmer, "The Black Addict: I. Methodology, Chronology of Addiction, and Overview of the Population," *American Journal of Drug and Alcohol Abuse* 3 (October 1976): 533.

36. David E. Smith and David J. Bentel, *Drug Abuse Information Project: Fifth Annual Report to the Legislature* (Sacramento, Calif.: Drug Abuse Information Project, 1971), p. 64.

37. In congressional testimony, Jerome Jaffe noted, ". . . in most of the large urban areas of the east and perhaps the midwest there would be an overrepresentation of black patients [in methadone maintenance programs]. However, in the southwest it would be Mexican-Americans." U.S. Congress, House Select Committee on Crime, *Narcotics Research*, Pt. 1, p. 234.

38. Bellis, *Methadone Evaluation*, p. 6.

39. Personal notes taken by the author at the 1971 Annual Conference on Methadone Maintenance Treatment.

40. For the theory of welfare as a means of regulating the poor to diffuse dissent, see Frances Fox Piven and Richard A. Cloward, *Regulating the Poor: The Functions of Public Welfare* (New York: Vintage Books, 1971).

41. Kenneth Clark, *Dark Ghetto: Dilemmas of Social Power* (New York: Harper and Row, 1965), p. 20.

42. U.S. Congress, Senate Committee on Labor and Public Welfare, *Narcotics and Alcoholism*, 92d Cong., 1st sess., Pt. 2, pp. 629, 607.

43. Ibid., p. 706.

44. Dole's support for methadone maintenance appears in a series of papers, including Vincent P. Dole and Marie E. Nyswander, "A Medical Treatment for Diacetylmorphine ('Heroin') Addiction," *Journal of the American Medical Association* 293 (August 23, 1965): 646–50; Vincent P. Dole and Marie E. Nyswander, "Rehabilitation of Heroin Addicts After Blockade with Methadone," *New York State Journal of Medicine* 66 (April 1966): 2011-17; Vincent P. Dole and Marie E. Nyswander, "Successful Treatment of 750 Criminal Drug Addicts," *Journal of the American Medical Association* 206 (December 16, 1968): 2711; and, most recently, Vincent P. Dole, "Addictive Behavior," *Scientific American* 243 (December, 1980): 138-51. See also Jaffe's highly supportive collection of papers in Jerome H. Jaffe, ed., *A Review of the Approaches to the Problem of Compulsive Narcotics Use* (Springfield, Ill.: Charles C. Thomas, Inc., 1968).

45. U.S. Congress, House Select Committee on Crime, *Narcotics Research*, Pt. 1, p. 234.

46. U.S. Congress, Senate Committee on Labor and Public Welfare, *Drug Dependence*. 92d Cong., 1st sess., 1971, p. 129.

47. Ibid.

48. Prim is quoted in *The Journal* (May 1, 1975), p. 1.

49. U.S. Congress, Senate, *Narcotics and Alcoholism*, Pt. 1, p. 122.

50. Ramirez's testimony is quoted in Zwerin, *Silent Sound of Needles*, p. 207.

51. Casriel's testimony appears in U.S. Congress, Senate Committee on Labor and Public Welfare, *Alcoholism and Narcotics*, 91st Cong., 1st sess., 1969-1970, Pt. IV, p. 787.

52. Ibid., p. 793.

53. Dole is quoted in "Methadone Maintenance: How Much, For Whom, For How Long?" *Medical World News* (March 17, 1972), p. 54.

54. U.S. Congress, Senate, *Drug Dependence*, pp. 333-34.

55. Dole's statement on smoking quoted in Richard C. Schroeder, *The Politics of Drugs: Marijuana to Mainlining* (Washington, D.C.: Congressional Quarterly, Inc., 1975), p. 93.

56. U.S. Congress, Senate, *Drug Dependence*, p. 119.

57. Quoted in "The Authors," *Scientific American* 243 (December 1980): 14.

58. Richard H. Blum et al., *Society and Drugs* (San Francisco: Jossey-Bass, 1970), p. 302.

59. Carol H. Weiss, "Policy Research in the University: Practical Aid or Academic Exercise?" *Policy Studies Journal* 4 (Spring 1976): 226-27.

60. Donfeld memorandum to Nixon quoted in Epstein, "The Krogh File," p. 117.

61. U.S. Congress, Senate, *Drug Dependence*, p. 172.
62. Donfeld is quoted in Epstein, "The Krogh File," p. 117.
63. Donfeld quoted in ibid., p. 118.
64. Domestic Council Option Paper quoted in ibid., p. 119.
65. Krogh quoted in ibid.
66. For reports on the apparent drop in heroinism, see Robert L. DuPont, "Coming to Grips With an Urban Heroin Addiction Epidemic," *Journal of the American Medical Association* 223 (January 1, 1973): 46-48; Robert L. DuPont and Mark H. Greene, "Patterns of Heroin Addiction in the District of Columbia," in *Fifth National Conference on Methadone Treatment: Proceedings, 1973*, ed. National Association for the Prevention of Addiction to Narcotics (New York: National Association for the Prevention of Addiction to Narcotics, 1973), pp. 786-93; Jerome H. Jaffe, "As Far as Heroin Is Concerned, The Worst Is Over," *Psychology Today* (August 1973), pp. 68-85; William I. Barton, "Narcotics-Related Deaths Decrease in 1972 from the Number of Narcotics-Related Deaths in 1971," *International Journal of the Addictions* 9 (Winter 1974): 513-29; and Robert L. DuPont, "Overview of Drug Abuse," in *Developments in the Field of Drug Abuse: Proceedings of the National Drug Abuse Conference—1974*, ed. Edward C. Senay, Vernon Shorty, and Harold Alksne (Cambridge, Mass.: Schenkman Publishing Co., 1974), pp. 26-31.
67. "Nixon Signs Drug Bill, Warns Bureaucrats," *Long Beach Independent Press-Telegram* (March 21, 1972), p. A-1.
68. DuPont and Greene, "Patterns of Heroin Addiction," p. 786.
69. Jaffe, "The Worst is Over," p. 68.
70. 1972 crime decrease detailed in "First Drop in Crime in 17 Years Noted," *Los Angeles Times* (October 4, 1974), Pt. I, p. 6.
71. "D.C. Police Say Major Crimes Down," *Long Beach Independent Press-Telegram*, (March 31, 1972), p. A-6.
72. Harold Pepinsky accused the Washington, D.C. police of manufacturing the crime rate decline through artifice. See his "The Growth of Crime in the United States," *Annals of the American Academy of Political and Social Science* 423 (January 1976): 23-30.
73. KABC-TV Newsfilm, March 26, 1972.
74. The former attorney general is quoted in "Kleindienst Tells Anaheim Meeting Crime Controlled," *Long Beach Independent Press-Telegram*, (October 19, 1972), p. A-18.
75. Ibid.

5

Victory Was Not Around the Corner

In the midst of the Nixon administration self-congratulation, and as opinion surveys indicated that the heroin issue had moved to the back burner of public concern, Mexican brown heroin and heroin transshipped through Mexico flooded across the U.S.-Mexico border.[1] Referring to the flow of Mexican heroin into the United States, Representative Lester Wolff (D-NY), chairman of the House Select Committee on Narcotics Abuse and Control, said in 1977 that, "The problem looks almost insurmountable—the future does look very bleak."[2] The Mexico-U.S. border was a Maginot Line being outflanked, outflown and infiltrated by people bringing in tons of heroin each year.

RETURN OF THE "HEROIN PROBLEM"

Coincident with the leveling off of federal funding for addiction treatment services, students of drug abuse began warning that the heroin problem was returning in full force. DuPont, for example, said in 1976 that ". . . the epidemic is continuing." In fact, he went on, "it never ended."[3]

Moreover, the crime rate decline appeared to be short-lived. By 1973, serious crime spurted up 6 percent,[4] and in 1974 serious crimes rose 18 percent, the largest increase in fifty years.[5]

All this occurred as financial stress was making addiction treatment funding exceedingly vulnerable. Compared to narcotic law enforcement, NIDA and addiction treatment were new entries into the federal budgetary arena and as such lacked long-established ties to powerful congressional committees and the money pipeline. Quite simply, the addiction treatment "subgovernment"[6] was weak compared to drug law enforcement. By 1975, federal treatment monies were going down while federal drug law enforcement expenditures were going up.[7] At the state level, in 1976 New York cut its addiction treatment budget from $136 million to $78 million, and California considered slashing its $70 million addiction treatment and rehabilitation budget by 30 percent.

DuPont, addressing the North American Congress on Alcoholism and Drug Problems in 1974, conceded that:

> A year ago we had talked about turning the corner [on heroin]. I don't think realistically we can talk about ending the problem. The idea was that we were going to wage a war on drug abuse and that if we just put enough troops and enough armament into the battle, we would have a victory and there would no longer be a problem. The better analogy now would be to weeding a garden. . . . It's a constant problem and we have to keep at [heroin addiction] all the time.[8]

A report to Nixon in 1973 implied a "decreasing rate of increase" in heroin use:

> . . . by 1969-1970 the rising curve of more new addicts each year had *flattened out*. . . . It should be emphasized that any such trend would be for the U.S. as a whole. It would not mean that the epidemic had peaked in every community in the country. In some, the problem might *still be worsening*.[9] [Emphasis added]

This kind of "decreasing rate of increase" was a tactical political maneuver first engineered by Attorney General John Mitchell, who proclaimed "decreasing increase" as a reliable index of victory in the Nixon administration's war on crime. This measure allows bureaucrats and line programs (addiction treatment and drug law enforcement service deliverers) to claim victory in their fight against crime or addiction without threatening the continued funding of their organizations. Treatment and law enforcement programs and personnel are pleased most with a simultaneous decrease *and* increase in addiction, seemingly a logical impossibility.

DuPont stated that he was "wrong" about the apparent reduction of heroin use in Washington, D.C., and New York City in 1973.

Announcing a new series of reports on heroin-use indicators, he said he "made a mistake" in suggesting that heroin-use rates had peaked in the 1960s and receded by 1972. He also admitted his methodological error of extrapolating data for the entire nation from temporary and regional data derived from Washington, D.C., and New York City. Said DuPont, "What at that time [1973] was described by me as well as others as a true, national trend [of reduced heroin abuse] turned out to be regional and temporary."[10] He went on: "We know from a number of sources that 1973 was a low point in terms of the last five or six years in the heroin problem. But we now have clear evidence that since 1973 the heroin use problem in the U.S. has deteriorated."[11]

The year 1973 was a recessive period in terms of heroin-use patterns. Though national estimates of the prevalence of heroin addiction all involve assumptions that are not supportable by external criteria, from all indications 1973 *was* a low point. The heroin flow from Indochina into the U.S. did decline rapidly when the U.S. military was defeated in Indochina, but not due to any success on the part of Nixon's drug treatment and law enforcement offensive. It may have been due more to the withdrawal of American Central Intelligence Agency (CIA) officers and operatives, who had been so instrumental in getting Indochinese opium off on the first leg of its journey to the U.S. Gradually, the heroin supply from the Golden Triangle in Southeast Asia dried up, with the exception of opium from Thailand, where the CIA and U.S. forces remained. The mistake, however, was in believing that the recession in importation and use was anything but temporary.

THE FEDERAL GOVERNMENT'S CURRENT INCIDENCE AND PREVALENCE MODEL

The federal government's most recent incidence and prevalence model is built around medical examiners' reprots on heroin-related deaths, emergency-room episodes involving heroin, serum hepatitis data, reports on the price and purity level of heroin, state and local law enforcement data, and client-load statistics from federally supported addiction treatment programs. By 1974 these data pointed to:

1. Increased potency of street heroin in certain areas;
2. Increased seizures of Mexican (brown) heroin and Asian (white) heroin;
3. Increased numbers of heroin-related deaths;
4. Increased detection of heroin-positive urines in arrestee, parolee and probationer populations;
5. Steady to rising demand for addiction treatment;
6. Rising property crime rates, crimes usually associated with heroin addiction.

The apparent increase in heroinism implied that the "heroin problem" had not been stabilized and continued to grow, however gradually.[12]

WORLDWIDE HEROIN ABUSE

Heroin abuse is increasing significantly in Hong Kong, Burma, Pakistan, Thailand, and in Europe.[13] In Thailand, for example, there were an estimated 600,000 heroin addicts in 1976, up from 300,000 in 1970.[14] A key White House narcotics policy advisor said in 1976 that there was a ". . . world-wide heroin epidemic."[15]

When Nixon and others proclaimed in 1973 that this nation had turned the corner and was winning the war on heroin, they were alluding to what was only a twist in the road. Apparently, while the generals were inspiring new insignia, the battle was being lost in the trenches. The Nixon campaign to stamp out heroin abuse probably had a more marked effect on public opinion than on addiction, since the most reliable data available indicate that the incidence and prevalence of drug misuse of all kinds in America, including heroin, is now at an all-time high.

TREATMENT POLICY UNDER THE FORD ADMINISTRATION

The presidency of Gerald R. Ford was a welcome antidote to the Nixon administration. In May 1975 Ford told Congress that "Recent evidence suggests an increase in the availability and use of dangerous drugs in spite of the creation of special federal agencies and massive federal funding during the past six years."[16]

His approach, however, was to concentrate mainly on heroin trafficking. While he said that five thousand persons died of drug overdose in 1975 and that thousands more ". . . only go through the motions of living," Ford's major emphasis was on drug law enforcement measures to reduce the supplies of heroin available to addicts.[17] The main thrust of his attack was a proposal to set mandatory minimum sentences for a variety of offenses, including "dealing in hard drugs."[18]

RELIANCE ON DRUG LAW ENFORCEMENT

In April 1976 Ford sent Congress a six-page, single-spaced message on "drug abuse" emphasizing bigger and better drug law enforcement. He proposed a "new and more aggressive campaign" against heroin and spoke of his" . . . deep concern about this problem and my personal commitment to do something about it." In his 1976 State of the Union Address he said:

> The sale of hard drugs is on the increase again. I have directed all agencies of the federal government to step up enforcement efforts against those who deal in drugs. . . . Hard drugs degrade the spirit as they destroy the body of their users.[19]

In pushing his law enforcement attack on heroin, Ford told a Texas audience:

> I do not believe we have yet succeeded in making it tough enough for drug traffickers. As far as I am concerned, the people who traffic in hard drugs are nothing less than merchants of death and should be put behind bars for a long, long time.[20]

Finally, in his acceptance speech at the Republican National Convention in Kansas City in May 1976 he proposed ". . . a program to crack down on crime and illegal drugs. . . ."[21]

The Ford administration, under leadership of the Domestic Council, produced yet another White Paper on the whole issue of federal heroin addiction policy. The document, like its predecessors, contained neither startling nor new data. It did, however, implicitly acknowledge defects in the federal approach to heroin control: "We now know that the very real progress made [against heroin] in the early 1970s was, in the main, temporary and regional."[22] The progress was regional because federal treatment and law enforcement funds poured into cities like New York and Washington, not into suburbs and the American Southwest. Moreover, as one source of heroin supply was shut down, new ones developed. If nothing else, this White Paper admitted what many in the field had long known: the elimination of heroin addiction or drug misuse in general may be impossible through legislative fiat and may even be beyond the reach of policy altogether.

THE CARTER ADMINISTRATION'S APPROACH TO HEROIN

After the U.S. withdrawal from Indochina, heroin availability and use in the U.S. did decline, sufficiently so that President Carter could proclaim on January 21, 1980:

> At the beginning of my administration there were over a half million heroin addicts in the United States. Our continued emphasis on reducing the supply of heroin, as well as providing the treatment and rehabilitation of its victims, has reduced the addict population to 380,000.[23]

Reportedly, the supply of heroin available in the U.S. also had plummeted to a ten-year low of four metric tons.[24] As governor of Georgia, Jimmy Carter, like Nixon, established an agency operating out of his office to coordinate all drug abuse control activities in the state. Peter G. Bourne, later Carter's special assistant in charge of federal narcotic policy, told me in 1975,

> For a long time [Carter] has shared with you and me a deep concern about the drug abusers in America. As President, I believe he would bring a whole new humanitarian focus to bear in dealing with . . . drug abuse.[25]

Each of the three presidents prior to Mr. Reagan—Nixon, Ford and Carter—has had his own resident psychiatrist doubling as sounding board in times of psychic need and narcotics policy adviser. For Nixon, it was Jerome Jaffe, then Robert DuPont. Ford had the ever-present DuPont, who showed himself to be a fixture as administrations came and went. For Carter it was Peter G. Bourne: psychiatrist in the White House.[26] He was brought in as director of the new Office of Drug Abuse Policy (ODAP) by Carter who said that Bourne had become perhaps "the world's foremost expert on drugs; their origin, their processing, their sale, their use, their effect on the human body, how they might be controlled."[27] Bourne had served in the Special Action Office for Drug Abuse Prevention (SAODAP) during the Nixon administration.

In 1977 Bourne said the time had come to "reexamine the question of whether we ought to decriminalize heroin and set up treatment centers to dispense heroin legally."[28] "We are exploring, not advocating decriminalization," added Bourne, who noted that "politically [heroin decriminalization] is a very hot issue."[29] The issue was so hot, in fact, that after making his "decriminalization" statement, Bourne recanted, saying the idea of a heroin maintenance program seemed "less viable."

Nevertheless, Bourne said the President

> . . . took a personal interest in [addiction treatment] programs and read a great deal, and became extremely knowledgeable about drug abuse. In fact, a lot of the time I got worried he was getting to know a lot more about it than I did, which was a bit disconcerting.[30]

With this kind of interest in the White House, Bourne said, ". . . it really forces the rest of the country to examine the pros and cons of issues in a much more practical way."[31]

Unfortunately, Bourne's White House career ended in 1978 when he resigned after being accused of supplying drug prescriptions to members of the White House staff.[32] A Washington woman was arrested while attempting to buy the drug Quaalude with an allegedly illegal prescription signed by Bourne.[33] Quaalude is a potent drug used to produce sleep or daytime sedation. Jack Anderson even alleged he had affidavits attesting to Bourne's *own* drug use.[34] Even so, radical proposals for heroin maintenance reappeared. The National League of Cities passed a resolution recommending a study of heroin maintenance. The Massachusetts Council of Churches urged heroin maintenance for confirmed addicts. A group of old-fashioned citizens banded together as a grand jury in San Diego and, headed by a foreman who was a retired Marine Corps general, proposed distribution of free or low-cost heroin "to certified addicts with no attempt at rehabilitation."

Heroin maintenance seemed out of the question under President Carter, however. Regarding marijuana, a more benign substance, he said, ". . . we ought to be very strong in eliminating the influx of marijuana into the country, heavy on the pushers. I don't favor the use of marijuana at all. The medical effects of persistent use of marijuana still concern me very much."[35]

With such an attitude toward a substance like marijuana, Carter never recommended heroin decriminalization. When asked by a questioner in his 1977 televised phone-in "talk show," whether he thought criminalization of heroin was unjust to addicts, Carter said, "Not to me," and went on to add that heroin and cocaine were the "most debilitating drugs in our society." He did not mention alcohol abuse, the number one drug problem in America.

RONALD REAGAN ASSUMES THE PRESIDENCY AND THE GOLDEN CRESCENT REPLACES THE GOLDEN TRIANGLE

On inauguration day, January 20, 1981, President Ronald Reagan's wife Nancy told the press that just as other First Ladies had their own pet projects, her's would be "getting teenagers off drugs."[36] Upon assuming office, however, the President and his wife faced an influx of potent heroin unequalled in U.S. history. Far from the tide turning, victory over heroin in the 1980s appeared to be more illusive than ever before.

By 1981 the encouraging statistics of the late 1970s were ancient history. The heroin supply was on the rise, coming from new sources, and its use had jumped dramatically. America is now, said a high-level law enforcement official, "about to enter another heroin hell."[37] This time the heroin is coming from the Golden Crescent area of Southwest Asia. The Newark, New Jersey, office of the DEA, for one, reports that "the known quantities of Golden Crescent heroin on the streets have suddenly jumped by 600 percent."[38] In Chicago, the police there reportedly expected 10 percent more addicts in 1980 because of the influx of heroin from the Golden Crescent. In New York State, admissions to drug treatment programs in 1980 were up 26 percent.[39] In Washington, D.C., medical examiner James Luke has recorded an increase in the number of deaths from heroin overdose from seven in 1978 to forty-three in the first nine months of 1980. Much of the heroin there seems to be coming from the Golden Crescent, and Alyce Gulatte of the Drug Abuse Institute at Howard University says that it "is destroying the city."[40]

In a 1974 book, Catharine Lamour and Michel Lamberti wrote that Afghanistan and northwestern Pakistan were a "source of opium as yet virtually untapped."[41] That was in 1972. By the time of the Reagan presidency, this source had been tapped and heroin produced from Afghan,[42] Pakistani,[43] and even Iranian[44] opium was flowing abundantly into Western Europe and the United States.

Not surprisingly, the unleashing of this opium flow from Afghanistan coincided perfectly with the arrival of the CIA on the Afghan-Pakistan border—to support and arm the tribes who were both producing opium and fighting the Russian invaders—all in the name of the fight against Communism. Anti-Communist . . . U.S.-supplied "rebels" . . . heroin . . .the CIA: all have a familiar ring. One is reminded of the Hmong tribes in Laos who, during the Vietnam War, were recruited by the CIA for mercenary armies. In exchange, the CIA provided them with planes and helicopters to transport their opium.[45]

Hoag Levins of the *Philadelphia* magazine asked a "high level law enforcement official in Washington" in an off-the-record interview about the U.S. government response to the recent influx of Golden Crescent heroin. The official said,

> You have the administration tiptoeing around this like it's a land mine. The issue of opium and heroin in Afghanistan is explosive. . . . In the State of the Union speech, the President mentioned drug abuse but he was very careful to avoid mentioning Afghanistan, even though Afghanistan is where things are *really* happening right now. He said something like he was worried about "drugs from Iran and Asia," but he specifically avoided dropping Afghanistan in there because the White House is worried that that will cause the media to ask an obvious question: "Why aren't we

taking a more critical look at the arms we are now shipping to gangs of drug runners who are obviously going to use them to increase the efficiency of their drug smuggling operation?"[46]

President Reagan now faces the same policy problem. David G. Canaday, special agent in charge of the DEA's Washington, D.C. office, has stated that the DEA cannot do anything about the heroin influx from the Golden Crescent because "we have virtually no diplomatic ties in that part of the world."[47] Perhaps the real reason, however, for the DEA's inability to prevent the flow of drugs from the Golden Crescent is that the opium growing tribes there are not to be "annoyed" because of their opposition to the Russian-backed Afghan government. Therefore, the DEA decided to withdraw all of its agents from the Afghan-Pakistan border area.[48] At the same time, the CIA, which is aiding these very tribes that grow the poppy for U.S. heroin, is expanding its operations in the area.

The Golden Crescent, with its expanding CIA presence, produced an estimated 1,000 metric tons of opium in 1979; 300 tons in Afghanistan, and some 700 tons in Pakistan, most of it in the border area between the two countries.[49] In contrast, Mexico's opium produce was estimated at only 10 tons in 1979. The 300 tons of opium produced in Afghanistan translates roughly into 30 tons of nearly pure heroin; the Pakistani crop 70 tons, for a grand yearly total of 100 tons of heroin. Some 60 tons of pure heroin from the Golden Crescent is now becoming available in the United States. And for the first time, the Afghan opium is being exported in large quantities to the U.S., thanks partially to the CIA-supported tribal "freedom fighters" who are shooting it out with the Soviet-dominated Afghan government. It's the politics of heroin all over again. Just as the CIA's "secret war" in Laos resulted in hundreds of thousands of heroin addicts at home, the CIA's "secret war" in Afghanistan promises to keep heroin readily available at the street level in America.

It is doubtful that the Reagan administration, faced with the complex politics and economics of this situation, will come up with an innovative twist to claim victory in the battle with demon heroin. All this, no doubt, will leave Reagan's federal heroin control policy mired in the twin tracks of the bygone Nixon era: hit and miss politically dictated law enforcement efforts to curtail supplies of the drug and treatment of addicts based on the medical model, mainly methadone maintenance, to reduce demand for heroin.

NOTES

1. "All Nations Threatened," *The Journal* (May 1, 1976), p. 1; also, "Heroin a Global Game," *The Journal* (October 1, 1976), p. 8.

2. Congressman Wolff quoted in *Science*, "Flow of Narcotics Uninterrupted," 192 (April 1977): 509.

3. "Heroin Use in U.S. Reported on Rise," *Los Angeles Times* (March 17, 1976), Pt. I, p. 4.

4. "First Drop in Crime in 17 Years Noted," *Los Angeles Times*, (October 4, 1974), Pt. I, p. 6.

5. "74 Crime Rate Up by 18%, FBI Report Says," *Los Angeles Times*, (December 10, 1965), Pt. I, p. 1.

6. "Subgovernments," or "whirlpools" of policymaking activity involve long-established interrelationships between executive branch agencies, legislative committees and subcommittees, and interested pressure groups. See J. Leiper Freeman, *The Political Process: Executive Bureau-Legislative-Committee Relations*, rev. ed. (New York: Random House, 1965).

7. Sybil Cline, *The Federal Drug Abuse Budget for Fiscal Year 1975* (Washington, D.C.: The Drug Abuse Council, Inc., 1974); also Sybil Cline and Carl Akins, "Federal Policy and Budget for Drug Abuse—FY 1976," in *Governmental Response to Drug Abuse*, ed. The Drug Abuse Council (Washington, D.C.: The Drug Abuse Council, Inc., 1975).

8. DuPont quoted in "Heroin Use in the U.S. on Increase Again," *Los Angeles Times*, (December 13, 1974), Pt. I, p. 1.

9. U.S. President, Strategy Council on Drug Abuse, *Federal Strategy for Drug Abuse and Drug Traffic Prevention: 1973* (Washington, D.C.: U.S. Government Printing Office, 1974), p. 1.

10. Quoted in "New Data Expose High Heroin Use," *The Journal*, (April 1, 1976), p. 1.

11. Ibid.

12. See Mark H. Greene, "The Resurgence of Heroin Abuse in the District of Columbia," *American Journal of Drug and Alcohol Abuse* 2 (April 1975): 141-64. In late 1978 and in 1979, as the "Mexican connection"

began drying up, the Middle Eastern nations of Afghanistan, Pakistan, and Iran were becoming major sources of heroin exported to Western Europe and the United States. See "Mideast Feared Heroin Source," *Long Beach Independent Press-Telegram*, (October 12, 1979), p. A-20.

13. "Heroin a Global Game," *The Journal*, (October 1, 1976), p. 8.

14. "All Nations Threatened," *The Journal* (May 1, 1976), p. 6.

15. Ibid., p. 5.

16. Ford quoted in Richard C. Schroeder, *The Politics of Drugs: Marijuana to Mainlining* (Washington, D.C.: Congressional Quarterly, Inc., 1975), p. 10.

17. Ford's emphasis on drug law enforcement is outlined in National Association of State Drug Abuse Program Coordinators, *Legislative Alerts Monthly Reports*, October 1976, p. 8.

18. Ford quoted in "Of two Minds About Crime," *The New Republic* (May 1, 1976), p. 1.

19. "State of Union Text: Condition is Better, But Not Good Enough," *Los Angeles Times* (January 21, 1976), Pt. I, p. 16.

20. Quoted in National Association of State Drug Abuse Program Coordinators, *Legislative Alerts Monthly Reports*, April 1976, p. 1.

21. ABC-TV Newsfilm, May 19, 1976.

22. "The War is Past, the Problem is as Big as Ever," *Science*, 190 (November 1975): 638.

23. Hoag Levins, "The Kabul Connection," *Philadelphia*, August 1980, p. 114.

24. *Newsweek*, March 10, 1980, p. 36.

25. Personal communications from Peter G. Bourne, June 19, 1975.

26. See Constance Holden, "Peter G. Bourne: Psychiatrist in the White House," *Science* 197 (August 5, 1977): 539-42.

27 The President is quoted in "Carter Remarks Provide Clues to Attitude on Science Advice," *Science* 196 (June 17, 1977): 1300.

28. "Georgians on Staff," *Los Angeles Times*, January 7, 1977, Pt. II, p. 9.

29. Ibid.

30. "Carter Will Listen Says Bourne," *The Journal*, January 1, 1977, p. 4.

31. Ibid.

32. "When the Grass Smoking Is in the White House, a Different Aroma Rises," *Los Angeles Times*, July 27, 1978, Pt. II, p. 7.

33. "Drug Arrest Tied to White House Health Adviser," *Los Angeles Times*, July 19, 1978, Pt I, p. 20; *see also* Patrick Anderson, *High in America: The True Story Behind NORML and the Politics of Marijuana* (New York: The Viking Press, 1981) pp. 6–8, 191–200.

34. "When the Grass Smoking Is in the White House," *Los Angeles Times*, July 27, 1978, Pt. II, p. 7.

35. "Carter Credits Wife for Son's Quitting Marijuana," *Los Angeles Times*, October 18, 1976, Pt. I, p. 3.

36. KABC-TV Newsfilm, January 20, 1981.

37. Levins, "The Kabul Connection," p. 202.

38. Ibid., p. 203.

39. *Black Enterprise*, August 1980, p. 39.

40. Quoted in *Washington Post*, September 28, 1980, p. A–9.

41. Catherine Lamour and Michel R. Lamberti, *The International Connection: Opium From Growers to Pushers* (New York: Pantheon Books, 1974), p. 177.

42. See Konrad Ege, "CIA Rebels Supply U.S. Heroin," *CounterSpy*, November 1980, p. 16.

43. "Pakistani Opium Harvest Stirs Concern," *Los Angeles Times*, April 26, 1978, Part IV, p. 1.

44. "Traffic of Drugs in Iran Soars," *Long Beach Independent Press-Telegram*, January 3, 1981, p. A-6.

45. See the detailed account by Alfred W. McCoy, with Cathleen B. Read and Leonard P. Adams, II, *The Politics of Heroin in Southeast Asia* (New York: Harper & Row, 1972).

46. Quoted in Levins, "The Kabul Connection," p. 202.

47. Quoted in *Washington Post*, September 28, 1980, p. A-9.

48. Levins " The Kabul Connection," p. 202.

49. Ege, "CIA Rebels," p. 17; on Afghan heroin in Europe, *see "West Germany Heroin Overdoses Increase,"* Long Beach Independent Press-Telegram, May 24, 1981, p. A-3.

PART II

HEROIN ADDICTION TREATMENT AND ITS OUTCOME

6 Goal Achievement Analysis of Methadone Maintenance

What have been the results of addiction treatment programs? How do the results compare with the goals that were set? Have we garnered any plausible material that can assist in future treatment programming? Presumably, the most prominent objective of any treatment program is somehow to eliminate the reason an addict needed treatment. Whether such changes are achieved is the most important question for evaluative research.

THE GOALS OF METHADONE MAINTENANCE

What are the exact, current behavioral criteria for client "success" in methadone maintenance treatment? Judged by these goals, how successful are these programs? Though consensus on the aims of treatment modalities is difficult to achieve, there is wide agreement on these goals of methadone maintenance:

1. *To attract* as many street addicts as possible into maintenance treatment[1]
2. *To retain* as many clients as possible in treatment[2]
3. *To transfer* the addict's dependence from heroin to maintenance doses of clinic methadone[3]
4. *To reduce/eliminate illicit drug use* among clients[4]
5. *To reduce the number of serious crimes* committed by clients[5]
6. *To rehabilitate clients vocationally*, defined as enabling them to secure and maintain a job[6]

7. *Ultimately to detoxify* methadone clients and keep them narcotic-free[7]

With these criteria, how successful have methadone programs been in reforming their clients?

GOAL #1: TO ATTRACT STREET ADDICTS INTO MAINTENANCE TREATMENT

Early proponents of methadone felt sure addicts would literally flock into treatment.[8] Have the data borne out optimistic predictions concerning the attractiveness of maintenance therapy?

Most heroin and other opiate addicts in America are *not* in methadone maintenance programs. With less than 85,000 addicts being maintained on methadone, and an estimated 500,000 to 600,000 persons in the United States using heroin daily, the ability of methadone clinics to attract addicts into treatment is questionable. Methadone programs today have little appeal to communities in which they exist or to the majority of addicts on the streets. After an initial dramatic growth period, for example, New York City clinics are now receiving decreasing numbers of new applications for treatment.[9] A similar pattern exists in California. Word from East Los Angeles, San Diego, San Jose and San Francisco is that waiting lists for methadone therapy have all but disappeared.

Why has methadone maintenance been accepted by only a fraction of the nation's total addicted population? There are several explanations. One is that the stringent regulations and controls imposed by the FDA, DEA and state and local monitoring agencies make the regimen unpalatable to most street addicts and succeed in keeping them away.

Regulations do not encourage methadone use as much as they try to *limit* and *decrease* its use among program clientele. For example, California's regulations governing methadone maintenance clinics mandate that:

> . . . *maintenance treatment dosage should be low* to minimize sedation, decrease withdrawal symptoms, and reduce the potential for diversion of take-home medication. Deviations from such average maintenance treatment dosage shall be noted by the physician, with reasons for such deviations, in the patient's medical record. A daily dosage above 80 mg.

shall be justified by the physician. . . . A daily dosage above 120 milligrams requires the prior approval of the [state]. . . . *Dosages above 160 mg. are prohibited.*[10] [Emphasis added]

Unfortunately, addicts, by their very nature, are repelled by such regulations. For the addict, if a little dope is good, more is better.

Dosage-limitation controls mandated by federal and state policy and enforced by clinics are based on the fear of giving out narcotics to addicts, especially by government at taxpayers' expense. This is a major ambiguity in methadone maintenance policy design: The policy at once calls for substituting a legal narcotic for an illegal one while keeping the methadone dosage so low that it is unsatisfying to addicts. The policy both attracts and repels. This situation contrasts with the early days of maintenance therapy under Dole and Nyswander when dosages ranged from 100 to 200 mg. per day, thus very satisfying to the addict-patients being studied and reported. Average dosage today in most clinics is around 35 mg a day—a low dose. Street addicts know this and think twice before resorting to government-sponsored methadone maintenance.

Strict "take-home" dosage requirements also deter potential clients from entering treatment. By keeping dosages low and enforcing strict take-home rules, officials hoped that diversion of clinic methadone into the streets for illicit use would be curtailed.

Diversion of clinic methadone has been a problem. One clinic in southern California could not account for 6,000 mg of methadone bulk powder, which disappeared between weighing the incoming batch and dissolving it in solution. A northern California program "lost" 70,000 mg of methadone. Such situations, with attendant media publicity and numerous reports over the past fifteen years of methadone-related overdoses on the streets, have led to strict intra-clinic controls, which make coming to the clinic an unpalatable experience for most clients. The policy dilemma is that the strict regulations designed to prevent diversion and ensure "rehabilitation" are the very ones that deter most self-respecting addicts from entering treatment in the first place.

To qualify for take-home dosages an addict-client has to be "good" as defined in government regulations. California, a liberal state, puts it this way: "[The program] shall provide take-home dosages of methadone . . . only when the patient is satisfactorily adhering to the requirements of this treatment program."[11] The requirement that all clients return to their clinic a minimum of two or three times per week and many of them every day for as long as they remain in treatment has driven many successful patients back to the streets and has erected a significant barrier for entry for potential clients.

Another purpose of take-home regulations is to reduce diversion and to keep methadone dosage levels as low as possible, and no programs may provide take-homes to a client whose daily dosage is above 100 mg. Take-home privileges thus depend on keeping one's dosage low. Potential clients know that if they want a satisfying dose of methadone (above 100 mg), there will be no take-homes, and they must attend the clinic 7 days a week, 365 days a year, indefinitely. Is being chained to this legal narcotics supply any better than slavery to an illegal one? Thousands of addicts think not.

Goldstein, a Stanford proponent of "low-dose" methadone programs, tried to prove that methadone clients really desire lower doses, not higher ones. Here is his research protocol:

> At the beginning of the [study] an open dosage self-adjustment protocol was instituted. Patients were then *given the opportunity to change their dosage [up or down]* by 5 mg once a week. The ceiling dosage was set at 120 mg. . . . *patients on dosages higher than 50 mg were allowed no take-home privileges.*[12] [Emphasis added]

What kind of behavior modification is this? Naturally he "found" that most patients selected doses under 50 mg, just as he wanted to prove. Clients did not opt to go over 50 mg, for they would lose all take-home privileges if they did and would have to come to the clinic every day. Goldstein claimed on the basis of his observations that "Patients on methadone clearly do not behave in the manner of morphine addicts in Lexington studies who typically took all the morphine they could get."[13]

But did Goldstein's clients stay under 50 mg because they were satisfied with the lower dose? Or did they stay under 50 mg because, if they went higher, they would be forced to attend the clinic 7 days a week, 365 days a year? Experience validates the latter conclusion.

Clients *detest* coming to overcrowded clinics where they are viewed by staff and local residents as freaks. Goldstein's conclusions, based on questionable research methods and not corrected through years of publications led to nationwide methadone dosage schedules in the range of 30 mg to 50 mg a day, a dosage too low for many potential clients. They prefer continued heroin use where they can at least regulate their own doses without penalty beyond that of increased drug costs.

Regulations dictate that to receive any take-homes at all, a client must:

1. Observe all program rules and regulations.
2. Demonstrate "substantial progress in rehabilitation" by "participating actively" in maintenance program "activities."
3. Demonstrate he is not using drugs improperly.
4. Give no indication of misusing his methadone (that is, not taking it).
5. Demonstrate he is participating in an "education, vocational or homemaking activity."

No addict-patient gets take-homes until he has "satisfactorily adhered to these requirements for at least ninety days." Many street addicts feel they could never follow all these rules, so they do not enter treatment. After three months of "good behavior" on the program, the regulations permit one take-home a week. Following six months of "satisfactory adherence to the requirements of [the] program, the patient may be permitted not more than a two day take-home dosage supply." So, six months into the program the client still must report to the clinic five days a week. Finally, after two full years of not breaking any rules, a client is allowed a dosage supply sufficient to last five days; he must attend the clinic only twice a week to pick up his methadone and submit a urine sample.

The overall impact of these strict take-home requirements is to make methadone maintenance unattractive to most heroin users. Once on the program, if a client breaks any rules he is moved backward to a schedule of fewer take-homes each week until such time as he can "prove" to program staff he is "adhering to the rules and regulations."

Urinalysis regulations and procedures deter new applicants. Strict requirements in this area are designed to ensure that addicts are (1) taking their clinic methadone, and (2) not using unprescribed drugs. Programs are required by federal and state law to test urine for presence of the following drugs at least twice a week for as long as clients remain in treatment:

1. Methadone
2. Morphine
3. Codeine
4. Amphetamine
5. Methamphetime
6. Phenobarbital
7. Pentobarbital
8. Secobarbital

If a client fails to supply a urine sample when ordered to do so by clinic staff, he is considered to be "dirty," and the presumption is recorded in the client's record to be used as reason for involuntary detoxification procedures or restrictions of take-home privileges. A clinic staff member must accompany the client to the toilet and actually observe the act of urination. This is a demeaning experience for client and observer alike. Says one female observer: "I don't like to supervise [urine] tests. I just don't feel right about it. It's an invasion of privacy to watch somebody else urinate."[14] Clients know observers do not like watching them urinate, and often seize this opportunity to "beat" or cheat on a test. Says one addict:

> I wouldn't dig standing out there observing someone else's penis. This is one of the reasons all these dudes beat the test. This guy taking these specimens would go in there and give you a bottle. He would turn around and look up at the sky, and that's when the guys who were beating the test had their chance.[15]

The tests are spurious not only in methadone clinics. The overall accuracy rate of drug screening laboratories performing urinalyses is fairly low.[16] The whole urine-testing system is intensely disliked by addicts, many of whom are on probation or parole and must test anyway as a condition of their releases.

Another factor driving away potential methadone clients is that they know maintenance policy dictates ultimate detoxification from methadone and abstinence from narcotics and other drugs. The regulations in California, for example, require programs to state their plans for ultimately detoxifying all clients. In every state, special justification is required to keep a client on methadone maintenance for more than two years. Knowing this, many street addicts never apply, since they feel they may need narcotics indefinitely to remain comfortable. Coping with abstinence is unthinkable for them.

The individual and group counseling offered in methadone clinics, sometimes provided by methadone-addicted staff members, places unrelenting pressure on the client to detoxify. Constant harangues on detoxification throughout treatment are enough to send many addict-clients back into the streets. Those who have yet to enter treatment know what to expect through the grapevine.

Government-enforced client selection criteria limit the types of addicts who are eligible for methadone treatment. This is another factor inhibiting the programs' attractiveness. First, all applicants must prove, with official records, a history of at least two years of addiction to heroin or other morphine-like drugs (morphine, methadone or any natural or synthetic opiate). Second, to be eligible, the addict must prove two or more "treatment failures," usually detoxification in a program or jail with subsequent relapse to regular narcotic use. Untreated or noncriminal addicts are thus excluded from program enrollment. Third, all applicants must be eighteen or older, even though some users experience onset of addiction as early as age nine, ten, or eleven. Fourth, to get into methadone treatment, an applicant has to present evidence of *current* addiction to morphine-like drugs, including signs of withdrawal. Addicts thus are forced to continue using heroin to qualify for maintenance therapy—another irrationality of methadone policy. "Clean" addicts sometimes inject heroin just to ensure entry into maintenance therapy.

All these strict eligibility requirements were devised to assuage the demand by methadone critics that maintenance be restricted to only the "hardest-core" addicts. Younger "experimenters" with shorter, unproven addiction histories are excluded from treatment. These admission policies have succeeded in their intent, but many bona fide narcotic addicts are still excluded from treatment because they do no meet eligibility criteria.

Attraction Power: Summary

Because of these strict regulations and the clinic system for dispensing methadone, the attitude of most street heroin addicts toward methadone programs is much less receptive today than it was ten or even five years ago. Most users reject methadone therapy because they find the regimen too demanding. They would encounter rigid, unreasonable and intolerable program rules, which claim to be helping them but in fact punish them for acting like addicts—the very reason they are supposed to be in treatment in the first place. In addition, cynical, suspicious and unsympathetic staff attitudes and behavior are a significant deterrent to entry into treatment. Potential applicants know that if they do not submit to regular "counseling" by staff, they can be dropped from treatment. And if they do not adopt white middle-class norms like going to college, working at a steady job, or keeping house, there is also the possibility of involuntary detoxification. Manipulation of their lives while in treatment even extends to their political beliefs and activities. A clinic in New York required clients to remove any political buttons before they were given their methadone.[17] Who needs it?

GOAL #2: TO RETAIN AS MANY CLIENTS AS POSSIBLE

Are methadone maintenance programs successful as measured by retention in treatment? Are they able to hold those addicts who do enroll? There is a positive correlation between retention in the program and positive client outcome.

Client Factors Related to Retention

Client background variables such as age are related to retention. Older clients are much more likely to remain in therapy than younger ones.[18] Perhaps the former have had more negative experiences as a consequence of illegal heroin use and are simply tired of the street life. Significantly, in the early methadone programs, which reported such successful results, the average client age was thirty-three to thirty-five years, fairly old for an addict. By selecting a disproportionately older group of addicts, these early experimental programs enrolled clients who would respond particularly well in terms of staying on the program. The patients of Dole and Nyswander, for example, averaged around thirty-three years in age, and early reports showed that 90 percent of them were retained in treatment. Did the Dole/Nyswander client selection criteria produce higher retention rates by admitting older addicts?

Race/ethnicity also is associated with retention. Hispanics appear more likely to remain in methadone therapy than Anglos,[19] who have higher retention rates than blacks.[20] Significantly, the early Dole/Nyswander program embodied mostly white persons.

In fact, the Dole/Nyswander clients were unrepresentative of most street addicts arrested in New York City, and this may have contributed to the likelihood of being retained in treatment. For instance, of 1,233 applicants for the Morris J. Bernstein Institute's early experimental methadone program, after exhaustive screening only 521 were finally admitted to maintenance therapy. These addicts tended to be older, white and less involved with criminal activities than the total pool of known addicts in New York City.[21] This differs from the popular belief that the Dole/Nyswander program enlisted only the most severe hard-core addicts, only the most "hopeless" cases. Table 6.1 compares patients on the early Dole/Nyswander program with addicts listed on the New York City Narcotic Registry (all addicts ever arrested in New York City).

Moreover, since they volunteered and remained on a waiting list for six months to a year, Dole/Nyswander's applicants displayed a strong motivation toward remaining in methadone therapy. Thus, motivation may have been a factor in the early high-retention methadone programs. The existence of long waiting periods for treatment in the past, particularly at those university-affiliated methadone programs from which most published research emanates, is an effective screening device that produces more highly motivated clients entering methadone therapy—clients more likely to *remain* in treatment.

Client health also is related to retention in treatment. Unhealthy clients are more likely to be retained than healthy ones.[22] Older addicts are less healthy, since they have been using adulterated

Table 6.1
Comparison of Average New York City Addicts with Dole/Nyswander Patients

	DOLE/NYSWANDER PATIENTS	NEW YORK CITY REGISTRY
Mean age	33	28
Over 30	68%	34%
Ethnic composition:		
White	48%	25%
Black	33	47
Puerto Rican	18	27

SOURCE: Paul Cushman et al., "Methadone Maintenance Treatment of Narcotic Addiction: A Unit of Medical Care Based on Over 50,000 Patient Treatment Years," *American Journal of Drug and Alcohol Abuse* 3 (April 1976).

street heroin under unsterile conditions for longer periods of time. By admitting older addicts, the early, apparently more successful programs were admitting a preponderance of less healthy people—addicts who are "sick and tired of being sick and tired," and thus more likely to remain in treatment.

Program Factors Affecting Retention

Beyond client background variables, program characteristics also appear related to retention. For example, high-dose programs (over 60 mg per day) have better retention rates than low-dose programs. Significantly, the initial programs like those of Dole and Nyswander were high-dose regimens and had high retention rates. Later programs adopted lower dosage schedules and today are experiencing significant numbers of dropouts.[23] Addicts on high-dose maintenance may be more insulated from reality, anxiety and tension than those on doses lower than 60 mg. The early programs, which noted retention rates over 90 percent, provided dosages in excess of 150 mg and sometimes more than 200 mg a day, amounts now against the law.

Adams and his colleagues, studying causes of client dropout, found six primary reasons for client-precipitated termination:

1. Objections to way program is run (rules and regulations, low dosage)
2. Complaints about another client in the program
3. Payment difficulties
4. Inability to see program physicians
5. Job conflict with clinic hours of operation
6. Side effects produced by methadone maintenance[24]

The early Dole/Nyswander methadone maintenance program claimed an amazingly high retention rate of 98 percent.[25] By 1969 they reported that 82 percent of all patients ever accepted into the program had remained on methadone maintenance.[26] Because of the enormous expansion of the Dole/Nyswander program in 1969, however, most of the clients in the "retained" category had actually been admitted to treatment only six months before the Gearing evaluation. When groups of patients who had been in the program for more than a year are analyzed, a much lower retention rate is obtained. For example, of the Dole/Nyswander cohort admitted thirty-three months before the Gearing evaluation of their program, and of the cohort admitted forty-eight months before the evaluation, only 58 percent were retained.[27] The magnitude of the *actual* rate of attrition was partially masked by the large numbers of newly admitted clients.[28]

To compare Dole and Nyswander's retention results with more recent trends in methadone programs, I examined the retention rates in four large California maintenance clinics. In 1973 these programs had a 70 percent retention rate, which is extremely high.[29] This means that of all clients ever admitted, seven out of ten were still in treatment when the evaluation was conducted.

In my 1976 study I defined *continuous retention* as the uninterrupted length of stay in the program. Based on a continuous retention rate curve, an analysis of the data confirmed that nearly 50 percent of all addict-patients "split" in less than six months. The average length of stay for all clients ever admitted was only eight months. Of all clients ever admitted to the four clinics studied, about 70 percent had terminated for one reason or another. Most terminations were "unfavorable" ones—dropouts, failures to abide by program rules, arrests and incarcerations.

Thus, my study contradicted the earlier 70 percent retention rate computed for the same clinics. I found a diametric opposite: *70 percent dropped out*. For whatever reasons, every year these clinics are achieving progressively lower retention rates.

Recent statistics from New York City confirm my data. Dole's original 98 percent retention rate has not been repeated since. In the three-year period from 1970 to 1973 the program census in New York jumped to 35,000, while the retention rate fell from 98 percent to 61 percent. By 1976 the census in New York programs was about 24,000, and the retention rate was 59 percent and falling. Program discharges in New York later exceeded admissions.[30] Newman and his colleagues found that for 17,008 total admissions to the New York City Methadone Maintenance Treatment Program, the combined retention rate had dropped to 50 percent.[31] These declining retention rates are a reflection of client dissatisfaction with more recent low-dose methadone therapy in overcrowded, inhumane clinics comparable to "filling stations" where addicts come in and gas up on dope.

Retention: Summary

With drop-out rates increasing dramatically, it is doubtful whether methadone maintenance through a rigidly controlled system of clinic dispensaries can *ever* achieve the same highly favorable retention rates noted by earlier investigators. High drop-out rates affect client outcome, since the quantity and intensity of program ancillary services, such as counseling or job development/placement, depend directly on the amount of time spent in maintenance treatment. No rehabilitation services can be expected to have an impact unless clients remain in therapy long enough to benefit from them. Unfortunately, clients today are remaining in treatment for shorter periods than ever before in the history of methadone maintenance.

GOAL #3: TO TRANSFER ADDICTION FROM HEROIN TO METHADONE

A twenty-eight-year-old Los Angeles woman surrendered to the FBI and admitted committing thirty bank robberies over a three-month period in which she netted close to $30,000. At her arraignment hearing she told the judge she was still using heroin, despite being on methadone maintenance for a year. "Taking methadone is supposed to keep you off heroin," said the judge. "Yeh, it's supposed to, but it don't," she replied.[32] "Dual addiction" situations like this prompt the question: How successful are methadone maintenance programs in transferring client addiction from illegal heroin to clinic methadone?

The Theory of Transference

The obvious goal of methadone maintenance is to get street addicts off heroin—not partially, not sporadically, but to cut the umbilical cord to heroin totally and immediately. The theory is that methadone substitution gives clients the opportunity to discontinue using street heroin without experiencing withdrawal. It works both ways: Methadone can be abruptly discontinued without any withdrawal symptoms by substituting heroin.

Substituting methadone for heroin, the addict is immediately freed (if the dosage is sufficient) from all pressure to secure heroin and can then focus on other problems, like getting his family back together, obtaining a job, and so on.

But transferring the client from heroin to oral methadone is difficult without major personal changes. First, methadone clients have to "cut loose" former friends and associates who are still enmeshed in the heroin-using subculture. Second, they must get away from locations in which heroin is readily available, and this is hard to do when relatives and close friends are often addicts. Third, methadone clients should not use other drugs like amphetamines, barbiturates, cocaine or alcohol. Without these "lifestyle" changes, transferring addiction from heroin to clinic doses of methadone is difficult if not impossible. But without abstinence from heroin, these lifestyle changes are impossible.

The mechanics of transferring addiction from heroin to methadone is not difficult. Most programs utilize the "loading dose" mechanism for stabilization of clients on methadone after abrupt heroin withdrawal. The client is given 10 mg doses of methadone at thirty minute intervals under supervision of a physician until central nervous system depressant effects are noted.

Program physicians then usually subtract 20 percent from this initial "loading dose" and maintain the client at that level, with reduction downward over the course of therapy.

Successful transfer of addiction from heroin to methadone is measured regularly by urinalysis to detect morphine sulfate and, less often, by physical examination of clients to detect cutaneous stigmata of parenteral heroin use.

The goal of the New York City program under Dole/Nyswander was to get clients to stop using heroin, as measured by repeated "clean" urine specimens. Based on urinalysis, Dole and Nyswander initially reported that among 120 clients admitted to their program, ". . . heroin use has been stopped consistently."[33] Five years later, reporting on 25,000 maintenance cases in New York, Dole concluded that ". . . even in the worst cases the regular use of heroin was stopped while the patients were taking their daily doses of methadone."[34]

The Dole/Nyswander program, however, may not have been as effective as it claimed in transferring addiction from heroin to methadone. For example, the statement that "heroin use has been stopped consistently" by clients was based on a subjective interpretation of what constitutes heroin "use." According to their own studies, urinalysis samplings revealed that 45 percent of Dole and Nyswander's patients took heroin at least once while receiving methadone, and 15 percent continued to use heroin repeatedly.[35] The number of reported successes would have been even lower if a substantial number of those who persisted in heroin use had not been discharged for failure to comply with the rules and omitted from the statistical picture as well. Thus, there was a selective "self-cleansing" process at work in the early Dole/Nyswander program whereby "dirty" clients were discharged or dropped out of therapy and out of subsequent analyses as well.

Dole explained the 45 percent one-time detection rate and the 15 percent continuous heroin use rate by contending that since methadone works as an "anti-narcotic" by "blockading" the euphoria induced by heroin, those who continued to take heroin were merely "testing" the "blockade" rather than "using heroin" per se. If, however, "using heroin" is defined simply as injecting the drug—which can be detected by accurate urinalysis—it cannot be maintained that methadone treatment "stopped" heroin use and that their program successfully transferred addiction from heroin to oral methadone.

GOAL #4: TO REDUCE OR ELIMINATE ILLICIT DRUG USE AMONG CLIENTS

Is there an association between methadone maintenance and discontinued use of illicit drugs among clients? Based on weekly urinalysis reports, how many methadone maintenance addict-patients abstain from using nonprescribed drugs? What client background variables and program factors appear related to reduced or eliminated illicit drug use among methadone clients? And what is the relationship between alcohol use and methadone therapy? And perhaps most important, what is the overall quality of research in this area? Are reports on client drug use accurate and reliable, or are they methodologically inadequate or self-serving measures of program "effectiveness"? These are important questions. It is a cherished bit of medical folklore that once on methadone, addicts stop using illegal drugs.

Urinalysis

Methadone maintenance programs, like probation and parole agencies, rely almost exclusively on urinalysis to determine illicit drug use among clients. Program staff are neither trained or inclined to look for post-injection cutaneous stigmata of intravenous heroin use. Neither are they expert in detecting neurological signs of illicit drug intoxication, especially in clients already sedated by methadone.

Various methods are used by urinalysis laboratories, including thin-layer gas chromatography and other spectrophoto-fluorometric methods. What these sophisticated drug-screening techniques have in common is total and complete unreliability. Sohn, for example, sent artificially treated urine specimens to 146 government-licensed drug-screening laboratories to check the reliability of their results as performance indicators for clients on methadone maintenance. The labs were wrong in 45.2 percent of the tests. Their overall accuracy rate was only 39 percent.[36]

Inaccurate results were mostly "false-positives" (clean urine reported inaccurately as dirty) and "false-negatives" (dirty urine reported inaccurately as clean).

In another study with similar results, Sohn and associates could only conclude that:

> These [laboratory] studies do not engender a high degree of confidence in the ability of licensed laboratories to consistently achieve accurate results, particularly where their day-to-day performance is concerned. . . . Routine daily performance would be anticipated to be considerably poorer [than results achieved in the study, which were based on a spot random check of labs].[37]

The whole intent of urine testing is to monitor whether or not clients are "cheating" on the program, defined as using nonprescription drugs or not taking their clinic methadone. Such tests, however, are untrustworthy indicators of drug use. A serious question is thus raised as to the validity of published results in terms of both positive and negative findings among methadone maintenance populations.

Illicit Drug Use on Methadone

Gorsuch reported that with methadone maintenance, opiate use among clients decreases sharply.[38] Gearing, in an evaluation of the Dole/Nyswander program, reported that "chronic abuse of drugs such as barbiturates, amphetamines, and more recently cocaine are evident in approximately 10% of the patients."[39] Although her study admits that a continuing "problem" with abuse of other non-opiates and alcohol exists and that discharge of individuals for these offenses continues, Gearing's evaluation included no discussion of heroin cheating or of possible discharges for continued heroin use.

Wieland and Chambers, in a study sample of clients drawn from the Philadelphia methadone program, found that 28.1 percent of them were detected by urinalysis to be occasional "cheaters" with heroin.[40] But in a review of the same program, Heyman reported that over 50 percent of her 162-patient sample submitted specimens positive for heroin in more than half their tests.[41]

In a recent study of methadone programs in New York City, Cushman and his colleagues noted:

> Finding of urinary morphine [in patients in treatment] was 3.9%. Data suggest that heroin use was low in these patients and substantiate the high degree of success that [Beth Israel Medical Center and the New York City Methadone Maintenance Treatment Program] have achieved regarding the goal of assisting patients to diminish or discontinue heroin or related drug use.[42]

However, in 1971 an independent check of client cheating patterns on the New York City program was conducted, and the results contradict Cushman. A random sample of forty addict-patients was selected from those clients in treatment more than six months and receiving more than 60 mg of methadone a day (a high dose). It was found that 82.5 percent used other detectable drugs, excluding marijuana and psychedelics: 77.5 percent used heroin; 73 percent used barbiturates; 25 percent used amphetamines; and 22.5 percent were using all three of these in combination.[43]

Dobbs, in a random sample of a hundred clients enrolled in the Washington, D.C. methadone maintenance program, found "the majority" of them still using heroin. Clients in treatment longest showed evidence of a higher rate of heroin use than recent enrollees.[44]

Results on illegal drug use thus vary widely. Three factors might explain the variance. First, strict admission requirements for the Dole/Nyswander New York City program may have skewed their "clean" results. For example, applicants were required to have a five-year history of using injected opiates, not a two-year addiction history required under current policy. This led to older clients who may have been closer to spontaneously "maturing out" of heroin use and less likely than younger, less involved addicts to abuse illegal drugs while on maintenance.

Second, only those persons who used either opiates exclusively or opiates with nonaddicting drugs were accepted into the early New York programs. Those who used barbiturates together with opiates, or who used alcohol heavily, were excluded from treatment. Early Dole/Nyswander study samples reported in the literature thus excluded users of multiple drugs and alcoholics. These clients are more common in treatment today because the quality of street heroin has declined over the past ten years. At least regarding drug use, then, Dole/Nyswander study groups were easier to treat: even though they were heroin addicts, they did not have multiple addiction histories like many later cohorts. Staff at the New York program themselves felt that for people with ". . . mixed addictions, the experience is not so good, the prognosis for success on methadone is poor."[45]

Third, if a member of the applicant's household, such as a husband or wife, was also addicted, the Dole/Nyswander program required the spouse to enroll in treatment as well. This eliminated the situation, common among later treatment groups, in which either the husband or wife (or lover or partner) is on methadone and the spouse continues using heroin. Under such conditions, the methadone-maintained spouse often relapses under the temptation and uses heroin regularly or occasionally.

In an attempt to gain a more complete picture of reports in the literature on "cheating" patterns among methadone maintenance clients, I surveyed urinalysis results from a large methadone clinic in California obtained between March 10 and June 20, 1975. The results in this investigation refer to dirty *urines*, not dirty *clients*. According to the clinic testing schedule, 1,280 samples of urine should have been submitted over the study period but only 919 were actually obtained. Of these 919 samples, 662 (72 percent) were free of nonprescribed opiates, amphetamines or barbiturates. Fifty-seven percent of the 257 "dirty" urine specimens contained morphine sulfate, the metabolite of heroin. This "cheating" pattern represents a more serious problem than merely failure to abide by program rules. Drugs taken in combination with methadone produce a synergistic effect and can result in overdose.

Combining the laboratory reports indicating the presence of illegal drugs with the 361 samples that should have been collected but were not, 48.2 percent of the total required urine samples may have contained illicit drugs. This 48.2 percent is the mean value, with a range of 41 percent in June 1975 to 60 percent in May 1975. A tentative conclusion is that if all samples required could have been analyzed, perhaps half of them would have tested positive for illegal drugs in addition to methadone metabolite.

From the numbers of dirty clients or dirty urines, it is obvious that anywhere from 10 to 60 percent of all clients on methadone maintenance continue using illicit drugs. Methadone maintenance does effect some reduction in during-treatment heroin use, but to what extent maintenance decreases the use of other drugs is unknown.

Alcoholism among Methadone Clients

Alcohol abuse by methadone clients has been the subject of attention. Bihari reported that alcohol has become the ". . . major drug of abuse among patients on methadone maintenance in New York City, both in prevalence and gravity."[46] Scott and his colleagues, studying alcohol use patterns among clients in a New Mexico methadone clinic, found "widespread alcoholism." One-fourth of the clients in the program were diagnosed as alcoholics, and the investigators concluded that:

> . . . alcoholism is the major health complication of methadone maintenance patients. . . . It largely develops following program admission. These findings give heavy support to the concept of the addictive personality.[47]

In 1976 Siassi and Alston found that 46 percent of the clients enrolled in a methadone program scored in the alcoholism range of the Michigan Alcoholism Screen Test (MAST). The authors say such data indicate that ". . . patients continue to have serious difficulties while maintained on methadone."[48]

It is possible that while they may be using heroin less, significant elements of a new lifestyle still elude many addict-patients. Problems of moodiness, loneliness and poor self-image may persist, and alcohol can dull such feelings. Gorsuch found that alcohol abuse decreased among clients in every other treatment modality *except* methadone maintenance.[49]

Illicit Drug Use: Summary

Many methadone clients continue using illegal drugs and alcohol. Those who desist are at an age where they might be expected to discontinue or decrease heroin use without narcotic substitution.[50] It is therefore reasonable to question the effect of methadone alone in "reducing" the use of narcotics for all clients. Older heroin addicts are much more likely to have exhausted their superficial veins through repeated intravenous injections and, therefore, are more likely to content themselves with the oral substitute methadone. Client characteristics therefore may be a more important independent variable than program factors in decreasing heroin use while in treatment. Further, substantial numbers of clients seek to potentiate the effects of low-dose methadone with other illegal drugs such as marijuana, cocaine and legal alcohol.

GOAL #5: TO REDUCE THE NUMBER OF SERIOUS CRIMES COMMITTED BY CLIENTS

Reduced criminal behavior seems to be the main social inducement for expansion and continuation of addiction treatment programs. However, an addict's criminal behavior may be less a function of a simple need to finance a heroin habit than part of a lifelong deviant behavior pattern. There are addicts who become criminals and criminals who become addicts.

Nearly all studies of methadone maintenance populations show significant reductions in criminal activity from pretreatment levels. But are these decreases program effects or are they attributable to other variables like client age or research bias?

The Dole/Nyswander Criminality Data

The most impressive and widely publicized statistics by Dole/Nyswander suggested that criminal behavior of addicts in their program had been "virtually eliminated."[51] They claimed 98 percent during-treatment decrease in "arrests" and a 90 percent decrease in "convictions." Their overall success rate in ending the "criminal activities" of their study group was 94 percent.[52]

Cushman and others in a study of the Beth Israel and New York City programs found an 88.5 percent decline in conviction rates compared to pretreatment levels.[53] In a separate evaluation of those programs Gearing found that arrests during the first year in treatment were 75 percent less than during the one year preceding treatment.[54] Of the 2,170 clients in the original sample, however, Gearing pared her sample down to 200 remaining clients. Thus, "positive outcomes" with reference to reduced criminality were confined to a constricted remaining sample, not the total program admissions.

In the Dole/Nyswander, Cushman, and Gearing data all clients in the Beth Israel and New York City programs who persisted in criminal activities were dropped from treatment very early. These "failures" were not included in the statistical appraisals. Thus, the 90 percent drop in convictions is less significant in view of the fact that any client convicted of a narcotic-related crime was promptly terminated from the Beth Israel and New York City programs. Thus, the study groups that were analyzed consisted of clients who had never been convicted and the 10 percent who had been convicted once and then immediately expelled from treatment. This appears to be preferential loading of the study populations with noncriminal addicts, more "successful" clients.

There are other faulty conclusions from these criminality data. For example, does the 90 percent reduction in arrests noted by Dole mean that methadone therapy, in and of itself, *caused* the result? Not necessarily. Incarceration measures not only client behavior, but police,[55]prosecutorial,[56] and judicial behavior as well.[57] Discretion undergirds the entire criminal justice system,[58] and in an age of "assembly-line justice"[59] some judges may tend to go easier on methadone clients, especially when the charge is internal possession—the most likely one among addicts. In fact, methadone maintenance clients are less likely to be arrested, prosecuted or imprisoned because of the very fact that they are in treatment. Patch and associates noted:

> Positive attitudes by local law enforcement authorities towards the methadone program . . . result in a "go easy" attitude toward criminal offenders with law enforcement recognition that continued treatment . . . could have more positive benefits for the patient and society than arrest.[60]

Thus, Dole and Nyswander's 98 percent decrease in arrests during treatment and 90 percent decrease in convictions do not mean that treatment in and of itself resulted in a lower actual crime rate among their clients. Variations in law enforcement activity, rather than methadone per se, may have been a causal factor.

The claim that methadone maintenance resulted in 94 percent of the addict-patients being arrest-free their first year in treatment is less impressive because 80 percent were arrest-free in the one year *prior* to their admission. The improvement in the arrest-free record was thus only 14 percent, not 94 percent. If 20 percent of the clients had been arrested during the year prior to admission but 6 percent arrested after they were in the program three months or longer, there is some indication that treatment resulted in reduction of arrests. Methadone does reduce arrests, but not to the degree it was believed.

Moreover, rather than relying on police and official records of postadmission criminal activity, most studies, including the Dole/Nyswander reports, depend heavily on the records of criminal activity by clients compiled by program counselors (who are mainly ex-addicts) from client self-reports, legal aid notes or rumor. This may lead to substantial underreporting of criminal charges, since there is ". . . a great discrepancy between self-reported crime and officially reported crime" among methadone patients.[61] Since these rates are based on different and sometimes unreliable information sources, they vary from one study to another. Moreover, a great discrepancy exists between officially reported crime and actual crime.

Many studies showing reduced criminality among methadone clients err in comparing crime rates across incomparable time periods. This is a methodological mistake, according to some students of methadone maintenance.[62] For example, the at-risk period prior to entry into methadone treatment may be a minimum of fourteen to nineteen years, while the period during treatment is not likely to exceed four or five years. This temporal incomparability ". . . makes it impossible to draw adequate conclusions attesting to methadone's direct relation to crime reduction."[63]

A problem that renders most crime-reduction studies of methadone populations suspect is that previous research has tended to attribute the reduction in criminality among clients *solely* to programmatic aspects of methadone therapy. As Jaffe noted:

> It is perhaps unreasonable to infer that methadone by itself produces change in lifestyle. Changes in criminal activity [are not necessarily] measures of the effectiveness of oral maintenance procedures.[64]

Intervening variables such as race, age, sex, social class, length of addiction, polydrug abuse patterns, addiction of spouse and residential patterns have been ignored as independent variables by all but a small number of studies.[65] Such a research strategy eventuated in a widely accepted conclusion that methadone maintenance directly and solely leads to a decrease in criminal behavior and that its effects are generally constant in different types and classes of clients.

Among *client variables*, the decline in criminal behavior may be more contingent upon age than on the drug methadone. The most crime-prone age group in American society is between eighteen and twenty-four. With or without methadone, men and women seem to decrease criminal activity in their thirties. Since the average age of Dole/Nyswander clients was well into their thirties, methadone therapy was begun at the very age when they might be *expected* to discontinue or reduce criminal behavior. Would the Dole/Nyswander crime-reduction data be valid for a treatment population of younger addicts?

Client Criminality: Summary

The crime-control claims of methadone maintenance programs are overrated. Methadone maintenance does reduce arrests and convictions for illegal acts directly related to heroin use, but its impact on criminal behavior is far smaller among those addicts who possess criminal behavior patterns that predate onset of addiction—criminals who become addicts. Thus, methadone maintenance relieves the "crime-to-get-money-for-dope" syndrome (if the dosage is sufficient), but the crime of all clients is not reduced. Criminal activity always remains in some methadone-treated criminals-turned-addicts.

GOAL #6: TO REHABILITATE CLIENTS VOCATIONALLY

Measures of success in methadone maintenance include "social rehabilitation," usually defined as the ability of a methadone-maintained client to find and hold a job. Less stringent definitions of employment include school involvement and "homemaking" activities. However, employment opportunities are sparse for many in America today; for lower-class heroin and methadone addicts they do not exist. A major premise of methadone policy and programs is that clients are not merely being shifted from one addictive substance to another; they *can* function, they *can* work. How successful are methadone maintenance programs as measured by the employment criterion?

Factors Related to Successful Employment

The extent to which a methadone maintenance client is able to secure a legitimate job is a highly variable treatment outcome. Much depends on *client characteristics* (like age, sex, addiction history, race, social class and motivation), *program factors* (such as dosage level, pressure to secure a job, clinic job development/placement efforts), and on *availability of employment* opportunities in the community. Methadone itself is not always the most relevant factor. Ross, for example, found a significant relationship between employment and client residential patterns:

> When we looked at the place of residence of [unemployed clients] . . . we found that they were all still residents [in a high heroin use area of Detroit]. When we looked at employed [clients] we found that 65% of them *ference, 1973,* ed. National Association for the Prevention of Addiction to relation between employment and change of address.[66]

In this study, residential mobility, interacting with methadone, paralleled successful employment. It is important, then, to know if any improvement in employment status is due to the therapeutic regimen and not to other, circumstantial variables.

Early Dole/Nyswander Employment Data. Dole and Nyswander's data showed gradual employment improvement while in treatment. For example, 66 percent of the study group was employed after one year's treatment, and 78 percent after four years in the program.[67] This employment rate applied only to clients *remaining* in treatment. If discharged clients and program dropouts are included, a much lower employment rate is obtained. For example, of the total number of clients entering the New York programs four years before their 1968 study, only 45 percent were employed (contrasted to 78 percent of those retained in treatment).

Similarly, Scher and his colleagues, reporting on a declining sample of remaining patients, reported 88 percent of their clients working, in school, or "housewifing."[68]

Early cohorts in the Dole/Nyswander New York programs succeeded in becoming classified as "socially productive" (job, school or homemaking) to a much higher extent than later cohorts. Part of the reason for the difference over time lies in the relative ease with which methadone-treated addicts were able to secure some kind of employment in the booming job market of the early 1960s. Also, the early studies may have included a larger number of potentially employable and employed clients by some sort of self-cleansing process and preferential loading of study populations with more employed and employable clients. Thus, higher employment rates may have resulted from manipulating treatment program intake procedures. Also, in the early programs a great deal more effort was made to find jobs for clients than in later programs nationwide.

Suffice it to say that the early maintenance programs produced heartening employment statistics, which indicated the efficacy of maintenance treatment and which were accepted by policymakers at all levels of government. Most employment studies are subject to the same critique concerning remaining samples in that they dealt only with the current remaining sample of addict-patients and not the total one from which it was drawn. Employment rates become significantly lower if all program admissions are included. Sechrest and Dunkley, reporting on methadone clients in California, said that although those who remain in treatment tend to do better employment-wise, dropouts ". . . are simply not performing in the legitimate job market."[69]

Dole and Nyswander reported that ". . . the majority of patients have become productive citizens."[70] But 25 to 30 percent of all methadone clients nationwide are employed when they enter methadone therapy. So the actual rates of employment improvement during treatment would be somewhat lower than those reported by Dole/Nyswander. Moreover, the Hawthorne Effect may have been at work on the early subjects: With all the high-powered professional attention focused on them, clients may simply have been motivated to "do better" in the employment realm.[71]

Most studies utilize liberal definitions of employment, such as school attendance or "housewifing."[72] Some would argue whether school attendance or "housewifing" are real employment. If full-time employment were to be considered separate from school attendance and homemaking, employment rates would be significantly lower than the rates claimed by numerous researchers. For example, Cushman and associates reported that in 1974 in the Beth Israel methadone program a total of 61 percent were employed, in school, or homemakers.[73] If employment alone is considered, the rate falls to 44 percent, a less impressive figure, particularly when compared to the fact that 43 percent of the same client population of 5,153 were on welfare. These figures resemble those for the New York City Methadone Maintenance Treatment Program: 41.5 percent were employed, but 49.8 percent were on welfare (Table 6.2). Some studies reported that *increased* dependence on welfare is associated with methadone treatment. In a study of Philadelphia addict-patients, in the first year of treatment only 12 to 15 percent of them were on welfare. In 1971, 21 percent were on welfare, and by 1972 over 50 percent were on welfare.[74] These data are consistent with the figures from Cushman and associates in Table 6.2.

Table 6.2
Social and Economic Activities of Methadone-Treated Patients in Two Consecutive Months in 1974

	Number	*Employed(%)*	*Welfare(%)*	*School(%)*	*Homemaker(%)*
New York City MMTP	11,700	41.5	49.8	5.1	8.3
Beth Israel	5,153	44.0	43.0	6.0	11.0

SOURCE: Paul Cushman et al., "Methadone Maintenance Treatment of Narcotic Addiction: A Unit of Medical Care Based on Over 50,000 Patient Treatment Years," *American Journal of Drug and Alcohol Abuse* 3 (April 1976).

Kinds of Jobs Held

When employment status is used as an outcome criterion, it is usually dichotomized as "yes-employed" or "no-unemployed." No consideration is given to type of job or the client's level of job performance, whether it is a full- or part-time job, and the length of stay on each job held. Should a client who mows lawns twice a week be classified with one who works a full-time, five-day-a-week job? Employment statistics are almost never broken down to present a detailed picture of the kinds of jobs held. When these data are uncovered, the nature and quality of jobs held by methadone clients tend to be poor.

Jobs are often viewed by some clients with marked ambivalence, tolerated as a concession to external pressure and abandoned when problems arise or other pursuits beckon. Johnson and his colleagues, for example, noted that in the Cambridge, Massachusetts, methadone treatment program when summer arrived there was a ". . . flurry of job resignations."[75] Further, of those clients in school, this report noted that their performance ". . . was often marginal."[76]

In most maintenance programs the information regarding employment status is derived wholly through self-reports. Few programs or evaluations of them demand objective evidence such as wage check stubs, time sheets, union books or employer verification. While contacting the employer interferes with a client's right of privacy and may cost the client his job, some type of objective employment status verification is necessary to validate client self-reports.

When starting samples rather than remaining ones are analyzed, when paying jobs are differentiated from school attendance or homemaking, and when employment figures indicate types of jobs held, the employment picture among methadone addicts is not so bright. Overall employment levels and welfare indices reflect the apparent failure of methadone programs to influence the vast majority of clients in the economic domain.[77] Admittedly, the most impressive during-treatment employment results are obtained with maintenance treatment (as opposed to drug-free treatment modalities), but the data indicate that substantial numbers of methadone clients remain unemployed, underemployed and dependent on public assistance and in-kind benefits like Medicaid.

Employer Attitudes toward Methadone Addicts

Beyond the client and program factors related to employment, potential employers tend to be prejudiced against persons undergoing methadone treatment. Methadone maintenance is a relatively recent development in treatment for heroin addiction. Most employers feel that using methadone in place of heroin is simply substituting one debilitating narcotic for another. They assert, to some extent correctly, that methadone maintenance fails significantly to remedy the basic problems of heroin addiction, that a methadone addict possesses the underlying "weakness" that caused him to turn to narcotics in the first place, and that such a person, while on methadone, may revert to heroin or turn to other drugs or alcohol abuse.

These employers also contend, and again to a degree correctly, that methadone impairs physical and mental performance, even if patients faithfully refrain from heroin or other illicit drug or alcohol abuse. If methadone maintenance is associated with euphoria, drowsiness, inattention, departure from concrete reality and showing of reaction time, the client may be a poor employee. Many work operations involve serious problems of safety for the public and other employees, and to employ methadone addicts could be imprudent. Would you like your bus driver or motorman to be on methadone? Many employers therefore claim that it is administratively necessary to have blanket exclusionary policies with respect to hiring methadone-maintained addicts.

Public entities, such as special districts, may not legally bar persons from employment for reasons which have no rational relationship to the demands of the jobs to be performed. To do so is a violation of both the due process and equal protection clauses of the 14th Amendment. Private employers, however, are still not subject to these restraints.

Heroin Dealers Maintained on Methadone

A factor never addressed in employment studies of methadone populations is the degree to which clients engage in illegal money-making activities. Many large-scale heroin and other drug dealers are themselves on methadone maintenance. They drive up to the clinics in expensive cars wearing expensive jewelry and expensive clothes. Where does this affluent forty-year-old unemployed, uneducated addict get all the money? By being on methadone, these dealers are not forced to dip into their own goods, leaving them more heroin to sell and consequently, greater profits.

Employment: Summary

What we see, then, in most methadone maintenance treatment programs today is a large group of disadvantaged, unemployed and underemployed narcotics addicts, almost half of whom are dependent on public assistance. Why work? The typical addict in methadone treatment, whose social class stands as a barrier to employment opportunity and whose constant hustling for heroin made legitimate work experience difficult to gain in the first place, is content with 50 mg of free methadone, a welfare check, a bottle of cold wine and color television all day long. The system has solved his problems for him. Many times addicts can be seen leaving a methadone clinic and heading straight for the nearest liquor store on their way home to another day of doing absolutely nothing.

GOAL #7: ULTIMATE DETOXIFICATION AND CONTINUED NARCOTIC ABSTINENCE

Are methadone addicts successful in breaking the methadone habit without returning to either heroin use or methadone treatment? Federal and state regulations governing maintenance programs *require* ultimate detoxification from methadone. The pressure to detoxify comes from the value placed on an opiate-free existence. What is the success rate in detoxification from methadone to maintenance? Are there certain client factors associated with successful or unsuccessful detoxification?

Berger and Schwegler studied seventeen clients who *voluntarily* attempted detoxification from methadone maintenance. The study sample excluded program dropouts and involuntary terminations. Keeping in mind the fact that duration of methadone treatment is highly associated with the ability of a person to refrain from narcotic use after detoxification,[78] Berger and Schwegler found that only nine long-term clients (53 percent) "succeeded."[79] The rest relapsed to heroin and were readmitted to maintenance therapy. The "successful" group, however, was more employed, less welfare-dependent, more middle-class, better educated, less criminally inclined, "cleaner" during treatment as measured by urinalysis, and were shorter-term heroin addicts than the "unsuccessful" group. Better-off addicts with shorter addiction histories stand a better chance of remaining abstinent following detoxification than less well-off, harder-core addicts. Schut and his colleagues also noted that detoxified methadone addicts who remained "totally abstinent" were usually white, better-educated and not separated from their spouses.[80]

Cushman and Dole studied detoxification in a "well-rehabilitated," selected group of methadone addicts. Thirty-eight (79 percent) of the forty-eight addict-patients studied were ". . . successfully detoxified, functioning well, and were drug-free when studied months after their last methadone treatment."[81] Twenty-one percent returned to maintenance therapy because of heroin use or withdrawal symptoms associated with detoxification from clinic methodone. The Cushman/Dole study group, however, was confined solely to "well-rehabilitated" methadone clients who detoxified *voluntarily*. That is, they were not program dropouts, nor were they involuntary detoxifications.

Similarly, Riordan and colleagues studied thirty-eight clients who had "successfully detoxified" from methadone maintenance. Their study group was limited to those clients ready for "good standing detoxification," that is, those in the program at least three months, with clean urine records during treatment, and with no criminal justice system involvement over the course of therapy. Obviously, this was a preferentially loaded remaining sample, not a total starting sample. Predictably, they found that a ". . . substantial number of these detoxified clients were drug-free, employed and uninvolved in the criminal justice system since detoxification."[82] Almost half of those who did relapse became reinvolved in methadone treatment. Riordan and colleagues' study, like most others, failed to examine alcohol abuse after detoxification from methadone. Moreover, all these outcome studies of detoxified methadone addicts rely on client self-reported data concerning drug use.

In a more accurate follow-up study, Stimmel and Rabin were able to obtain interviews with 168 of 198 detoxified methadone clients (85 percent). The sample included both starting and remaining patients, and the investigators divided their follow-up data according to type of discharge, either voluntary or involuntary. Ninety-two percent of those who were discharged from the maintenance program for "violation of rules" reverted to opiate use on follow-up. Of those whose enrollment was terminated by arrest, 91 percent were unable to maintain narcotic abstinence. A full 85.9 percent of persons who *voluntarily* discontinued methadone maintenance were also unable to stay "clean." Of all clients interviewed, only 17 percent were heroin-free at the time of interview. These findings, said Stimmel and Rabin, ". . . suggest that many persons will be unable to maintain the abstinent state. Detoxification and abstinence therefore should not be the sole goal of persons on methadone therapy."[83]

More recently, Stimmel and colleagues followed 269 "successfully detoxified" maintenance clients (their sample excluded dropouts). They found that 58 percent had returned to heroin use, and 8 percent were either in jail or deceased.[84]

A thorough review of the methadone detoxification literature reveals that if all detoxification cases are examined—both voluntary *and* involuntary—relapse rates are consistently in the range of 60 to 95 percent. Relapse rates predictably go down when "voluntary" detoxifications only are studied or when study groups are confined to small remaining rather than large starting samples.

Reasons for Failure Following Detoxification

It has often been charged that methadone maintenance and the medical model in general treat the symptoms of narcotic addiction rather than its causes, which may be beyond the reach of medical and policy science. Why do so many detoxified methadone addicts relapse? Jackman hypothesized that as methadone dosages are gradually reduced, clients are not nearly as well insulated from reality, anxiety and stress as they were on a higher, fixed dosage.[85] It is this reentry into the real world that tends to result in relapse to heroin use or return into methadone treatment. Typically, as methadone dosage is lowered in the process of the standard slow withdrawal schedule, it reaches a range of approximately 30 mg to 10 mg, when clients begin to reexperience the outside world emotionally with all its pain, tension and anxiety. At this point, narcotic craving typically returns, and relapse almost inevitably follows. For most clients methadone maintenance is an either/or proposition: either a lifetime on methadone (which the regulations preclude) or detoxification and eventual relapse.

In the frenzied search for the best way to "get the addict off the stuff," few have had the temerity to question the medical or empirical basis for concluding that detoxification must be the universal final goal of methadone maintenance treatment. We appear to be back where we were at the beginning, with detoxification the prevalent approach to narcotic addiction.

CONCLUSIONS ON METHADONE MAINTENANCE THERAPY

Available data from methadone maintenance outcome studies are compatible with two diametrically opposed views of this treatment modality. The "pro" view, and the one generally accepted by policymakers, is that methadone maintenance interrupts a vicious cycle of heroin addiction with its concomitant criminal activity to support the habit, resulting in a methadone-maintained blockade from heroin hunger. The addict, according to this view, is then able to turn his energies to being socially productive and developing a "rehabilitated lifestyle." Methadone maintenance has saved the lives of many street addicts.

The "anti" methadone group posits that methadone maintenance is simply the substitution of a legal addiction for an illegal one, its effects are just as detrimental as those of heroin, and methadone only relieves the addict of the inflated expenses of maintaining his criminal addiction. Criminality is not significantly affected by oral methadone maintenance; addicts continue to engage in crime although they are arrested less frequently for drug-related crimes such as possession of heroin. Comparing arrest rates immediately prior to entry into methadone treatment, when narcotic tolerance pushes them up to a lifetime peak, with the rate after enrollment is fallacious. Comparing postenrollment rates with rates sometime prior to enrollment may not show any marked change in criminality. It is possible that criminals-turned-addicts (rather than addict-criminals) maintained on methadone may be able to give up the hasty scuffle of mugging, pickpocketing, shoplifting and mail theft for the more lucrative fields of car theft, confidence games and burglary. Such a criminal career "upgrading" is never reflected in any statistics on crime committed by methadone-maintained clients.

The data presented in this chapter allow for some accommodation of these two contradictory viewpoints. Methadone maintenance is not as effective a treatment modality as was once believed. There is still a need for much more scientifically valid and relevant research in this area. When the results of such investigations beome known, the likelihood is that methadone maintenance, when compared to simple detoxification, residential treatment and aftercare counseling, will not be the panacea pronounced by its early scientific and political supporters.

In the interim, methadone maintenance is the kind of policy choice that cannot easily be retracted. What would happen, for example, if all methadone maintenance programs were abolished forthwith? More than eighty thousand methadone addicts would hit the streets in search of a fix. Can the public at large or local and national officials allow such a policy retrenchment? One doubts whether they would, and methadone maintenance programs will remain with us for some time.

NOTES

1.On the attraction goal of maintenance, see Robert G. Newman and Sylvia Bashkow, "Arrest Histories Before and After Admission to an Ambulatory Detoxification Program," in *Fifth National Conference on Methadone Treatment: Proceedings, 1973*, ed. National Association for the Prevention of Addiction to Narcotics (New York: National Association for the Prevention of Addiction to Narcotics, 1973), p. 106; Richard J. Cohen, "Treatment Seeking Behavior: Or Who Goes Where For What, and What Happens Then," in *Developments in the Field of Drug Abuse: Proceedings of the National Drug Abuse Conference—1974*, eds. Edward C. Senay, Vernon Shorty and Harold Alksne (Cambridge, Mass: Schenkman Publishing Co., 1974), pp. 347-55; Vincent P. Dole and Marie E. Nyswander, "Methadone Maintenance Treatment: A Ten-Year Perspective," *Journal of the American Medical Association* 235 (May 10, 1976): 2117-19; and Vincent P. Dole, "Addictive Behavior," *Scientific American* 243 (December, 1980): 138-51.

2. For client retention as a goal, see Richard G. Adams et al., "Heroin Addicts on Methadone Replacement: A Study of Dropouts," *International Journal of the Addictions* 6 (Summer 1971): 269-77; William D. Martin, "Commentary on the Second National Conference on Methadone Treatment," *International Journal of the Addictions* 5 (September 1970): 545-51; Urban F. Bass, III, and Barry S. Brown, "Methadone Maintenance and Methadone Detoxification: A Comparison of Retention Rates and Client Characteristics," *International Journal of the Addictions* 8 (December 1973): 889-95; Cohen, "Treatment Seeking Behavior," pp. 347-55; Thomas Henchy, Byron Eckerson and Jesse L. Paez, "The Relationship Between Age and/or Negative Experiences and Success on a Methadone Maintenance Program," *International Journal of the Addictions* 9 (April 1974): 221-27; S. Lofchie et al., "Early Performance As Predictor of Treatment Outcome in a Methadone Maintenance Program," in *Developments in the Field of Drug Abuse*, ed. Senay et al., pp. 153-70; George W. Joe and D. Dwayne Simpson, "Retention in Treatment of Drug Users: 1971-1972 DARP Admissions," *American Journal of Drug and Alcohol Abuse* 2 (January 1975): 63-72; Dole and Nyswander, "Methadone Maintenance Treatment," pp. 2117-19; and Robert G. Newman, A. Tytun and Sylvia Bashkow, "Retention of Patients in the Patients in the New York City Methadone Maintenance Treatment Program," *International Journal of the Addictions* 11 (October 1976): 905–31.

3. On the transference of addiction from street heroin to legal methadone, see Vincent P. Dole and Marie E. Nyswander, "A Medical Treatment for Diacetylmorphine ('Heroin') Addiction," *Journal of the American Medical Association* 193 (August 23, 1965): 646-50; Vincent P. Dole and Marie E. Nyswander, "Rehabilitation of Heroin Addicts After Blockade with Methadone," *New York State Journal of Medicine* 66 (April 1966): 2011-17; Vincent P. Dole and Marie E. Nyswander, "Heroin Addiction: A Metabolic Disease," *Archives of Internal Medicine* 120 (July 1967): 19-24; Vincent P. Dole and Marie E. Nyswander, "Successful Treatment of 750 Criminal Drug Addicts," *Journal of the American Medical Association* 206 (December 16, 1968): 2711; and Dole, "Addictive Behavior," *Scientific American* 243 (December, 1980): 138-51.

4. On discontinuance of illegal drug use in methadone therapy, see Dole and Nyswander, "A Medical Treatment for Addiction," pp. 646-50; Dole and Nyswander, "Rehabilitation of Heroin Addicts," pp. 2011-17;

Dole and Nyswander, "Heroin Addiction: A Metabolic Disease," pp. 19-24; Dole and Nyswander, "Successful Treatment," p. 2711; Stuart Ross, "A Study of Living and Residence Patterns of Former Heroin Addicts as a Result of Their Participation in a Methadone Treatment Program," in *Fifth National Conference, 1973,* ed. National Association for the Prevention of Addiction to Narcotics, pp. 554-61; Dale K. Sechrest and Thomas E. Dunckley, "A One-Year Follow-Up of Methadone Patients on Drug Use, Criminal Behavior, and Wages Earned," in *Fifth National Conference, 1973,* ed. National Association for the Prevention of Addiction to Narcotics, pp. 1290-303; Robert C. Wolfe, "Methadone Maintenance as a Medical Treatment: The Continuing Need for Controlled Clinical Study," in *Fifth National Conference, 1973,* ed. National Association for the Prevention of Addiction to Narcotics, pp. 723-27; Lois R. Chatham and S. B. Sells, "Evaluation of Treatment for Drug Abuse Based on the Joint NIMH-TCU Drug Abuse Reporting Program (DARP)," in *Developments in the Field of Drug Abuse,* ed. Senay et al., pp. 102-9; Thomas J. Cox and Bill Longwell, "Reliability of Interview Data Concerning Current Heroin Use From Heroin Addicts on Methadone," *International Journal of the Addictions* 9 (January 1974): 161-65; Richard L. Gorsuch, "The Impact of Drug Treatment on During-Treatment Criteria: 1971-1972 DARP Admissions," *American Journal of Drug and Alcohol Abuse* 2 (January 1975): 73-98.

5. For crime reduction as a goal of methadone therapy, see Sechrest and Dunckley, "A One-Year Follow-Up of Methadone Patients," pp. 1290-303; Wolfe, "Methadone Maintenance as Medical Treatment," pp. 723-27; Ross, "Living and Residence Patterns of Former Addicts," pp. 554-61; Chatham and Sells, "Evaluation of Treatment," pp. 102-9; William P. Collins and William P. Kelly, Jr., "Methadone Treatment and Crime Reduction—Differential Impact: An Analysis and A Case Study," in *Developments in the Field of Drug Abuse,* ed. Senay et al., pp. 143-47; Gorsuch, "The Impact of Drug Treatment," p. 73-98; and Dole and Nyswander, "Rehabilitation of Heroin Addicts," pp. 2011-17. Others note that the criminal justice system tends to "go easy" on methadone clients who commit crimes, thus making the programs seem more successful than they really are. See Wayne R. LaFave, *Arrest: The Decision to Take a Suspect into Custody* (Boston: Little, Brown and Co., 1964); Frank Miller, *Prosecution: The Decision to Charge a Suspect with a Crime* (Boston: Little, Brown and Co., 1969), chapters 14-16; and James Klonoski and Robert Mendelsohn, eds. *The Politics of Local Justice* (Boston: Little, Brown and Co., 1970), chapters 1-2.

6. For analyses of whether or not maintenance is successful in terms of the vocational rehabilitation criterion, see Martin, "Commentary," pp. 545-51; Ross, "Living and Residence Patterns of Former Addicts," pp. 554-61; Sechrest and Dunckley, "A One-Year Follow-up of Methadone Patients," pp. 1290-303; Wolfe, "Methadone Maintenance as Medical Treatment," pp. 723-27; Burt Johnson et al., "Clinical Experiences with Methadone Maintenance in Young Adults: The Public Health Approach Versus the Individual Perspective," in *Fifth National Conference, 1973*, ed. National Association for the Prevention of Addiction to Narcotics, pp. 601-9; Chatham and Sells, "Evaluation of Treatment," pp. 102-9; and Thomas P. Griesa, "Carl Beazer v. New York City Transit Authority," *Contemporary Drug Problems* 4 (Fall 1975): 360-65.

7. For ultimate detoxification as a primary goal of methadone therapy, see Vincent P. Dole, Marie E. Nyswander and Mary Jeanne Kreek, "Narcotics Blockade," *Archives of Internal Medicine* 118 (October 1966): 304-9; Paul Cushman, Jr., and Vincent P. Dole, "Detoxification of Well Rehabilitated Methadone Maintained Patients," in *Fifth National Conference, 1973*, ed. National Association for the Prevention of Addiction to Narcotics, pp. 262-69; Herbert Berger and Michael J. Schwegler, "Voluntary Detoxification of Patients on Methadone Maintenance," *International Journal of the Addictions* 8 (December 1973): 1043-47; Barry Stimmel, Joel Rabin, and Carol Engel, "The Prognosis of Patients Detoxified From Methadone Maintenance: A Follow-Up Study," in *Fifth National Conference, 1973*, ed. National Association for the Prevention of Addiction to Narcotics, pp. 270-74; Wohlmuth Schut, Barbara Naglin, and Karen File, "Identification of 'Successful' Patients in a Methadone Maintenance Program Based on Weekly Urinalysis Reports," in *Fifth National Conference, 1973*, ed. National Association for the Prevention of Addiction to Narcotics, pp. 1066-69; John N. Chappel, "Methadone and Chemotherapy in Drug Addiction: Genocidal or Lifesaving?" *Journal of the American Medical Association* 228 (May 6, 1974): 725-28; Paul Cushman, Jr., "Detoxification of Rehabilitated Methadone Patients: Frequency and Predictors of Long-Term Success," *American Journal of Drug and Alcohol Abuse* 1 (September 1974): 393-408; Paul Cushman, Jr., "Detoxification from Methadone Maintenance," *Journal of the American Medical Association 236 (November 8, 1976): 2171;* Joel Rabin and Barry Stimmel, "A Follow-Up of Patients Discharged From Methadone Maintenance," in *Developments in the Field of Drug Abuse*, ed. Senay et al., pp. 171-76; and Barry Stimmel, J. Goldberg and M. Cohen, "Ability to Remain Abstinent After Methadone Detoxification: A Six Year Study," *Journal of the American Medical Association* 237 (March 21, 1977): 1216-20.

8. See Morris Ploscowe, "Some Basic Problems in Drug Addiction and Suggestions for Research," in *Drug Addiction: Crime or Disease? Interim and Final Reports of the Joint Committee of the American Bar Association and The American Medical Association on Narcotic Drugs*, ed. Advisory Committee to the Federal Bureau of Narcotics (Bloomington, Ind.: Indiana University Press, 1961), pp. 103-7; and Alfred R. Lindesmith, "Traffic In Dope," *The Nation* (April 21, 1956), pp. 337-39.

9. Dole and Nyswander, "Methadone Maintenance Treatment," pp. 2117-19.

10. California State Department of Mental Hygiene, *Methadone Maintenance Regulations* (Sacramento, Calif.: Department of Mental Hygiene, March 1973), p. 28.

11. Ibid., p. 30.

12. Avram Goldstein, Ralph W. Hansteen, and William H. Horns, "Control of Methadone Dosage by Patients," *Journal of the American Medical Association* 234 (November 17, 1975): 734.

13. Ibid., p. 735.

14. Quoted in Virginia Lewis et al., "Nalline and Urine Test in Narcotics Detection: A Critical Overview," *International Journal of the Addictions* 8 (January 1973): 169.

15. Quoted in ibid.

16. David Sohn, "Analysis for Drugs of Abuse: The Validity of Reported Results in Relation to Performance Testing," *International Journal of the Addictions* 8 (February 1973): 72.

17. Richard Kunnes, *The American Heroin Empire: Power, Profits, and Politics* (New York: Dodd, Mead and Co., 1972), p. 114.

18. See Henchy, "Relationship Between Age and Negative Experiences on Methadone;" Lofchie, "Early Performance as a Predictor of Outcome;" and Joe and Simpson, "Retention in Treatment."

19. Henchy, Eckerson and Paez, "Relationship Between Age and Negative Experiences on Methadone."

20. Joe and Simpson, "Retention in Treatment," pp. 63-72.

21. M. E. Perkins, "Survey of Methadone Maintenance Treatment Programs," *American Journal of Psychiatry* 126 (April 10, 1970): 33-39.

22. Henchy, Eckerson and Paez, "Relationship Between Age and Negative Experiences on Methadone."

23. Robert G. Newman, "Methadone Maintenance: It Ain't What It Used To Be," in *Developments in the Field of Drug Abuse*, ed. Senay et al., pp. 51-55.

24. Adams et al., "Heroin Addicts on Methadone: Dropouts," p. 269.

25. Dole et al., "Narcotics Blockade."

26. Reported in Frances R. Gearing, "Successes and Failures in Methadone Maintenance Treatment of Heroin Addiction in New York City," U.S. Public Health Services Publication #2172 (Washington, D.C.: U.S. Government Printing Office, 1971), pp. 2-16.

27. Ibid.

28. For excellent critiques of the Gearing and Dole/Nyswander data, see J. V. DeLong, "Treatment and Rehabilitation," in *Dealing With Drug Abuse*, ed. The Ford Foundation (New York: The Ford Foundation, 1973), p. 176; and Edward Jay Epstein, "Methadone: The Forlorn Hope," *The Public Interest* 36 (Summer 1974): 3-24.

29. Sechrest and Dunckley, "A One-Year Follow-Up of Methadone Patients," pp. 1290-303.

30. Reported in Dole and Nyswander, "Methadone Maintenance Treatment," 2117-19.

31. Newman, Tytun, and Bashkow, "Retention of Patients in Maintenance Treatment," pp. 905-31.

32. "Woman Sought for 30 Robberies Turns Self In," *Los Angeles Times* (January 14, 1977), Pt. I, p. 4.

33. Dole and Nyswander, "Rehabilitation of Heroin Addicts," p. 2016.

34. Vincent P. Dole, "Methadone Maintenance Treatment for 25,000 Heroin Addicts," *Journal of the American Medical Association* 215 (February 23, 1971): 1333.

35. Dole and Nyswander, "Successful Treatment of 750 Drug Addicts," p. 2711.

36. Sohn, "Analysis for Drugs of Abuse," p. 72.

37. David Sohn et al., "Management of Ancillary Facilities Within Methadone Maintenance Treatment Program: Quality Control of the Laboratory and the Pharmacy," in National Association for the Prevention of Addiction to Narcotics, *Fifth National Conference, 1973*, p. 1081. Paul Blachly, an addiction treatment specialist, says that ". . . routine urine testing in methadone programs is an extreme waste of money. There is no evidence presented of cost-effectiveness with regard to helping rehabilitate patients, and every physician who has had much experience with these programs feels that, on a routine basis, they are a great waste of resources." See his Letter to the Editor, *Journal of the American Medical Association* 238 (July 4, 1977): 27.

38. Gorsuch, "The Impact of Drug Treatment," p. 75.

39. Gearing, "Successes and Failures in Maintenance Treatment," p. 10.

40. William F. Wieland and Carl D. Chambers, "Methadone Maintenance: A Comparison of Two Stabilization Techniques," *International Journal of the Addictions* 5 (September 1970): 9.

41. Florence Heyman, "Methadone Maintenance as Law and Order," *Society* 9 (June 1972): 25.

42. Paul Cushman et al., "Methadone Maintenance Treatment of Narcotic Addiction: A Unit of Medical Care Based on Over 50,000 Patient Treatment Years," *American Journal of Drug and Alcohol Abuse* 3 (April 1976): 226.

43. Heyman, "Methadone Maintenance as Law and Order," p. 25.

44. William H. Dobbs, "Methadone Treatment of Heroin Addicts: Early Results Provide More Questions Than Answers," *Journal of the American Medical Association* 218 (December 6, 1971): 1536-41.

45. Raymond M. Glasscote et al., eds. *The Treatment of Drug Abuse: Programs, Problems, Prospects* (Washington, D.C.: Joint Information Service of the American Psychiatric Association and the National Association for Mental Health, 1972), p. 73.

46. Bernard Bihari, "Alcoholism in M.M.T.P. Patients: Etiological Factors and Treatment Approaches," in *Fifth National Conference, 1973,* ed. National Association for the Prevention of Addiction to Narcotics, p. 288.

47. Neil R. Scott, Walter W. Winslow and David G. Gorman, "Epidemiology of Alcoholism in a Methadone Maintenance Program," in *Fifth National Conference, 1973,* ed. National Association for the Prevention of Addiction to Narcotics, p. 286.

48. Iradj Siassi and Dominick C. Alston, "Methadone Maintenance and the Problem with Alcohol," *American Journal of Drug and Alcohol Abuse* 3 (April 1976): 273.

49. Gorsuch, "The Impact of Drug Treatment," p. 76.

50. See Richard N. Bale et al., "Methadone Treatment Versus Therapeutic Communities: Preliminary Results of a Randomized Study in Progress," in *Fifth National Conference, 1973,* ed. National Association for the Prevention of Addiction to Narcotics, p. 1028.

51. Dole and Nyswander, "Rehabilitation of Heroin Addicts," p. 2017.

52. Dole and Nyswander, "Successful Treatment," pp. 2708, 2710.

53. Cushman et al., "Methadone Maintenance Treatment: 50,000 Patient Years," p. 227.

54. Gearing, "Successes and Failures in Maintenance Treatment," pp. 2-16.

55. On police discretion, especially in relation to clients enrolled in methadone therapy, see LaFave, *Arrest*; and James Q. Wilson, *Varieties of Police Behavior: The Management of Law and Order in Eight Communities* (New York: Atheneum, 1971), chapter 4.

56. On the leniency prosecutors display toward addicts enrolled in methadone therapy, see Donald E. Newman, *Conviction: The Determi-*

nation of Guilt or Innocence Without Trial (Boston: Little, Brown and Co., 1966), pp. 60-79; Miller, *Prosecution*, chapters 14-16; David W. Neubauer, *Criminal Justice in Middle America* (Morristown, N.J.: General Learning Press, 1974), pp. 117-18; and Michael A. Mulkey, "Adjudication as the Administrative Procedures of Charging and Plea Bargaining: The Roles of Prosecution and Defense," in *Crime and Criminal Justice*, ed. John A. Gardiner and Michael A. Mulkey (Lexington, Mass.: Lexington Books, D.C. Health and Co., 1975), pp. 121-30.

57. On judicial leniency toward methadone clients, see G. Hayim, "Changes in the Behavior of Addicts: A One-Year Follow-Up Study of Methadone Treatment," mimeographed, 1972.

58. Klonoski and Mendelsohn, eds. *The Politics of Local Justice*, chapters 1-2.

59. The term "assembly-line justice" is from Abraham Blumberg, *Criminal Justice* (Chicago: Quadrangle Books, Inc., 1967); also, on crowded court calendars pushing judges to go easy on addicts enrolled in treatment, see Jonathan Casper, *American Criminal Justice* (Englewood Cliffs, N.J.: Prentice-Hall, 1972); Herbert Jacob and James Eisenstein, *Felony Justice* (Boston: Little, Brown and Co., 1976); and Herbert Jacob and James Eisenstein, "Sentences and Other Sanctions in the Criminal Courts of Baltimore, Chicago, and Detroit," *Political Science Quarterly*, 90 (Winter 1975-1976): 617-36.

60. Vernon D. Patch et al., "Heroin Addicts and Violent Crime," in *Fifth National Conference*, 1973, ed. National Association for the Prevention of Addiction to Narcotics, p. 387.

61. Collins and Kelly, "Methadone Treatment and Crime Reduction," p. 146.

62. For an examination of this methodological error, see James F. Maddux and Charles L. Bowden, "Critique of Success with Methadone Maintenance," *American Journal of Psychiatry* 129 (October 1972): 440-46; Jordan M. Scher et al., "Overemployment, Mobility, and Rehabilitation in Methadone Maintenance," in *Fifth National Conference, 1973*, ed. National Association for the Prevention of Addiction to Narcotics, p. 846; Wolfe, "Methadone Maintenance as Medical Treatment," p. 726; and Collins and Kelly, "Methadone Treatment and Crime Reduction," p. 146.

63. Collins and Kelly, "Methadone Treatment and Crime Reduction," p. 146.

64. Quoted in Epstein, "Methadone: The Forlorn Hope," p. 13.

65. A few studies pay close attention to intervening variables beyond the simple administration of methadone. See, for example, Bale et al., "Methadone Treatment Versus Therapuetic Communities," p. 1028; Ross, "A Study of Living and Residence Patterns of Former Addicts," p. 555;

Henchy, Eckerson and Paez, "Relationship Between Age and Negative Experiences on Methadone," p. 225; and Lofchie et al., "Early Performance as a Predictor of Outcome," p. 157-58.

66. Ross, "A Study of Living and Residence Patterns of Former Addicts," p. 558.

67. Dole and Nyswander, "Successful Treatment," p. 2711.

68. Scher et al., "Overemployment, Mobility, and Rehabilitation," pp. 847-48.

69. Sechrest and Dunckley, "One-Year Follow-Up of Methadone Patients," p. 1300.

70. Dole and Nyswander, "Successful Treatment," p. 2711.

71. For the experimental industrial study that originally induced the "Hawthorne Effect," see F. J. Roethlisberger and W. J. Dickson, *Management and the Worker* (Cambridge, Mass.: Harvard University Press, 1939).

72. See Dole and Nyswander's wide definition of employment in their "Successful Treatment," p. 2711.

73. Cushman et al., "Methadone Maintenance Treatment: 50,000 Patient Years," pp. 221-27.

74. Heyman, "Methadone Maintenance as Law and Order," p. 25.

75. Johnson et al., "Clinical Experiences with Methadone Maintenance," p. 607.

76. Ibid.

77. The same conclusion is reached by Chatham and Sells, "Evaluation of Treatment for Drug Abuse," p. 107.

78. On the relationship between time in treatment and success, see Stimmel, Goldberg and Cohen, "Ability to Remain Abstinent," p. 1216.

79. Berger and Schwegler, "Voluntary Detoxification," pp. 1043-45.

80. Schut, Naglin and File, "Identification of 'Successful' Patients in a Methadone Program," pp. 1067-68.

81. Cushman and Dole, "Detoxification of Well Rehabilitated Methadone Maintained Patients," p. 747.

82. C. E. Riordan et al., "Successful Detoxification From Methadone Maintenance," *Journal of the American Medical Association* 235 (June 14, 1976): 2004.

83. Barry Stimmel and Joel Rabin, "The Ability to Remain Abstinent Upon Leaving Methadone Maintenance: A Prospective Study," *American Journal of Drug and Alcohol Abuse* 1 (July 1974): 379-80.

84. Stimmel, Goldberg and Cohen, "Ability to Remain Abstinent," p. 1216.

85. Jay M. Jackman, "A Hypothesis Concerning the Difficulty of Withdrawal from Maintenance on Methadone," in *Fifth National Conference, 1973*, ed. National Association for the Prevention of Addiction to Narcotics, pp. 472-73.

7

Heroin Detoxification and Aftercare Counseling

Heroin detoxification, as defined here, is dispensing, for a period of less than twenty-one days, decreasing doses of methadone or other symptomatic medication to an addict in an in- or outpatient setting in order to alleviate the acute physiological and psychological effects incident to withdrawal from chronic narcotic use. It is a method of bringing the individual to a drug-free state within such a period.

TREATMENT PROCESS AND OUTCOME GOALS

Most detoxification programs, which must be licensed to operate by appropriate government agencies, have two broad categories of goals. First, during-treatment *process goals*, are measurable at the time of discharge from treatment, mainly to maximize the number of heroin addicts who successfully complete in- or outpatient detoxification treatment.

Second are posttreatment *outcome goals*, which are measurable only after program discharge. The outcome goal analyzed here is to minimize the number of clients who relapse to regular narcotic use following discharge from in- or outpatient detoxification.

HISTORY OF DETOXIFICATION TREATMENT

Addicts, of course, have detoxified themselves for years by gradually reducing their own narcotic dosage. I have "kicked" more than fifty heroin habits in this manner. By the late 1800s physicians were generally treating morphine and heroin addiction by gradually reducing the amount of the drug they gave to the patient. How well this gradual withdrawal treatment worked then is not known; there are no follow-up data available. Nevertheless, from the mid-nineteenth century until well into the 1940s physicians continued to tell one another that simple detoxification and perhaps a few weeks of aftercare was the most effective "cure" for opiate addiction.

Lexington and Ft. Worth: "Narcotic Farms"

The first large-scale inpatient heroin detoxification program in the United States was at the U.S. Public Health Service narcotics hospital in Lexington, Kentucky. A similar hospital at Ft. Worth, Texas, was authorized in the legislation that created the Lexington facility.

When these two hospitals were established in the mid-1930s, knowledge about addiction and narcotics was rudimentary. During this period the procedure for medically assisted withdrawal was first being worked out. Begun in the flush of New Deal optimism, both hospitals are now considered abject failures. Neither of them is treating addicts on a large scale.

In a follow-up of 12,000 addicts discharged from Lexington, Vaillant explored the relation of inpatient detoxification to client outcome following discharge. He defined "success" as posttreatment narcotic abstinence outside the institution. Within a year of discharge, however, more than 90 percent of his study group relapsed to regular narcotic use.[1] The "success" rate, as measured by heroin relapse, was 10 percent. Detoxification did not suppress postdischarge "narcotic hunger" or "craving."

Robert Felix, M.D., former director of NIMH and a physician at Lexington from 1936 to 1941, confirms Vaillant's findings: "If we got a 10% [postdischarge] nonrelapse rate, we felt very good about it."[2]

Retention in Treatment

Detoxification programs must be able to keep their addict-patients in order to treat them. What percentage of cases are retained until they complete their detoxification regimen? Raynes and his colleagues in a random sample of a hundred addicts detoxified at Boston City Hospital noted a 48 percent "split" rate prior to program completion: "Of the 100 patients . . . only 52 completed detoxification while 48 failed to finish the regimen leaving 'Against Medical Advice.' "[3]

Metropolitan State Hospital's heroin detoxification ward in Norwalk, California, has a "split" rate of around 35 percent. Some detoxification units have managed to drop this attrition rate to as low as 10 percent.[4] Attrition rates in detoxification depend primarily on four variables: (1) type and amount of medication dispensed to control withdrawal, (2) staff attitudes toward clients, (3) client background variables, including level of motivation and severity of habit, and (4) the length of the actual detoxification regimen.

Retention in treatment is important, since time-in-treatment is associated with postdischarge narcotic use. Raynes and his colleagues compared postdischarge heroin use by patients satisfactorily completing detoxification to patients who "split" prior to formal discharge. Comparing completers to splitters, they concluded: "One year after treatment seven of the 'Complete' group were heroin-free (13.4%) while only two of the 'Incomplete' group were heroin free (4.2%)."[5] Thus, program completers did slightly better after discharge than splitters.

Postdischarge Outcome

An investigation by Washington, D.C.'s Narcotic Treatment Administration showed that in-hospital detoxification was successful in only about 3 percent of their cases. Based on the high relapse rate following discharge, this study concluded that inpatient detoxification is ". . . a difficult modality in which to achieve a large measure of success. . . . [It] does not achieve the great deal of success we would like to see. . . ."[6]

Raynes and his colleagues followed a combined group of splitters and completers and found a combined relapse rate of 91.3 percent. They could only conclude that "With general hospital inpatient treatment costing upward of $110 a day, it is evident that this modality of treatment has poor cost effectiveness."[7]

Abramowitz and Pantleo followed sixteen urban heroin addicts detoxified with methadone in a Denver hospital to assess the impact of the program on postdischarge heroin use. They found that ". . . methadone withdrawal intervention typically had only a minor impact on the drug use of the addict exposed to it."[8]

RESULTS OF OUTPATIENT DETOXIFICATION

With such poor results in expensive hospital settings, clinicians and government funding sources have turned to outpatient, ambulatory detoxification of heroin addicts. It was predicted that relapse rates would be about the same for both modalities, but that treatment costs could be cut as much as 80 percent by utilizing outpatient instead of in-hospital detoxification. What are the results of outpatient detoxification compared to the inpatient modality? Are the relapse rates similar?

Gudeman and associates in a comparative follow-up study found a slightly lower relapse rate for inpatient heroin detoxification cases than those exposed to outpatient treatment. The combined relapse rate for both modalities, however, was 90 percent within one year of program discharge.[9] These results are similar to those achieved by Raynes and his colleagues.[10] Gay and his colleagues also found a 90 percent relapse rate following discharge from an outpatient detoxification program in San Francisco.[11] This program, however, used symptomatic medication such as minor tranquilizers to control the withdrawal syndrome. Experience indicates their program probably had an exceptionally high "split" rate because addicts generally prefer easing withdrawal with a narcotic rather than with nonnarcotic symptom relievers such as strong or weak tranquilizers, muscle relaxants, stool softeners or more esoteric techniques like acupuncture.

Tennant attempted to detoxify eighteen heroin addicts on an ambulatory regimen using acupuncture, electrical stimulation and staplepuncture. He compared this group to two similar groups, one detoxified with methadone and the other with Darvon-N (propoxyphene napsylate, a mild analgesic structurally related to methadone). In only one person (5 percent) of the group treated with acupuncture or staplepuncture was complete detoxification achieved, compared with thirteen and ten persons, respectively, in the other two groups.[12]

Canada followed 157 discharged clients detoxified on an outpatient basis using methadone and noted that only ten of them (7 percent) were "clean"—narcotic-free—six months after program discharge. He concluded that a ". . . short term program with ambulatory patients . . . does not produce favorable results."[13]

O'Mally and associates similarly found little success, as measured by relapse, with outpatient detoxification of heroin addicts.[14] Tennant and Silsby explored relapse rates for twenty-one young heroin addicts admitted to an outpatient heroin detoxification program using methadone to control withdrawal syndrome. The treatment regimen was seven days, a standard one in this modality. The findings of the study were characteristic:

> Eight (38%) did not finish detoxification. After 6 months, only 2 (9.5%) were found to be heroin-free. Although low-dose methadone detoxification can easily be accomplished on a short-term ambulatory basis, the high relapse rate to opiate use indicates this procedure should only be used with selected, motivated people.[15]

Most detoxification programs, however, do not attempt to weed out "motivated" treatment applicants from unmotivated ones; whoever applies for detoxification usually is admitted. I have admitted some clients to inpatient and outpatient detoxification each more than thirty times.

In a large outpatient sample Werner and her colleagues reported the experience of New York City's huge outpatient detoxification program, organized to save taxpayers' dollars by eliminating the need for hospitalization. Of 21,764 patients who started detoxification treatment, only 51 percent completed the full seven-day regimen. Thus, the program had poorer retention power than most inpatient programs. It was also less successful in terms of reducing during-treatment drug use among the client population. Of the 51 percent remaining in treatment, 27 percent submitted urine samples positive for heroin on either the sixth or final seventh day of treatment.[16] These results support the conclusion that significant numbers of clients being detoxified on an ambulatory basis continue using heroin throughout the treatment episode.

Comparative results based on relapse indicate that inpatient detoxification may be slightly more effective than outpatient withdrawal.[17] Hospitalization is especially successful in keeping addict-patients more heroin-free during the regimen. The clinician can be fairly certain that most clients are not using illicit drugs while hospitalized for detoxification. It is another story when clients are free in the streets, attending a detoxification clinic daily for decreasing doses of methadone.

Wilson and colleagues compared relapse rates for outpatient versus inpatient detoxification using methadone and found

> . . . little benefit from either treatment approach and no significant differences between the treatments. But the cost of outpatient detoxification can be done for 10% the cost of in-hospital treatment without significantly altering effectiveness of treatment [as measured by post-discharge relapse].[18]

SUMMARY

Outcome studies paint a gloomy picture for detoxification from heroin, the oldest "cure" for narcotic addiction. The overwhelming finding is that even if detoxification is achieved without the client "splitting," relapse nearly always follows discharge because the addict reexperiences reality with all its inevitable conflicts, frustrations and anxieties.

Detoxification as a Contributor to Addiction

Detoxification programs might even contribute to heroinism. The easy availability of methadone-assisted detoxification today, especially in exotic hospital settings where addicts are cared for in the fullest sense, may actually *encourage* further heroin use: The addict finally reaches that point in his heroin use where tolerance develops, euphoria is lost, and he has to hustle every waking hour just to stave off withdrawal. The addiction is no longer fun. Then he enters a detoxification ward and is comfortably withdrawn from heroin. Detoxification is made so easy, compared to "cold turkey," that addicts are not confronted with the negatively reinforcing pharmacological and physiological aspects of addiction.

What has been the train of events? The treatment system has solved the addict's problems for him: the problems of lost euphoria, of the high cost of obtaining several grains of heroin daily, of physiological dependence. Detoxification simply reduces the addict's tolerance so that he can once again experience heroin euphoria at an affordable price.

This kind of "cure" or "treatment" may, then, actually support addiction as much as it ameliorates it. Program staffs should not be surprised or miffed when addicts leave the detoxification ward and inject heroin within a few minutes or hours.

AFTERCARE COUNSELING

Aftercare counseling programs constitute about 30 percent of the addiction treatment client "slots" available in the United States. These outpatient, drug-free counseling services get most of their clients directly from in- and outpatient heroin detoxification units. Aftercare counseling programs are not residential, they do not use methadone or other drugs, and their main treatment goal is abstinence. They are postdetoxification counseling and casework services designed to reform heroin addicts. Reform in such programs is measured through during- and posttreatment reduction/termination of (1) heroin use, and (2) criminality, as well as getting and holding a legitimate job.

THE ABSTINENCE GOAL

The manifest treatment goal of all aftercare programs is drug abstinence generally, including alcohol. One program says, "The goal [of aftercare] is to interrupt the abuse of drugs, embarking the abusers on a course of treatment . . . [geared toward returning the abuser to the community symptom-free."[19] Another large, publicly funded aftercare program in the Los Angeles area says its major goal is to ". . . free the drug user from his habit so that he will . . . stop using illegal drugs and/or narcotics and will not begin to use them again. . . ."[20]

Unfortunately, neither of these aftercare centers has ever conducted a post discharge follow-up study to determine just how many and what kinds of clients stay drug-free after discharge. The largest aftercare program in southern California states simply that its goal is "heroin abstinence."[21] They cannot measure goal achievement, however, since they too have eschewed systematic post-discharge follow-up of aftercare clients.

TYPES OF AFTERCARE PROGRAMS

Two broad types of aftercare programs have emerged since the Nixon administration targeted them for increased funding: (1) day-care centers, where addicts spend a good portion of each day in various forms of "therapy," and (2) drop-in or "walk-in" centers where clients are free to use services on an "as-needed" basis, usually at least once a month to be called an active client. Drop-in centers are by far the more numerous.

Therapy

Aftercare program philosophies generally see heroin addiction in terms of the standard medical model: addicts are sick, physically, mentally and/or socially, and compulsive heroin use is but a symptom of this "disease." The focus is on the individual user rather than on environmental conditions that may be associated with addiction. "Therapy" is eclectic, embracing individual, group, family and crisis counseling, urine surveillance, job development/placement efforts, recreational activities and other ancillary services (such as educational and legal counseling and referrals to other programs).

Counseling

Traditional counseling is the most prominent element in the aftercare program regimen. It is aimed at strengthening the client's ability to cope with abstinence following detoxification. Short-term personal, family and job/school/legal problems related to heroin use or a return to heroin addiction are the main topics during these counseling sessions. For deeper, more complicated problems beyond the program's capability, clients are often referred to public and mental health services such as employment development, public assistance and psychiatric/psychological therapy at community mental health centers. Aftercare staff are supposed to monitor carefully the course of such referrals and incorporate the results into the counseling offered.

In most aftercare programs counselors sit back and give advice to addicts on a regularly scheduled appointment basis. This brand of "therapy" keeps few addicts off heroin. Counseling is talking; and a counselor can talk until his larynx gives out with little affect on a client's compulsive drug abuse.

Dissatisfaction with this "talking" approach has led some aftercare programs to adopt a "doing" orientation or "field casework" model whereby counselors are transformed into hip street workers who go out and meet clients on their own turf, literally walking them through the details of the mundane, work a day world of abstinence: applying for jobs, starting a bank account, getting enrolled in school, joining the Navy, filing for divorce, getting back into a detoxification program after relapse to heroin. The idea behind this casework approach is that "talk is cheap" and virtually useless in keeping addicts "clean." Action speaks louder than words.

The content, type and frequency of counseling or casework services vary depending on program goals, client characteristics and staff background, training and expertise. For example, "rap groups" are a popular offering by programs dealing with young "multiple-drug abusers" who use heroin occasionally, but who have not become addicted. These raps focus on personal problems, self-awareness, decision-making skills, values clarification and alternatives to drug use. They are mainly *prevention*-oriented. Programs treating older, hard-core heroin addicts are more inclined to employ traditional individual and family counseling, casework in the streets, or perhaps hard-attack group encounter sessions.

Federal policy requires aftercare programs to have a psychologist and psychiatrist on staff "to treat clients and provide supervisory training and evaluation of effectiveness of specific techniques."[22] Most programs, however, do not employ such professionals. Instead, they are staffed largely by recovered addicts, many of whom are barely off heroin themselves. Most addicts who "clean up" "get religion" and have a burning desire to work for a treatment program so they can help their less fortunate "partners." These "counselors" have a niche in aftercare programs because:

1. They provide necessary information to "straight" staff about street life and the addict subculture.

2. They relate to addicts and individuals trying to get off heroin in a way that academically trained professional staff cannot emulate because the latter lack personal experience in the "drug life."
3. They are often the first staff members to notice problems developing with clients.

Intra-staff conflicts within aftercare programs often get in the way of service provision. There is always jealousy and internecine conflict between "paraprofessional" or "experientially trained" ex-addict staff and professional, nonaddict employees. The professionals are often white, middle-class "social worker types." Conflicts between them and recovered addict staff are often rooted in squabbles over job status, inequalities in pay, job titles and actual duties.

Some professionals working in aftercare centers lack even rudimentary knowledge of addicts, addiction, psychology, medicine or social work, despite their academic training and impressive resumes. Ex-addict staff, despite their personal experience with heroin, generally lack the same kinds of knowledge. One professional staff member at an aftercare program, for example, told me the correct initial dosage of methadone in a heroin detoxification schedule should be 85 mg. This is too large a dose even for the most tolerant addict. It should be less than half that, and then only given in divided dosages of 20 mg each over a twenty-four hour period. Another university graduate counselor working with hard-core heroin addicts in an aftercare program said marijuana is "psychologically addictive," a contradiction in medical terminlogy—a nonsense term. Addiction is defined in terms of physiological tolerance, dependence and withdrawal, not as the desire to repeat a pleasurable experience such as that produced by pot ("habituation"). One can be psychologically *habituated* to grass, but not psychologically *addicted* to it. After my explanation, the counselor, who himself smokes the weed, agreed.

The principal problem of ex-addict staff (beyond conflicts with their professional supervisors) results from their lack of experience dealing with administrative bureaucracies. Especially difficult for them is the paperwork that funding sources require on every client, including extensive and detailed intake work-ups, client action plans detailing short- and long-term treatment goals and methods of achieving them, ongoing counseling notes relevant to those goals, discharge summaries and national, state and local reporting requirements like the complex federal CODAP system ("Client Oriented Data Acquisition Process"). This paperwork blizzard is often too much for ex-addict counselors to handle, and they quit in frustration.

There is a tendency among ex-addict workers in aftercare counseling centers to overidentify with clients, get on a "bummer," then "burn out" and quit after about a year of employment. Perhaps "burn-out" results from depressingly intense daily involvement with clients' problems—crises with which the counselor is all too familiar: "jumping back in the spoon" (relapse), police or other criminal justice system "hassles," family crises, "contracts" out on clients' lives, and so on. The "burn out" syndrome among the ex-addict staff often ends in resignation or termination and sometimes leads to more serious problems like family breakup and excessive drinking. Relapse to heroin use by such counselors is not uncommon and is known in the business as an occupational hazard.

Here is a "no drinking memo" issued to an aftercare counseling program staff by their executive director after numerous on-the-job drinking incidents:

> Effective immediately, drinking of alcoholic beverages while on program business or during normal working hours is prohibited. Further, employees will not report to work in an intoxicated condition . . . and will not attempt to contact other employees while in an intoxicated state. . . . The aforementioned action was prompted because:
>
> 1. Certain incidents have been attributed directly to the drinking of intoxicants.
> 2. Our business of federally funded "drug abuse treatment" should parallel our convictions. [Private file]

At this drug treatment program the boss himself drank during working hours and on several occasions was drunk on the job. Staff meetings occasionally held at his home during working hours were always attended by lavish liquor supplies. Staff members present usually got too drunk to return to work.

Drug dealing occurs in some aftercare programs. It can be expected, given the social context of ex-addict staffers mixing with addicted clients, many of whom are "holding" illegal drugs. Here is a secret memorandum issued by the director of one of the nation's largest aftercare programs after parents of clients complained to their congressman about rampant drug dealing at the program:

I. Problem for Staff Meeting Discussion: Drug Dealing at the Project and Possible Loss of Public Funding Because of It
   A. Drug sales on grounds to clients and minors
   B. Staff dealing drugs to other staff and to clients
   C. Possibility of drug overdoses on project grounds
   D. Staff being indifferent to drug problem (i.e., drinking on the job)
   E. Difficulty distinguishing clients from staff and clients from non-clients
   F. Use of program phones for setting up drug sales
   G. Community pressure to "clean up our act"
   H. Credibility in the community as a drug abuse treatment program
   I. Possible undercover at the project by FBI/DEA agents
   J. Physical intimidation/violence against staff with knowledge of drug sales on project grounds [Private file]

This program is in a "rough" part of the city. At my first day on the job there was a knife fight in the waiting room. Most staff members "hear no evil, see no evil, and speak no evil." The project is a world of its own filled daily with a mixture of clean and dirty clients and staff, Mexican Mafia, and other "loaded" clients squatting outside and spitting on the sidewalk. The anomaly is that this very "looseness" makes clients comfortable at the program and attracts new ones into treatment.

TREATMENT OUTCOME: RETENTION

Are aftercare programs able to keep their clientele in order to treat them? To find out, I analyzed three large federally supported aftercare centers over a one-year period to determine their combined attrition rate. During the study period a total of 743 detoxified heroin addicts were admitted to the programs and 431 of them (59 percent) were discharged.

The average length of stay among those who remained in treatment was only 3.2 months. Of the 431 discharges over the year, a full 80 percent were discharged "Treatment not Complete," that is, they either "split" or were terminated for failure to comply with program rules. Most of the discharges were for reasons unflattering to the programs. Such programs would appear to have little retention power, especially when compared with the money spent on them.

During-Treatment Outcome

There are no reliable posttreatment follow-up studies of aftercare program discharges. Experience indicates that most of these aftercare facilities have had negligible impact in terms of keeping their clients off heroin or other chemicals while in treatment. The final unit of service delivered is often readmission to a detoxification program following relapse during aftercare.

I studied during-treatment drug use among a representative sample of twenty-two "abstinent" clients enrolled in a federally supported aftercare program. They were asked to submit a urine sample voluntarily for qualitative drug-screen analysis. Three clients refused and walked out, and it may be assumed that the tests would have shown the use of nonprescribed drugs. Of the nineteen samples obtained and analyzed, ten (53 percent) were positive for morphine sulfate, the metabolite of heroin. If the three refusals are counted as "dirty" tests, 60 percent of the urines for a population active in treatment were "dirty." Further, urinalysis only detects drugs used within forty-eight hours. After that, drug metabolite has already been excreted from the body. Conceivably, more clients could have been using heroin or other drugs during treatment and were undetected through urine testing.

Since urinalysis results are notoriously inaccurate, at the time I took the samples I also physically examined each member of the study sample for postinjection cutaneous stigmata, including hematoma and thrombosis on the antecubital fossae of both arms, and neurologic signs of heroin intoxication like myosis, lethargy or mydriasis. Results were noted in their clinical records. At least two of these signs were noted in eight of the ten clients who tested "dirty," thus giving an 80 percent accuracy rate for the urinalysis results.

SUMMARY

For those few clients who remain in aftercare programs without "splitting," the majority continue using drugs: heroin, cocaine, amphetamines, barbiturates, marijuana and/or alcohol. Aftercare therapy does not generally suppress craving for heroin. Success at finding jobs for clients is often achieved by taking on ex-clients as staff members.

When aftercare programs do not "work," clients will sometimes voluntarily seek admission to a residential care facility, or be forced to enter one by a judge, parole or probation agent. Do residential treatment programs achieve any more success than aftercare programs in "curing" their clientele?

NOTES

1. George E. Vaillant, "A 12-Year Follow-Up of New York Narcotic Addicts: III. Some Social and Psychiatric Characteristics," *Archives of General Psychiatry* 15 (March 1966): 599-609.
2. Felix quoted in John Walsh, "Lexington Narcotics Hospital: A Special Sort of Alma Mater," *Science* 182 (December 7, 1973): 1005.
3. Anthony E. Raynes et al., "Evaluation of Hospital Detoxification Using Various Outcome Criteria," in *Fifth National Conference on Methadone Treatment: Proceedings, 1973*, ed. National Association for the Prevention of Addiction to Narcotics (New York: National Association for the Prevention of Addiction to Narcotics, 1973), p. 675.
4. David J. Bellis, "Progress Report Submitted to National Institute on Drug Abuse: 1973-1974," (Ontario, Calif.: West End Drug Abuse Control Coordinating Council, Inc., 1974), p. 6.
5. Raynes et al., "Evaluation of Hospital Detoxification," p. 676.
6. Raymond A. Lloyd et al., "Detoxification: What Makes the Difference?" in *Fifth National Conference, 1973*, ed. National Association for the Prevention of Addiction to Narcotics, pp. 278-79.

7. Raynes et al., Evaluation of Hospital Detoxification," pp. 676-77.

8. Stephen I. Abramowitz and Paul M. Pantleo, "The Effectiveness of Brief Methadone Withdrawal Among Urban Opiate Addicts," *International Journal of the Addictions* 7 (Winter 1972): 633.

9. J. E. Gudeman, R. F. Shader and T. S. Hemenway, "Methadone Withdrawal in the Treatment of Heroin Addiction," *Diseases of the Nervous System* 33 (March 1972): 297-303.

10. Raynes et al., "Evaluation of Hospital Detoxification," p. 676.

11. George R. Gay et al., "Short-Term Heroin Detoxification on an Outpatient Basis," *International Journal of the Addictions* 6 (April 1971): 641-64.

12. Forest S. Tennant, Jr., "Outpatient Heroin Detoxification with Acupuncture and Staplepuncture," *Western Journal of Medicine* 125 (September 1976): 191-94.

13. A. T. Canada, Jr., "Methadone in a 30-day Detoxification Program for Narcotic Addicts: A Critical Review," *International Journal of the Addictions* 7 (August 1972): 613.

14. J. E. O'Malley, W. H. Anderson and A. Lazare, "Failure of Outpatient Treatment of Drug Abuse: I Heroin," *American Journal of Psychiatry* 128 (May 1972): 856-68.

15. Forest S. Tennant, Jr., and H. Silsby, "Short-Term, Ambulatory Detoxification of Opiate Addicts Using Methadone," *International Journal of the Addictions* 9 (February 1974): 170.

16. Doris Werner et al., "Experience of a Large-Scale Ambulatory Detoxification Program," in *Fifth National Conference, 1973*, ed. National Association for the Prevention of Addiction to Narcotics, p. 692.

17. See the comparative study by Alex Richman et al., "Entry into Methadone Maintenance Programs: A Follow-Up Study of New York City Heroin Users Detoxified in 1961-1963," *American Journal of Public Health* 62 (June 1972): 1002-7.

18. B. K. Wilson, R. R. Elms and C. P. Thomas, "Outpatient vs. Hospital Methadone Detoxification: An Experimental Comparison," *International Journal of the Addictions* 10 (January 1975): 13, 24.

19. San Bernardino County Department of Mental Health, "Recommendations to County Board of Supervisors on Five-Year Drug Abuse Control Plan," (San Bernardino, Calif.: County Department of Mental Health, 1975, mimeographed), p. 8.

20. Santa Monica Bay Area Drug Abuse Council, Inc., "A Proposal to Provide Intake, Primary Care and Diversion Services for Drug Users in Santa Monica, West Los Angeles, Pacific Palisades and Malibu," (Santa

Monica, Calif.: Santa Monica Bay Area Drug Abuse Council, Inc., mimeographed), p. 13.

21. Narcotics Prevention Project, "Methadone Maintenance Letter of Intent," (Los Angeles: Narcotics Prevention Project, Inc., mimeographed), p. 2.

22. U.S. President, Special Action Office for Drug Abuse Prevention, *Outpatient Drug-Free Treatment Manual* (Washington, D.C.: U.S. Government Printing Office, 1974), p. 26.

8

Residential Programs and Jailhouse Therapeutic Communities

The failure of the standard addiction treatment modalities—detoxification and aftercare counseling—and the explosive increase in identified addicts in urban areas in the 1950s and 1960s spurred the search for alternative treatment methods. Methadone maintenance was one such modality. Another was the so-called "therapeutic community."

WHAT RESIDENTIAL TREATMENT IS

Residential treatment programs for heroin addicts were an integral part of the Nixon administration's comprehensive "multimodality" rehabilitation strategy and served to counter the claim that the government was relying solely on methadone maintenance. Residential programs have made extravagant and unsubstantiated claims about how they could "cure" most addicts.[1] Today these programs constitute only 6 percent of the total addiction treatment "slots" available in metropolitan areas, but a "therapeutic community movement" has developed, and these programs have generated publicity out of proportion to their numbers.

Called variously "therapeutic communities," "residentials," "half-way houses," "recovery houses," or simply "TC's," they can be defined as twenty-four hour, nonmedical residential care facilities designed to reform heroin addicts. Therapy is generally based on the medical model: addicts are presumed to be sick, suffering from an underlying personality disorder, of which compulsive heroin use is but a symptom.

Residential programs differ from each other primarily in their internal discipline structure and required length of stay. There are two kinds of disciplinary structures: programs with relatively demanding (high) or relatively undemanding (low) internal structures.[2] Length-of-stay requirements range from fourteen days to a lifetime, depending on whether the program is a short- or longer-term residential.[3]

HISTORY AND DEVELOPMENT OF THE RESIDENTIAL MOVEMENT

The term "therapeutic community" was coined first by British psychiatrist Maxwell Jones to describe a unique kind of ward milieu for hospitalized psychiatric patients where each patient is at once a therapist and a patient.[4] Most residential programs are based on some variant of this "milieu therapy" model.

Residentials also borrowed heavily from the philosophy developed by Alcoholics Anonymous, a variant of Christian redemption, built around the concept that alcohol or drug addiction reflects certain inherent psychological instabilities and character deformations. The pattern is as follows: the weakness, the temptation with heroin, the self-indulgence, the rise and fall, and the redemption through recognition and perception of oneself as a child of original sin. To be sure, weaknesses are spoken of in psychological rather than religious terms (except in religious residentials), but the whole religious journey of self-degradation, self-negation, the trip through hell, the public confession, the self-abasement, the blinding insight, the revival and the salvation is evoked.

Synanon was the first residential in the United States to gain wide publicity and academic attention.[5] Since it began in Santa Monica, California, in 1959, Synanon has addressed the problem of overcoming supposed ignorance among its clientele through a process of "mutual self-education." Its founders and residents insist that it is not so much a community of students or teachers as a community of "scholars," each learning and teaching at the same time. Residential programs tend to see themselves as simultaneous therapeutic and learning environments.

Synanon, however, differs from most residentials in three respects. First, it takes the position, almost unique among these programs, that the ambient society is so deficient, corrupt and unfeeling that the most authentic and rational choice for program "members" is to continue as residents of Synanon for the rest of their lives. Second, Synanon has moved away from strict focus on the drug-alcohol misuser toward a kind of "sensitivity" program for nonaddicts as well. Third, Synanon has never accepted government funding, because it does not want to be tied to government rules and regulations. Financial support comes mainly through client fees and various business enterprises that Synanon has spawned over the years.

Synanon has not shown much interest in outcome studies. Some informal evidence indicates that their recovery rate is low, especially among those who "split" and leave the facility. Charles Dederich, the cofounder of Synanon (and arrested in 1979 on an attempted murder charge), is said to believe that the relapse rate is 90 percent and that roughly one in ten has stayed "clean" outside the facility.[6] More comprehensive follow-up studies are not available for Synanon. The various Synanon spin-off residentials such as Daytop, Phoenix House and Odyssey House have taken more interest in evaluation studies, probably because they receive government grants and feel a need to "prove" their merit.

PHILOSOPHY OF RESIDENTIAL TREATMENT

What exactly is the philosophy of these residential treatment programs for heroin addicts? Upon what kinds of problems do they focus? Residentials adopt the medical model and focus on the client's inner life rather than on factors external to the individual that might stimulate and perpetuate opiate dependence.

Residentials, like most drug treatment programs, see addict-clients as arrested in their emotional development, as persons who have not yet grown up, in other words, as "babies." Programs thus operate on the standard medical assumption that addicts suffer from underlying personality defects. That their clients are sick and must submit to "rehabilitation" is the sacred, universal tenet of residential programs. In this pathogenic view, addicts are looked upon as "weaklings" and "snivelers" who cannot cope with life on its own terms without resorting to self-medication. Thus, the residential dogma does not presuppose sickness in the strict medical /physiological sense so much as plain stupidity and character weakness on the part of the habitue. Residential programs take the medical model of addiction as irrefutable gospel, and staff flaunt their newly acquired facility to "diagnose" clients in case records as "passive-dependent" personalities with "sociopathic tendencies."

THERAPEUTIC TECHNIQUES

"Therapy" in residential treatment programs consists of a varied set of individual and group transactions including focused individual and group counseling in addition to free-wheeling, unstructured group interactions, all conducted under a loose system of "behavior modification." The ultimate goal is to get the client to stop using drugs. In most residentials, behavior defined as desirable is rewarded with privileges, while infractions (or inertia in the program) are punished by removing privileges previously granted or by imposing tedious and disagreeable work assignments. Behavior modification is thus the operative underlying principle. One moves up the status hierarchy in the residential by proving to be "capable of positive change," as defined by staff and senior residents.

Role Disassociation

Residents, especially new ones, are immediately cut off from all contact with outside persons, including family. Clients are generally on restriction from several weeks to several months, unable to leave the facility and sometimes even forbidden to converse with fellow clients, especially those of the opposite sex. Most residentials see sexual maladjustment as a common problem among heroin addicts, and sexual relationships are usually denied. These are privileges to be "earned" through "good behavior."

The new enrollee is subjected to "degradation ceremonies"[7] of various sorts to erase outward manifistations of a sense of personal identity, especially a self-image as "junkie," "dope fiend," or "con."

Shaved heads or self-deprecating signs hung around the neck for rule infractions or "nightcreeps" by senior residents and staff to terrorize the new arrivals and keep them off guard are techniques employed by residentials to break down the client's self-concept. Total and complete role dissociation from former street life is attempted. Program staff insist clients should accept this kind of "reeducation" without complaint or even feeling that any injustice has been committed. Enrollees who oppose role disassociation (often harder-core addicts with longer addiction and prison backgrounds) are looked upon as demonstrating that they are still suffering from an internal "character disorder" and are "emotionally immature."

The Synanon Game

High-discipline programs usually employ the confrontive "Synanon game"—a leaderless group encounter session to create aggressive and provocative interchange, using ridicule, cross-examination and hostile attack. During these group assaults on individual residents in the "hot seat," especially newcomers, any castigation and ridicule appear to come from the whole community of clients. Facing this, it is difficult for the subject of attack to resist or defend himself. At this point, the resident on target must confront and be confronted with the "real reasons" for heroin use: a weak, rotten being, the black depths of "shithood" as a "dope fiend." In such sessions a client can demonstrate to staff that he is "learning" the cause of the "irresponsibility" that led to narcotic delinquency in the first place. That one is irresponsible is *never* open to question. One either plays the game and is rewarded with privilege and favorable discharge, or one "splits" from the program.

Staff members and senior residents usually facilitate these group encounter sessions, as well as provide individual counseling. Experience indicates that when these counselors use an especially intrusive, aggressive approach, frequently debasing and harshly confronting clients, they may do more harm than good. Counselors, many of whom are ex-addicts, tend to be impatient, authoritarian and demanding, usually insisting on immediate self-disclosure, emotional expression and attitude change from clients.

This intrusive, assertive therapeutic style works well for a few clients but may injure many more. Neurotic addicts, especially, tend to question their own judgement before questioning that of staff and resident leaders. A number of clients, yearning for a sense of belonging and something to believe in after removing the heroin from their lives, relinquish all independence and subjugate themselves to these staff and senior residents, accepting humiliation and total control over their lives even to the extent of accepting complete direction of their sex lives, outside work, incomes and, when permitted, medication.

Quite simply, the so-called "therapy" and "rehabilitation" practiced in most residentials are somewhat out of control. Thousands of untrained staff and residents in hundreds of residentials nationwide, many hardly off heroin themselves and under no legal or professional oversight, unleash their own brands of "therapy" on addicts, many of them under court-ordered mandatory treatment. These so-called therapists have catchy titles like "head counselor," "group leader," "game leader," "expeditor," and so on.

I terminated one such "head counselor" at a federally funded residential who forced female clients to engage in fellatio with him while he "pled their cases" to parole or probation officers over the telephone. The women complained, and the staff member later overdosed on heroin in his office after he was fired. The male "founder" and assistant director of another large federally supported all-female residential was having intercourse with an unkwnown number of his clients, most of them young heroin addicts, scared and unable to resist his advances. This came to my attention when one of them, a retarded fifteen-year-old, told me (and I later verified) that he had taken her to a motel, "screwed" her then "dumped her" beside the road with no money and no way back to his "therapeutic community." Incidents like these are not unique in residentials.

Funding sources like the National Institute on Drug Abuse, central state drug abuse agencies and county health departments, especially their monitors and "project officers," are unequipped to monitor closely the therapies and therapists in residentials twenty-four hours a day for effectiveness and ethical practice. Although the unproved claims of residentials are being challenged, dangerous practices still prevail in many of them. In 1975 not one of the four large residential programs in one California county operating under the aegis of the federal government had a bona fide psychologist or psychiatrist on staff, though they all waved the banner of formal psychology. Similar situations abound throughout the country.

RESIDENTIALS AND THE MENTAL HEALTH POWER ELITE

A number of residential program staff members, especially founders of such programs, are charismatic. These ex-addicts are politically adept and have a self-serving interest in the proliferation of residentials. A number of these people have mobilized considerable community and political support by promising to reduce drug misuse among youth. They have become skilled at manipulating the news media and do not hesitate to play on the natural fears of parents concerning drug abuse by their children. By offering parents and civic leaders simplistic, client-centered solutions to a complex problem like addiction, some residential programs have managed to accumulate a significant amount of political influence. They manipulate local, state and national government officials to utilize and expand their facilities by enlisting community drug hysteria. Eventually, some programs and their leaders have created situations where they are answerable to no one—licensing bureaus, housing or health regulations, fiscal auditors or scientific evaluators.

DO RESIDENTIAL PROGRAMS WORK? RETENTION AND OUTCOME

Are residential programs able to reform their addict-clients? Reform is generally defined as: (1) postdischarge narcotic abstinence, (2) reduced criminality, and (3) employment or school involvement. Scientific evaluations of residentials are few, since only a small minority of those responsible for residentials seem concerned about client follow-up and evaluative research.[8] Most residential program staffs lack the methodological and analytical skills to perform such evaluations. Moreover, they know that the briefest investigation would show failure to achieve overt goals.

RETENTION IN TREATMENT

Retention in treatment is a major process goal for residential programs, as it is for methadone maintenance, detoxification and aftercare centers. Are residentials able to hold their clients? Studies of residentials have found attrition rates over 80 percent prior to formal program completion or "graduation."[9]

In a typical study, Glaser found eighty-six of every hundred admissions to a large residential program terminating themselves against advice of staff. Most of them "split" within thirty days of admission.[10] Brill studied 2,110 consecutive admissions to Phoenix House, a residential in New York, and found a 96 percent drop-out rate. Of the 4 percent who finally "graduated," 25 percent had become paid staff members. As a result, Brill doubts that residential programs can ". . . return large numbers of residents to the community as rehabilitated or 'cured.' "[11]

The inescapable conclusion is that residentials are unable to retain substantial numbers of addict-clients in order to "treat" them. Those who do remain are highly motivated, and might have discontinued heroin use without the intervention of the program.

Retention in treatment is an important goal in any addiction treatment modality; everything else depends on it.[12] DeLeon and colleagues found that at Phoenix House, the longer a client stays, the larger the post-discharge reduction in arrests. Addicts with any time in Phoenix House, even those who "split," showed "sharp reductions" in criminal activity ". . . during and after leaving the program."[13]

Retention rates seem to be affected by two factors: program approach (high- or low-disciplinary structure) and client background variables. The more strict the program, the lower the percentage of clients retained in treatment.[14] Young, white, shorter-term addicts appear to stay longer in treatment than older, black/brown, longer-term addicts with more extensive histories of institutionalization.[15]

With high "split" rates and numbers of untreated street addicts running low in some communities, residentials are now concentrating on the youthful "multiple-drug abuser" or "polydrug abuser," the person who is using heroin sporadically in combination with other drugs or perhaps not using heroin at all. These clients are more likely to be retained in residential treatment than hard-core heroin addicts. A federally sponsored residential program in California was funded to "treat" the "adolescent and young adult, middle-class soft-drug use syndrome." Whether or not large sums of money should be spent on treating "soft drug" users is questionable. Should the federal government be funding Synanon-type residentials for pot smokers and occasional heroin users? To hold the newer "lightweight" clients, some programs have somewhat altered their treatment approach. No longer is the hard-attack encounter the primary therapeutic tool. A "softer," less confronting approach, designed not to scare clients away, prevails.[16]

Retention rates at New York's Odyssey House are instructive, for this program was heralded as the "Tiffany" of therapeutic communities. The program's founder, Judianne Densen-Gerber, calls her project ". . . the country's most successful program for curing drug addiction."[17] Is it? Or is there a vested interest in the background?

At Odyssey House only a quarter of all admissions stay longer than thirty days. After six months the figure falls to 9.7 percent retained. At one year the Odyssey retention rate is 5.6 percent. After eighteen months, the program's required length of stay in order to "graduate," only 2.8 percent of all admissions are retained. This is a 97.2 percent "split" rate.[18] Obviously, only the most motivated clients complete the prescribed treatment regimen. Could the same results have been acheived *without* the intervention of Odyssey House, where the cost per "graduate" is more than $20,000?

"Body Snatching"

With high attrition rates like these, residential programs, especially since their overexpansion during the Nixon era, constantly need new addicts to fill their beds, meet contractual client matrices and keep their grants. Since they have difficulty keeping clients, and because methadone maintenance poses a serious threat to their continued existence, many residentials actively solicit clients, called "body snatching" in the trade, or more respectably, "outreach."

For example, residentials seek the court-ordered "diversion" client, since clients who have been diverted into residentials in lieu of jail or prison are more likely to stay than voluntary ones. The reason is obvious: Such a resident stays because he tries to "beat a case" by making a favorable impression on the court or the staff members who ultimately provide feedback to the court—especially feedback on whether or not the client is still in treatment. Thus, preferential loading of residential client populations with diverted addicts can effectively boost retention power.

Virtually all residential treatment programs have formed and nurtured close alliances with various elements of the criminal justice system, and consider police, courts and corrections excellent sources for potential clients.[19] A large residential program in Pennsylvania, for example, says that ". . . in the past 2 years the majority of our clients have been admitted as a result of some immediate and direct action by one part or another of the criminal justice system."[20]

The largest addiction treatment intake unit in Los Angeles has a legal department which focuses primarily on diverting addicts out of jail into its in- and outpatient services, including two residentials. The program says its legal office is ". . . invaluable in bringing [program] clientele into treatment *and keeping them there. . . .*"[21] (Emphasis added) In the words of *The Godfather,* diversion offers the addict a choice he cannot refuse: remain in jail or "voluntarily" request release, which is conditioned on entering and remaining in a specified residential program. This can be bad when the program is bad.

In such diversion cases, is the residential program the agent of the client, the court or the community? Voluntary addiction treatment involves a therapeutic relationship in which the primary responsibility of the program or therapist is to the client alone. In an involuntary treatment setting (diversion), the program's primary responsibility is to some third party, usually a criminal court.[22] The objectives of most residentials who go to the criminal justice system for clients extend beyond simply "rehabilitation." Their aims include self-perpetuation and social control over addict criminals.

Addict diversion is particularly invidious when applied to the pretrial addict prisoner who pleads guilty at the preliminary hearing phase. It is, in effect, a plea bargain. Pretrial diversion clients are given the "choice" of treatment *prior* to being offered a trial. Thus they forfeit the opportunity to prove their innocence by accepting treatment in lieu of a trial. Addict-defendants in such cases are really forced to accept treatment that they generally do not want for a "disease" they often believe to be nonexistent. They are thus denied due process.

There is near-unanimous support for this kind of diversion among residential program directors and staff. Their motto appears to be: "Keep the beds full, at any cost." Some programs have used "bounty hunters" to find diversion clients who "split" prior to formal discharge. Others will pay a "finder's fee" for each new client brought in. One program paid $10 a head, and a former ex-addict staff member there had a stable of "recruiters" on the streets and in the jails looking for potential clients.

A 1974 survey found that most residential program directors see themselves as moving closer and closer to the criminal justice system as a source of clients.[23] Residential program staff and directors are thus quite frank about their commitment to perpetuate residentials through close alliance with the criminal justice system, particularly where the bulk of the staff are recovered addicts themselves. They have, like aftercare program staffs, found a niche and understandably are determined to hold it. When criticized, they staunchly defend goals of their programs, client recruitment methods and treatment results.

THE RELATIONSHIP OF TREATMENT TO OUTCOME

Recruiting and holding onto clients is one thing. In the end do residentials succeed in benefiting clients they manage to retain?

SUCCESS CRITERIA

Success critieria in client follow-up studies of residential programs vary. Drug use, criminality, social functioning of some kind and health are areas in which client status on follow-up is consistently examined. Closer scrutiny, however, reveals that while the categories are similar, the definitions of these outcome measures vary wildly.

In drug use, for example, some studies examine the use of illicit *and* licit drugs after discharge, demanding abstinence from the use of both as a criterion of "success." Another viewpoint holds that only reduction in the use of illegal drugs is evidence of "successful" residential treatment outcome.

In the area of subsequent criminality most outcome studies focus on arrest histories and arrest rates. Few studies examine wider criminal involvements. Where some studies utilize official records, others rely on client self-reported drug use, arrests or other pertinent data. Similar disparities at this level are evident in every category of outcome measurement.

Outcome Studies of Dropouts

Some studies attempt to demonstrate that residential programs are so successful they even achieve some success with dropouts. DeLeon and his colleagues determined the percentage of arrests for a sample of 254 clients who failed to complete the Phoenix House program. Even the dropouts, they concluded, ". . . showed sharp reductions in criminal activity during and after leaving the program. These changes relate to the rehabilitative aspects of the program."[24]

There are severe methodological problems with such studies. First, to conclude that postdischarge reductions in arrests were due to the rehabilitative aspects of the program is a self-serving assumption, since no control group or other standard of comparison was used to determine independent program impact on postdischarge arrest rates.

Second, postdischarge "arrests" as the only indicator of "criminality" is an inadequate measure. Victimization surveys, for example, which measure the true crime rate by asking population samples if they have been victims of crimes, indicate that reported crimes are not reliable indicators of total crimes committed. Arrests would seem to be an even poorer indicator, since most crimes are never cleared by an arrest. One victimization study found that 50 percent of all crimes in the nation's five largest cities were unreported to the police.[25] Was an unknown amount of lawbreaking, unknown to him and his colleagues, going on among DeLeon's study sample? In substance, a lower reported arrest rate does not mean a lower actual rate of crimes committed among the discharged clients interviewed.

A third glaring methodological error of the DeLeon study was that the New York City Narcotic Registry was used to validate client self-reported arrests. Arrests among the study group *outside* New York City did not appear in the registry.[26]

True, an unexplained relationship exists between residential treatment and positive outcome, even among dropouts. But untested assumptions, unreliable criminality indicators, and all the pitfalls of client self-reported data (no friends or relatives were interviewed to corroborate self-reported information) characterize the study.

Chambers and Inciardi, in a comprehensive residential follow-up study, used the following postdischarge behavioral variables in examining a group of clients who dropped out of Phoenix House between the third and eighteenth month of treatment:

1. Abstinence from drug use since discharge.
2. Arrest history since discharge.
3. Employment status at follow-up.

Was Phoenix House so effective that it even achieved some success with dropouts? "Twenty-seven percent of Phoenix House splitees can be considered as complete successes, 43.5% can be considered as marginally successful and 29.3% can be considered as failures."[27]

As with most similar reports, however, methodological problems beset the Chambers and Inciardi study. It was nonexperimental; no matched set of controls was compared with the treatment group to determine independent program effect. Nor was any other form of comparison used. Although it admittedly was a study of "dropouts," only clients in the program at least three months were included in the study group. Thus, *early* dropouts (the great majority of all admissions) were specifically excluded from the sample. Conclusions deduced from remaining rather than total starting samples are speculative and highly questionable. Of 182 individuals in the sample, only 92 were found and agreed to be interviewed. So almost one-half of the original group were unavailable for interviews. Generalizations from this small group applied to the total number of dropouts are tentative and conjectural. Those clients who could be found and agreed to be interviewed may have been the very ones who were most "successful," as evidenced by their availability and willingness to be interviewed. Further, all data for the study were self-reported by the ex-clients and therefore unreliable. There was no cross-checking to validate this information. Thus, the conclusions drawn from the Chambers and Inciardi study are scientifically unsound and, to a degree, self-serving.

Outcome Studies of Graduates

Another often-quoted residential treatment program follow-up study confined follow-up interviews to "successful graduates" of New York City's Daytop Village and predictably found a majority no longer "abusing drugs" or "committing crimes." Most were also working or in school.[28] Behavioral measures of success employed in this study were:

1. Postdischarge drug use.
2. Postdischarge alcohol use.
3. Arrest history since discharge.
4. "Prosocial involvement," defined as in school or working at follow-up.

The Collier and Hijazi investigation of Daytop Village concluded that the program had an independent, positive impact on the postdischarge behavior of program graduates, but this conclusion is marred by four methodological errors.

First, the study sample was biased and therefore unrepresentative of the total discharge population. The sample excluded all dropouts and focused instead only on program "graduates." Since most admissions to Phoenix House drop out prior to graduation, this is the same commonly repeated flaw of generalizing from remaining samples. Casriel and Amen, in their study of Phoenix House "graduates," committed this same error.[29]

Second, the Collier and Hijazi study was nonexperimental: No matched controls were used to determine if indeed it was the "treatment" that accounted for the ex-clients' success or if extraneous variables, particularly client characteristics like age, race or addiction history, accounted for the observed "reform." Some addicts undergo "spontaneous remission" of their addiction. Sick and tired of being sick and tired, they naturally begin to "mature out" of heroin addiction in their thirties without the ministrations of professional helpers.[30]

Third, arrests were utilized as the sole indicator of client criminality. The pitfall of this indicator is obvious. Fourth, follow-up interviews were conducted only nine months after program graduation. This is a very short period of time in which to make generalizations regarding the durability of observed behavioral change. Detoxified addicts should not be considered a "success" after only a few months of drug-free existence ". . . in view of the well-known relapse potential of detoxified addicts."[31] Vaillant suggested that at least *five years* is a more realistic minimum period to determine the persistence of client change.[32] This may be an unnecessarily stringent requirement. Nevertheless, the *probative* aspects of the Collier and Hijazi study taint its weak conclusions.

Pin and his colleagues studied three hundred graduates of Horizon House, another New York therapeutic community. Only 164 were actually found and interviewed; the rest were lost to follow-up. Of those interviewed one year after discharge, 64 percent had a job or were in school, 69.9 percent were "abstaining from drugs," and 64.5 percent had not been arrested.[33]

Like other studies, however, this one also omitted dropouts from the sample, interviewed only 164 of 300 clients in the original study group, used arrests as the sole indicator of subsequent criminality, relied exclusively on self-reported follow-up data, and interviewed clients within a year of discharge—a short period of time not comparable to the clients' more extensive drug-using histories prior to admission to treatment. The "success" rate that Pin and his colleagues found is thus debatable on methodological grounds and tells us virtually nothing about the overall success rate that the program achieved. Such is the case with almost every other residential outcome study.

CLIENT FACTORS AND SUCCESS

Reform observed in clients after discharge may be more attributable to client characteristics and research designs than to program impact. For example, the absence of detoxification procedures using methadone or other drugs at residentials may encourage only those addicts with weak heroin habits to seek admission. Further, many of the recorded postdischarge "successes" of residentials may never have been addicted to narcotics at all. A large number of them are middle-class pot smokers and runaways, not really disadvantaged, long-time heroin addicts.

It remains to be demonstrated whether therapy in drug-free residential programs is more effective than ". . . that found in the coercive or custodial types of facilities in terms of eventual rehabilitation of residents and return to the community."[34] In effect, residentials probably are no more effective than jails, prisons or community-based corrections such as probation.

CRC: A JAILHOUSE THERAPEUTIC COMMUNITY

Do jails and prisons reduce heroin use among addict-inmates after release? Incarceration and the cold turkey withdrawal that usually accompanies it is at least a negative reinforcer. The jail experience brings home to the addict the physiological consequences of repetitive heroin use. Perhaps this reinforcement is best summed up by the phrase, "if you want to play, you have to pay." The analysis here is confined to the California Rehabilitation Center (CRC) at Corona, on the outskirts of Los Angeles. It is representative of nationwide "civil commitment" programs for addicts.

In 1958 California pioneered civil commitment procedures for court-declared heroin addicts. In this way government authority can force an addict to take treatment, regardless of his wishes. The civil commitment program in California was an updated version of the old Lexington—Ft. Worth model: establishment of a "therapeutic milieu" within a locked custodial facility (CRC is a decommissioned World War II naval hospital).

In 1961 California opened the CRC facility amid much fanfare and high hopes of breaking the cycle of heroin addiction. By 1978, thousands of addicts later, CRC had come under fire from all directions and was itself suffering from severe withdrawal symptoms:

> . . . the CRC program is removing relatively few addicts from the streets of California. Only a small percentage of those committed to the program are being successfully rehabilitated. CRC is not preventing the spread of addiction [and] the elimination of the . . . program should be considered in view of its burden to the taxpayers.[35]

Although the stated purpose of CRC is to provide an enforced drug-free therapeutic community for the "psychological rehabilitation" of "criminal addicts," the institution is really a prison. This reduces the effect of what little the institution has to offer the committed addict. Labeling inmates "residents" and the institution a "rehabilitation center" does not alter the fact that CRC is, following Goffman's usage, a total institution, admission to which can only be described ". . . as a leaving off and a taking on, with the midpoint marked by physical nakedness."[36]

Entrance to CRC is what Goffman calls a "degradation ceremony": the new inmate is completely stripped, buttocks spread and a finger probing for narcotics is inserted into the anus (or vagina). Then the "resident" is gowned in prison garb. The result is total and complete role dispossession. Such skin and internal searches do not keep drugs out of CRC or other prisons. J. J. Johnson, a former "N-number" parole agent ("N-number" means a caseload of addicts only) said, "You can make a connection in CRC easier than you can on the street."[37] Howard McGarrey, a state parole supervisor in California's San Bernardino County, told the press, "Sure, we've got heroin [in CRC]. It is a constant source of concern to us. . . . as long as you run a minimum security institution, you're going to have the problem of drugs coming in."[38]

Edward Bunker, a brilliant addict-writer who served time in a therapeutic community at the Federal Correctional Institution, Terminal Island, said:

> Heroin is cheaper in Terminal Island than on the streets of Los Angeles. Narcotics is the number-one problem in this institution. . . . At least 40 inmates at Terminal Island are "hooked." Another 150 or more use heroin as they can afford it. . . . [I] spent $12,000 on narcotics within six months while imprisoned [at Terminal Island].[39]

Inmates no doubt use drugs to calm their anxieties while in institutions like CRC or Terminal Island. John Lopez, a former CRC resident, said: "Some of those cops at CRC are sicker than the inmates. You talk about hysteria and anxiety, man, CRC is full of it. I think the place should be fully exposed."[40] The guards in such institutions, said Bunker, have ". . . fixations on punishment [and] spend all their time trying to get some poor addict to urinate in a bottle."[41]

The drive to "get loaded" within such institutions leads inmates to use forbidden drugs, whether it is pruno, a sickening alcoholic concoction made from sandbagged breakfast prunes, or heroin, barbiturates or cocaine. I have interviewed a number of individuals who first developed heroin addiction *inside* prisons and jails, not an uncommon circumstance. Bunker says, "My first 'fix' was given me in jail. For every addict cured in jail, two dozen are created."[42]

"THERAPY" AT CRC

Inmates soon learn to despise CRC, like all prisons, and everything it claims to be doing for them. As a result, the so-called "therapeutic" aspects of the program, CRC's raison d' être, are dramatically curtailed by the very context of the institutional setting. CRC's tall wire fences and operative norms place a barrier between the addict-inmate and the outside world to which he or she one day is supposed to return "cured."

Group Counseling

Inmates, many of whom have been there before, know the quickest way out of CRC: "If you wanna walk, you gotta talk." The normal prison stance of "hold your mud," and "fight, fuck or hit the fence," is forgotten at CRC in order to impress counseling staff that one is "rehabilitated" and ready for release.

Group therapy sessions at CRC, which have their moments in terms of impact, are a standing joke among residents. Residents are well aware that one of the most important criteria for being released is to demonstrate in group sessions that one is aware of the "psychic disturbances" that the *staff* feels caused the narcotic addiction and, more important, that one is able to express in some kind of searching, groping or perhaps articulate fashion that this is the case. Group counseling provides one of the few occasions for serious dialogue between inmates and staff, but reports suggest that spectacular results should not be expected from such "therapeutic" encounters.[43]

Stigma

The approval of the treatment staff is critical for early departure from CRC, and this approval comes primarily from "good behavior" in the "therapeutic community." The manifest function of CRC is to make the addict's reentry into the non-heroin-using community smooth and successful. However, the very existence of CRC as a separate institution for addicts and the group sessions for addicts underscore the inmate's self-concept as a separate kind of person. By a kind of suggestion process, addicts eventually come to view themselves as sick. This creates an unanticipated and very undesirable side effect in CRC and other treatment programs as well: The addicts are trained to percieve themselves as a class of men and women apart. Commitment to CRC or any other treatment program automatically and retrospectively effects crucial modifications in the individual's self-identity. Labeling the inmate an addict-criminal is a positive step in his progress toward a true criminal career.[44] The effect of this stigma on addicts is such that their behavior becomes a self-fulfilling prophecy. Such treatment programs, especially in prisons, undermine the goal of reform.

STAFF PERCEPTIONS OF THE ADDICT WORLD

Though most inmates at CRC are working- or lower-class and half are Hispanic, the treatment staff is solidly middle-class and Anglo. The white, middle-class treatment counselor at CRC has the dominant and commanding view of the way "normal" life should be lived when the resident is released. The counselors have highly class-biased views on what constitutes "appropriate" behavior in the community of "normal" men and women, and the readiness of the inmate for release is based on these class-biased judgments. Most counselors have never seen the sprawling *barrios* of East Los Angeles or seen Watts at close hand, nor do they have a very sharply etched conception of pressures these communities exert on their returning citizens.

What benefits have been reaped by the millions of dollars poured into CRC and other civil commitment programs around the country? Few reviewers defend CRC. According to CRC's own figures, 20 percent of the addicts committed between 1961 and 1971 achieved a "success" accreditation: at least two drug-free years on the outside.[45] John Kramer, former research chief at CRC, said the program ". . . has had very little success in rehabilitating clients . . ."[46] and that "CRC does not help very many people stay away from heroin. . . . On the average CRC delays by perhaps a few months the return to heroin addiction."[47]

The majority of addicts in CRC are high school dropouts and do not possess the rudimentary qualifications for employment. Their parole agents do not spend much time seeking job opportunities for them upon release. A close friend of mine, who died from a massive heroin overdose several days out of CRC, was a three-time "graduate" of the institution. The "vocational training" he received in gardening at CRC was nothing that could have developed into a decent job on the outside (he was an excellent musician). CRC itself does not have much of a job development/placement program; residents are turned out to find employment on their own after release.

After the state of California spends more than $20,000 a year for each inmate at CRC, he is given about $100 at the gate and told to go home and report to his parole agent. Go home to what? To San Francisco, Los Angeles or San Diego where less than 20 percent will stay relatively "clean" during their first two years out of the institution? After release to middle-class parole agents holding bottles for urine samples and after standing cap-in-hand before wary employers unwilling to take a chance, the paroled CRC addict sees society as clothed in persistent harassment if not cruelest persecution. Relapse to heroin under such conditions is almost certain and understandable.

Clearly, then, CRC, like most non-custodial therapeutic communities, removes relatively few heroin addicts from the streets, and only a miniscule percentage of those committed to such treatment programs are successfully rehabilitated as measured by reduced drug use, reduced criminality and increased "stability."

SUMMARY

Most "scientific" outcome studies of residential programs are narcissistic and self-aggrandizing and have the primary funciton of legitimating program continuation. Many therapeutic communities conduct self-serving measurements of themselves, using research strategies crafted to prove that their particular programs "work." Outcome research on residential programs is so shoddy or, if carefully designed, so unkind to program impact, that funding sources have tended to overlook outcome altogether and to focus instead on treatment process—numbers of admissions, client-counselor contacts, discharges, and so on.

It would be surprising if objective evaluation showed that more than 5 percent of those who come into contact with residential treatment programs are enabled to lead a reasonably drug-free, socially productive life as a result of the programs. No residential program has ever graduated more than an insignificant fraction of those admitted. Under such conditions, most therapeutic communities could be eliminated without great loss, considering their minimal direct benefits (and possible harm) to clients and the high costs of their services.

NOTES

1. As examples see Paul A. Henningsen, *The Role of Therapeutic Communities in the National Plan to Treat the Drug Abuser* (Racine, Wisc.: The Johnson Foundation, 1973); and Judianne Densen-Gerber, *We Mainline Dreams* (New York: Penguin Books, 1974), the story of Odyssey House in New York City.

2. On classifying internal value structures of therapeutic communities, see Henry L. Lennard and Steven D. Allen, "The Treatment of Drug Addiction: Toward New Models," *International Journal of the Addictions* 8 (June 1973): 521-35; Jerome S. Miller, John Sensenig and Johnathan S. Raymond, "Value Structure as a Predictor of Type of Discharge Among Residential Addicts," *International Journal of the Addictions* 9 (January 1974): 127-36; Steven G. Cole and Lawrence R. James, "A Revised Treatment Typology Based on the DARP," *American Journal of Drug and Alcohol Abuse* 2 (January 1975):37-50; and Reginald G. Smart, "Outcome

Studies of Therapeutic Community and Halfway House Treatment for Addicts," *International Journal of the Addictions* 11 (February 1976): 143-59.

3. William S. Aron and Douglas Daily, "Short- and Long-Term Therapeutic Communities: A Follow-Up and Cost Effectiveness Comparison," *International Journal of the Addictions* 9 (October 1974): 619-36.

4. Maxwell Jones, *The Therapeutic Community* (New York: Basic Books, 1953); see also his later work, *Beyond the Therapeutic Community: Social Learning and Social Psychiatry* (New Haven, Conn.: Yale University Press, 1968).

5. For the story of Synanon's early years, see Lewis Yablonsky, *Synanon: The Tunnel Back* (Baltimore, Md.: Penguin Books, 1967).

6. Edward M. Brecher and Consumer Reports Editors, *Licit and Illicit Drugs* (Boston: Little, Brown and Co., 1972), pp. 135-39.

7. The term is Erving Goffman's, from *Asylums: Essays on the Social Situation of Mental Patients and Other Inmates* (New York: Anchor Books, 1961).

8. Stanley Einstein came to this conclusion after surveying residential directors. See his "Methadone Treatment: Views of Program Directors," in *Fifth National Conference on Methadone Treatment: Proceedings, 1973,* ed. National Association for the Prevention of Addiction to Narcotics (New York: National Association for the Prevention of Addiction to Narcotics, 1973), pp. 718-22.

9. For typical studies demonstrating high "split" rates, see Leon Brill, "Some Comments on the Paper 'Social Control in Therapeutic Communities' by Dan Waldorf," *International Journal of the Addictions* 6 (March 1971): 45-50; Dan Waldorf, "Social Control in Therapuetic Communities for the Treatment of Drug Addicts," *International Journal of the Addictions* 6 (March 1971): 29-44; Deborah Colburn and Kenneth Colburn, "Integrity House: The Addict as a Total Institution," *Society* 10 (May-June 1973): 39-45; Frederick B. Glaser, "Splitting: Attrition from a Drug-Free Therapeutic Community," *American Journal of Drug and Alcohol Abuse* 1 (December 1974): 329-48; David J. Bellis, "Jericho Home Evaluation," (Ontario, Calif.: West End Drug Abuse Control Coordinating Council, Inc., 1974); Vitali V. Rozynko and Kenneth B. Stein, "Social and Psychological Factors Associated with Length of Stay in a Drug Treatment Facility," *International Journal of the Addictions* 9 (December 1974): 873–78; and George W. Joe and D. Dwayne Simpson, "Retention in Treatment of Drug Users: 1971-1972 DARP Admissions," *American Journal of Drug and Alcohol Abuse* 2 (January 1975): 63-72.

10. Glaser, "Splitting," pp. 329-48.

11. Brill, "Some Comments," p. 48.

12. Time in treatment, for example, seems to be associated with client performance after discharge. See Emile Jean Pin, John M. Martin and John F. Walsh, "A Follow-Up Study of 300 Ex-Clients of a Drug-Free Narcotic Treatment Program in New York City," *American Journal of Drug and Alcohol Abuse* 3 (September 1976): 403-7.

13. George DeLeon, Sherry Holland, and Mitchell S. Rosenthal, "Phoenix House: Criminal Activity of Dropouts," *Journal of the American Medical Association* 222 (November 6, 1972): 686.

14. S. B. Sells et al., "A National Followup Study to Evaluate the Effectiveness of Drug Abuse Treatment: A Report on Cohort 1 of the DARP Five Years Later," *American Journal of Drug and Alcohol Abuse* 3 (October 1976): 545-50.

15. A number of studies explore the relationship between client characteristics and retention, including Aron and Daily, "Short- and Long-Term Therapeutic Communities"; George W. Joe and D. Dwayne Simpson, "Retention in Treatment of Drug Users: 1971-1972 DARP Admissions," *American Journal of Drug and Alcohol Abuse* 2 (January 1975): 63-72; and Rozynko and Stein, "Social and Psychological Factors Associated with Length of Stay."

16. On the change in treatment approach to hold "soft-core" opiate users in treatment, see Herbert J. Freudenberger, "The Therapeutic Community Revisited," *American Journal of Drug and Alcohol Abuse* 3 (January 1976): 33-42.

17. Densen-Gerber, *We Mainline Dreams*, p. 196.

18. Odyssey House retention data reported in "Is Odyssey House the Tiffany of TC's?" *The Journal*, (June 1, 1974), p. 5.

19. "Junkies are becoming a scarce commodity," say Thomas McCahill, Karen N. File, and Leonard Savitz, "On Counting (on) Addicts in the Criminal Justice System," in *Developments in the Field of Drug Abuse: Proceedings of the National Drug Abuse Conference—1974*, ed. Edward C. Senay, Vernon Shorty, and Harold Alksne (Cambridge, Mass.: Schendman Publishing Co., 1974), pp. 886-91.

20. Vincent J. Rinella, "Rehabilitation or Bust: The Impact of Criminal Justice System Referrals on the Treatment of Drug Addicts and Alcoholics in a Therapeutic Community (Eagleville's Experience)," *American Journal of Drug and Alcohol Abuse* 3 (January 1976): 550.

21. Narcotics Prevention Project, "Methadone Maintenance Letter of Intent," (Los Angeles: Narcotics Prevention Project, 1974, mimeographed), p. 3.

22. For the implications of diversion relevant to therapist-client relationships, see Robert G. Newman, "We'll Make Them an Offer They Can't Refuse," *Fifth National Conference, 1973*, ed. National Association for the Prevention of Addiction to Narcotics, pp. 96-99; Roger C. Smith, "Addiction, Coercion, and Treatment: Reflections on the Debate," in *Developments in the Field of Drug Abuse*, ed. Senay, Shorty, and Alksne, pp. 852-62; and Barbara Underwood, "The Conflict Between the Criminal Justice System and Addiction Rehabilitation Systems," *American Journal of Drug and Alcohol Abuse* 3 (January 1976): 59-61.

23. "Recommendations Designed to Help NY Programs Fulfill Their Stated Goals," *The Journal* (July 1, 1974), p. 1.

24. DeLeon, Holland and Rosenthal, "Phoenix House," p. 686.

25. See Kurt Weis and Michael E. Milakovich, "Political Misuses of Crime Rates," *Society* 10 (July/August 1973): 29; and the victimization survey reported in "Study Bares Profusion of Unreported Crime," *Long Beach Independent Press-Telegram* (April 27, 1972), p. A–18.

26. For a history and analysis of the New York City Narcotics Register, see J. J. Fishman, Donald P. Conwell, and Zili Amsel, "New York City Narcotics Register: A Brief History," *International Journal of the Addictions* 6 (July 1971): 561-69.

27. DeLeon, Holland and Rosenthal, "Phoenix House," p. 127.

28. Walter V. Collier and Yasser A. Hijazi, "A Follow-Up Study of Former Residents of a Therapeutic Community," *International Journal of the Addictions* 9 (December 1974): 819.

29. Daniel Casriel and George Amen, *Daytop: Three Addicts and Their Culture* (New York: Hill and Wang, Inc., 1971), chapters 1-3.

30. On spontaneous remission of narcotics addiction with onset of maturity, see Charles Winick, "Maturing Out of Narcotic Addiction," *United Nations Bulletin on Narcotics* 14 (January 1962): 1-7; and M. Snow, "Maturing Out of Narcotic Addiction in New York City," *International Journal of the Addictions* 8 (December 1973): 921-38. In fact, this is how most addicts "clean up," not through the ministrations of some program, but on their own.

31. This methodological warning comes from an experienced outcome researcher, Paul Cushman, Jr., "Detoxification from Methadone Maintenance," *Journal of the American Medical Association* 236 (November 8, 1976): 2171.

32. George Vaillant, "A 12-Year Follow-Up of New York Narcotic Addicts: III. Some Social and Psychiatric Characteristics," *Archives of General Psychiatry* 15 (March 1966): 599-609.

33. Pin, Martin and Walsh, "A Follow-up Study of 300 Ex-Clients," pp. 400, 403.

34. Brill, "Some Comments," p. 348.

35. Howard A. Katz, "California Rehabilitation Center: A Critical Look," *International Journal of the Addictions* 6 (September 1971): 550-51.

36. Goffman, *Asylums*, p. 18.

37. "California Rehabilitation Center," *Long Beach Independent Press-Telegram* (April 6, 1972), p. A–20.

38. McGarrey is quoted in ibid.

39. Edward Bunker, "Methadone in Prisons?" *The Nation* (November 8, 1975), p. 454.

40. Lopez's testimony appears in U.S. Congress, Senate Committee on Labor and Public Welfare, *Alcoholism and Narcotics*, 92d Cong., 1st sess., Pt 1, p. 110.

41. Bunker, "Methadone in Prisons?" p. 454.

42. Ibid.

43. On the failure of "counseling" in prisons, see Leslie T. Wilkins, *Evaluation of Penal Measures* (New York: Random House, 1969); Richard J. Carlson, "Rehabilitating Criminals," *The Center Magazine* (July/August 1973), pp. 27-31; Robert Sommer and Barbara A. Sommer, "Showcase Prisons: The Best are a Waste," *The Nation* (October 1974), pp. 369-72; Bunker, "Methadone in Prisons," pp. 454-55; and Robert Martinson, "What Works?—Questions and Answers About Prison Reform," *The Public Interest* 35 (Spring 1974): 22-54.

44. On labeling theory and its relation to heroin addiction, see Edwin M. Schur, *Crimes Without Victims* (Englewood Cliffs, N.J.: Prentice-Hall, 1965).

45. J. E. Berecochea, R. A. Bass and G. E. Sing, "Narcotic Addict Outpatient Program: One Year Followup," Research Report #33 (Sacramento, Calif.: California State Department of Corrections, 1971), pp. 6, 11, 33.

46. U.S. Congress, House Select Committee on Crime, *Narcotics Research, Rehabilitation, and Treatment*, 92d Cong., 1st sess., Pt. 2, p. 642.

47. This Kramer quote appears in "California Civil Commitment Program," *Los Angeles Times* (May 9, 1971), Pt. I, p.B.

9

The Drug Abuse-Industrial Complex

The money spent on treating heroin addicts is substantial. With the added costs of capturing, trying, convicting and incarcerating heroin distributors, users and abusers, the aggregate dollar outlay for controlling heroin supply and demand becomes enormous.

One reason the return on our investment in drug law enforcement and addiction treatment is so low is that addiction control strategies ignore the political and economic realities of (1) upper world groups who "fight heroin addiction," and (2) the functions of the underworld heroin market. Both factors help perpetuate heroin addiction. "Fighting heroin" creates pressure groups who develop vital interests in sustaining the addiction "problem" and vitiating attempts at policy reform such as heroin decriminalization, which might be the most rational approach.

An analysis of addiction treatment strategies and their outcomes should therefore elucidate the official "mission" in society of these programs, their manifest and intended purposes and consequences, and their latent functions—the covert goals and unintended consequences of heroin control efforts.

THE LATENT GOALS OF ADDICTION TREATMENT STRATEGIES

An agency or program originally created for one purpose frequently and insidiously acquires additional, often unplanned functions. Operations might then be influenced more by the acquired objectives than by the purposes that first motivated the establishment of the agency or program. Official goals are *manifest*, since they appear in legislation, directives or formal announcements under which programs are created or policy publicly justified. Actual goals must be inferred from the behavior of functionaries within organizations, in terms of the real objectives they seem to establish. Those interests and objectives often emerge different from the publicly proclaimed objectives and may appropriately be called *latent* goals. Robert K. Merton's thesis was that organizations and their personnel displace manifest goals and functions with latent goals and functions.[1]

The impact of addiction treatment policy and programs on reaching their formal, overt goals seems minimal. What, then, motivates people in these organizations? Is it only the goal of eliminating heroin abuse? Although the formal goal and manifest function of most addiction treatment and rehabilitation programs is ultimately to "self-destruct"—to be unnecessary—their covert goal and latent function is self-perpetuation, continually expending vast sums of public dollars on the interminable treatment of addicts in programs destined to fail. Worse is a current federal retrenchment in addiction treatment funding. Rehabilitation programs nationwide will fight a grim holding action, not getting much new money and desperately trying to keep their current funding. With a perennial economic squeeze organizational survival becomes paramount—a matter of bread and butter.

On January 17, 1961, in his farewell radio and television address to the American people, outgoing President Dwight D. Eisenhower coined the term "military-industrial complex":

> In the councils of government, we must guard against the acquisition of unwarranted influence, whether sought or unsought, by the military-industrial complex. The potential for the disastrous rise of misplaced power exists and will persist.[2]

Eisenhower did not allude to the nascent stages of a similar titanic complex in the social service field, "The education-poverty-mental health industrial complex,"[3] a social pork barrel consisting of a broad array of groups whose basic industry is ministering to the psychosocial problems of poverty. These are the service deliverers, the social or human services workers, the mental health professionals and the storefront lawyers—the "helping professions" and "caregivers" who depend on a steady flow of funds from labor-intensive federal programs designed to help the disadvantaged. This "social pork barrel," says Shapiro," . . . just like the military-industrial complex, makes thousands of workers dependent on the federal budget for their jobs and way of life."[4] Are our manpower and financial resources enriched or decimated by the compelling necessity of human services professionals feeding their families through government grants?

In 1973 Sonnenreich coined the term "drug abuse—industrial complex":

> About four years ago we spent a total of $66.4 million for the entire federal effort in the drug abuse area. . . . This year we have spent $796 million, and the budget estimates that have been submitted indicate that we will exceed the $1 billion mark. When we do so we become, for want of a better term, a drug abuse industrial complex.[5]

Sonnenreich referred to the combined economic effect of federal drug law enforcement and addiction treatment efforts. What kind of political and economic clout do these programs have in our communities?

DRUG LAW ENFORCEMENT: THE TURNKEY INDUSTRY

Federal outlays for fiscal year 1969 for all drug abuse-oriented programs, both law enforcement and treatment, was $81 million. Five years later, in 1974, the federal government spent $800 million on these efforts, a dramatic 1,000 percent increase. Obviously, the handling of addicts by police, courts and corrections is big business and has been since heroin and addiction were criminalized in 1914. It is estimated that over $600 million a year is spent to arrest, convict and incarcerate addicts and suppliers.

This "turnkey industry" is a profitable enterprise for customs agents, police, courts, correctional institutions, attorneys, and peripheral hangers-on like bail bondsmen, jail and prison construction contractors, urine-testing laboratories, and even some ex-offender programs. It provides thousands of jobs for middle-class

Americans. Though the stated goal of this turnkey industry is to self-destruct ("crush crime"), its unstated mission is self-maintenance. Quite simply, the criminal justice system *needs* addicts and has developed what Veblen called a "vested interest" in addiction. If crime and addiction were somehow to disappear tomorrow, many police officers and their ancillary personnel would be out of jobs. Chasing addicts and pushers provides federal, state and local drug law enforcement agencies and personnel with a reason for being.

Policy impacts are the effects a policy or program has on the target population and other features of the environment. Impacts are intended or unintended, anticipated or unanticipated. Policies and programs may not have their intended impact on a problem. "Spillover effects" represent the unanticipated consequences of policies and programs. Examples of unanticipated consequences of heroin criminalization illustrate the negative spillovers of narcotic control policy since 1914.

Undeniably, the criminalization of heroin has had a corrupting influence on the entire criminal justice system. Anti-narcotic laws provide a special incentive for the corruption of police, judicial and corrections personnel. People who have worked with intelligent and aggressive heroin addicts know of their cunning, their single-mindedness and their absolute amorality where their drug supply is concerned. Standard practices place the police officer who has a narcotics assignment in a continuing illegal relationship with a series of user/seller informants. The addict's desperate attention to his own needs and the officer's power over the addict make a tremendous risk for the honest police officer. The evidence is mounting that narcotics law enforcement officers, dealing as individuals with small-fry users and dealers, are vulnerable to corruption.

THE KNAPP COMMISSION

The New York City Police Department has been rocked by major narcotics scandals. In 1971 the Knapp Commission's ten-month-long investigation revealed the following corrupt practices among officers:[6]

1. Keeping money and/or narcotics confiscated at the time of arrest or raid
2. Selling narcotics to addict-informants in exchange for stolen goods
3. Passing confiscated heroin to police informants for sale to addicts
4. "Flaking," or planting heroin on narcotics suspects
5. "Padding," or adding to the quantity of narcotics found on an arrested person to upgrade an arrest
6. Storing heroin, needles and other drug paraphernalia in police lockers
7. Illegally tapping suspects' telephones
8. Accepting money or narcotics from suspected narcotics law violators as payment for the disclosure of official information
9. Financing heroin transactions
10. Determining the purity and strength of unfamiliar heroin they had seized by giving the narcotics to addict-informants to test on themselves
11. Kidnapping critical witnesses to prevent them from testifying
12. Providing armed protection for heroin dealers
13. Offering to obtain "hit men" to kill potential witnesses

Law enforcement agencies look good if (1) fewer crimes are reported, (2) a greater number of arrests are made—whether or not those arrested are important criminals, and (3) a higher percentage of convictions—whether or not the convictions are for important crimes or of important criminals—are obtained. The emphasis, in other words, is on quantity, not quality. The pressure on the police investigator is not to eradicate or reduce the traffic in heroin. It is to develop such an interrelationship that he can secure the number of arrests and convictions that will mark him and his department as good performers. Small-fry heroin users and dealers serve this need.

Myles Ambrose, former head of the U.S. Treasury Department's Bureau of Customs and President Nixon's first director of the Office of Drug Abuse Law Enforcement (ODALE), said that "Police corruption appears to be a factor in disappointing local and state drives against narcotics pushers."[7] He implied that local efforts to eliminate narcotics sellers were faltering because of police corruption. Former Attorney General John Mitchell, referring to the lack of effective local drug law enforcement efforts, alluded to corruption when he said that, ". . . the system of law enforcement has not worked out for various reasons I will not go into."[8]

The dramatic forays of police seizures are only a small part of total police activity against narcotics violators. The major, more routine, day-to-day work is so structured that it automatically fragments a narcotics detail and drives it into a position where illegal action is easy; legal action is difficult and sometimes close to impossible.

Corruption at Federal Level

Pervasive organized corruption of this kind runs to the federal level as well, mainly the Drug Enforcement Administration, the U.S. Border Patrol and the Customs Service. Charges against DEA include criticism for abandoning a probe into alleged heroin smuggling by Nixon contributor-billionaire Robert Vesco, a series of scandals involving DEA with filming narcotics suspects in sex traps, surveillance of U.S. mail, a bizarre catalog of assassination devices, an intramural bureaucratic war within the agency itself, and assorted other charges of graft, murder, heroin peddling and overzealous door smashing and gunslinging by DEA agents.

As a result, nearly all of DEA's top staff were shifted or removed from office. Perhaps for this reason the Carter administration considered abolishing DEA and redistributing its functions elsewhere in the Department of Justice and to the Treasury Department.[9] Internal corruption in this agency may be one reason it never decreased the heroin trade.

Some critics of DEA argue that protection of heroin profiteers is not caused by internal corruption in the heart of DEA but is, in fact, the *function* of DEA under present anti-narcotic laws. Narcotics enforcement does little more than preserve the monopoly of professionals in the heroin trade by making life difficult only for amateur and unorganized dealers who cannot afford big payoffs.[10] In this view, DEA is little more than a weak regulatory agency whose benign neglect rationalizes and legitimizes the big conglomerates in the huge heroin industry created by anti-narcotics laws.

Corruption goes beyond police and involves prosecutors, attorneys, bondsmen, certain judges and, allegedly, some state legislators.[11] Several large-scale heroin dealers in southern California told me that a prominent member of the California State Senate was once a "kingpin" of the heroin trade.

The punitive approach to the heroin problem, requiring increased police power, has led to gross infringement of constitutional liberties. Law enforcement agencies have committed excesses in the pursuit of evidence. These excesses, in turn, have evoked a judicial conterreaction in the form of restrictions upon the use of evidence, which are designed to discourage unconstitutional police practices.

A leading Supreme Court decision on entrapment was evoked by overzealous undercover agents in a narcotics case—*Sherman* v. *United States* (1958). Decisions involving admissibility of evidence arising from illegal arrests have been rendered most often in narcotics prosecutions—*Johnson* v. *United States* (1948) and *Draper* v. *United States* (1959). Legal restraints on lawful search and seizure have stemmed largely from litigation over the past fifty years concerning a variety of forms of physical intrusion by police in the course of obtaining evidence of violations of narcotics laws.[12] The same is true with respect to the developing law of wiretapping, bugging and other forms of electronic surveillance.[13] Indeed, probably no single phenomenon is more responsible for the whole pattern of judicial restraint on methods of law enforcement than the unfortunate experience with enforcing narcotic drug laws.

ADDICTION MONGERERS AND DRUG ABUSEOLOGISTS

Federal support for addiction treatment and rehabilitation rose from $28 million in 1969 to over $350 million in 1974. Like drug law enforcement organizations, addiction treatment programs and personnel that depend on government grants have an important economic stake in maintaining their hegemony. Such programs are big business. How committed are they to the politics and economics of organizational survival?

Psychiatrist Thomas Szasz says the addiction mongerers and drug abuseologists associated with treatment programs need to produce more and more heroin addicts in order to make themselves indispensable. Szasz calls this enterprise a "racket":

> Obviously, addiction has been the glamour stock of the late sixties and early seventies, and addiction mongering the only true growth industry in America during these years. . . . The whole business of addiction-mongering is a gigantic hoax, a socially and professionally validated racket. . . . [Addiction treatment is] . . . malicious medical meddling into personal habits, a pseudomedical enterprise that redefines personal preferences [using heroin] as a scientific and medical problem, concealing medical coercion as treatment and [thereby] creating an immense economic interest. . . .[14]

Treatment programs and their funding sources employ men and women, some in high-status jobs. They have a vested interest in the maintenance of their programs and, by extension, in perpetuating the supposed malady they are mandated to "cure." Even though their overt mission is to contain heroinism, they promote addiction through treatments that fail. Programs consistently cling to the status quo and resist innovations that might make them obsolete.

The executive director of a big treatment program recently asked me to write a "heroin maintenance" protocol for his agency to submit for possible funding. My interest was deflated when, after further clarification, all he really wanted was a standard cost-benefit analysis to legitimize his agency's huge annual expenditures on ineffective inpatient detoxification of heroin addicts. His intention was to demonstrate to funding sources that it was cheaper for them to pay for periodic in-hospital detoxification than to let addicts run freely in the community, where they would use more and more heroin and commit more crimes in support of the habit. Periodic detoxification, said the program director, at least keeps addicts off the streets for seven days every six months and reduces their tolerance to affordable levels so they can "maintain" themselves on smaller doses of illegal heroin for less money. What he meant by "modified heroin maintenance" was continued illicit heroin use (his idea of "heroin maintenance"), "modified" periodically by inpatient detoxification to reduce tolerance. I refused to write the protocol.

ADDICTION TREATMENT ROLES

There seems to be an increase in the "heroin problem" proportionate to the attention directed at its eradication. The larger the structure developed to treat addicts, the larger becomes the population of addicts needed to feed and support it. Treatment programs and the criminal justice system supply that need. And since their heroin control efforts have generally failed to cut supplies or reduce demand for the drug, an endless supply of heroin addicts is virtually guaranteed.

The interests of those in high-echelon occupational roles in these treatment organizations become more entrenched the longer the organizations persist and the more permanent becomes their funding. Scuttling these ineffective treatment programs and their sponsoring bureaucracies poses a real threat to those whose careers have been narrowly defined by treating heroin addicts. Thus, treatment programs and their funding sources have been a force of conservatism and resistance to reforms in laws and policies relating to the criminalization of heroin. With a vested interest like this, it is doubtful whether the heroin "crisis" will ever be "solved."

An examination of the industrial aspects of addiction treatment and rehabilitation must involve descriptions of work and occupations relevant to the enterprise. These job titles (which exclude law enforcement roles) are directly related to addiction treatment, rehabilitation and prevention/education and, though hardly exhaustive, the list represents the kinds of roles addiction treatment has spawned:

A. Treatment Program Management

1. Program directors
2. Deputy directors
3. Assistant directors
4. Clinical directors
5. Training specialists
6. Public information officers
7. Personnel directors
8. Fiscal control officers
9. Management assistants

B. Medical Treatment

1. Physicians
2. Nurses (RNs and LVNs)
3. Medical assistants
4. Psychiatrists
5. Laboratory technicians
6. Hospital administrators
7. Hospital deputy administrators
8. Hospital ancillary staff (dieticians, cleaning, and the like)
9. Pharmacists and pharmacy technicians

C. Community-based Treatment

1. Directors, counseling services
2. Therapeutic counselors
3. Group facilitators
4. Intake counselors
5. Vocational rehabilitation counselors
6. Social workers
7. Psychologists
8. Psychologist assistants
9. Psychiatric social workers

D. Community Program Support Personnel

1. Community organization specialists
2. Drug program development specialists
3. Mental health program development specialists
4. Addiction prevention/education specialists
5. Outreach counselors
6. Street caseworkers
7. Youth specialists
8. Day-care specialists
9. Recreation specialists
10. Family counselors
11. Attorneys

E. Addiction Prevention/Education

1. Education coordinators
2. Trainers
3. Drug counselors (in school)
4. Health counselors (in school)
5. Student aides (in school)

F. Training In Addiction Treatment And Rehabilitation

1. Training directors
2. Training program coordinators
3. Trainers/facilitators

G. Federal/State/Local Drug Abuse Treatment Authority

1. Agency directors, deputy directors and assistant directors
2. Chief administrators
3. Deputy administrators
4. Coordinators for education/prevention
5. Coordinators for treatment and rehabilitation
6. Coordinators for state planning
7. Coordinators for county planning
8. Coordinators for municipal planning
9. Community program monitoring/evaluation personnel

H. Research/Evaluation Personnel

1. Directors of evaluation and research
2. Research/evaluation assistants
3. Research Analysts
4. Research Assistants/statistical clerks
5. Epidemiologists (in program or academic setting)
6. Pharmacologists (in lab, program or academic setting)
7. Social scientists (in academic or program setting)
8. Toxicologists (in lab, program or academic setting)

I. Consultants and Lecturers In Addition Treatment/Prevention

1. Consultants—treatment
2. Consultants—rehabilitation
3. Consultants—prevention/education
4. Consultants—research/evaluation
5. Consultants—criminal justice
6. Consultants—state planning
7. Consultants—community planning
8. Consultants—training
9. Consultants—drugs in industry
10. Lecturers—drug abuse control policy
11. Lecturers—addiction treatment
12. Lecturers—addiction prevention
13. Lecturers—addicts and the law
14. Lecturers—addict behavior
15. Lecturers—biochemical research

What all these service deliverers want and need is more money, and they are determined to hang onto their positions, whether or not their ministrations cure addicts.

Another latent function performed by addiction treatment policies and programs is cooptation of potentially dissident minorities—black, brown and Asian—into established social service delivery systems of local communities. By this process marginal groups adopt the values and goals of the established elites to win benefits from the institutions controlled by elites.[15] Selznick used the relationship between the Tennessee Valley Authority and powerful groups within the valley to exemplify this type of cooptation.[16]

In some respects, addiction treatment and rehabilitation programs have replaced the community action agencies of President Johnson's "Great Society" as a means of coopting minority professionals and paraprofessionals into the "establishment." Just as there was a relationship between the War on Poverty and the "blackening" of urban social service bureaucracies,[17] there appears to be a direct association between the "heroin problem" and occupational entry of blacks, browns and Asians into the not-so-revolutionary health care delivery system.

PROFIT-MAKING COPORATIONS

Among other spin-off industries created by recent expansion of addiction treatment is the business of urine testing. The extent of urinalysis testing for drugs is largely unknown. Goldberg estimated that 15 million urine samples are analyzed yearly for the presence of drugs. Eight million are from methadone maintenance programs and five million from the military.[18] Undoubtedly these figures are low for today. Urinalysis for drugs has become a multimillion dollar industry and one of the chief economic beneficiaries of the burgeoning drug abuse industrial complex. Suffice it to say that all this testing supports a huge laboratory industry. It costs taxpayers about $25 million a year just to conduct required urinalyses on methadone maintenance cleints. Regarding urine testing in methadone maintenance programs, Paul Blachly focused on its industrial aspects by noting, ". . . once having been established as procedure, it is virtually impossible to stop this wasteful practice. By this time, to terminate the practice would put people out of work, and there is now a vested interest in maintaining the status quo."[19]

In the early 1970s Frederick Douglass Intermediate School in Harlem received a $125,000 federal grant to test the urine of all children in the fifth through eighth grades. Of thousands of samples, only two specimens were positive for illicit drugs. In Alabama, Governor Wallace's Commission on Drug Abuse recommended that the state test the urine of every junior and senior high school student at least once a year. The civil liberties implications of such testing programs will not be explored here. Given the unreliability of urinalyses (many urine samples appear to be "sink-tested"), the costs of testing would seem to outweigh the benefits.

DRUG ADVERTISING

Other profit makers in the addiction treatment industry include pharmaceutical manufacturers themselves, who provide drugs used to treat addiction, including *tons* of methadone hydrochloride each year. Drug companies not only make money treating addicts. They *create* addicts.

In their quest for profits, drug manufacturers are described by critics as ". . . pushers who push through promotion and advertising means to create a drug acculturated society ready to take drugs and often immune to their hazards."[20] The industry, of course, counters that the degree to which drug promotion through advertising affects either the prescribing practices of physicians or the degree of drug misuse by Americans is unknown. Contrary to the arguments of the pharmaceutical companies, repeated studies of prescribing practices have shown that doctors get their knowledge of drugs and suggestions as to their use from advertisements in medical journals and from the "detail men" who plug drugs in doctors' offices. Such advertising constantly recommends products to "treat" the sadness of death in the family, the nervousness of a child's first day at school, the apprehension of a visit to the dentist and other ordinary problems of everyday living.

Women, the elderly and other roles are constantly stereotyped in ads for psychotropic drugs which generally show greater appeal to emotion than advertisements for non-mood-altering drugs. Here, for example, is part of an ad for Abbot's Placidyl, a hypnotic similar to chloral hydrate ("knock-out drops"):

> The night has a thousand whys. The answers used to come easy. But lately everything's becoming a problem. She can't understand why her husband has to work late, why her son has to wear his hair so long, why the price of hamburger changes every time she goes to the supermarket. And now there is a new problem: she can't fall asleep. This patient needs help. She needs Placidyl.[21]

For the elderly who appear depressed, CIBA, Inc., offers Ritalin, a stimulant related to amphetamine: "Before treatment, the geriatric patient was withdrawn, apathetic. Ritalin will bring your elderly patient out of his apathetic/withdrawn senile behavior."[22] And into what frame of mind? CIBA notes the following possible adverse reactions to Ritalin: nervousness; insomnia; hypersensitivity (including skin rash, uticaria, fever, arthralgia, exfoliative dermatitis, erythema multiforme with necrotizing vasculitis, and thrombocytopenic purpura); anorexia; nausea; dizziness; palpitations; headache; dyskinesia; blood pressure elevations or hypotension; tachycardia; angina; cardiac arrhythmia; and weight loss. Ritalin is also recommended as adjunctive therapy for minimal brain dysfunction in children. Thousands of youngsters are given Ritalin or amphetamines to alter classroom behavior. Critics charge that physicians, school authorities and drug manufacturers under the guise of "helping" children, are using chemicals to control them—drugging for deportment, as it were.[23]

Drug companies employ persuasive lobbying techniques creating an almost impenetrable legal framework that protects them. Both consumers and physicians are captives of this industry. It is estimated that Roche Laboratories, Inc., alone spent about a quarter billion dollars in the 1960s for the promotion of just two tranquilizers—Librium and Valium—which subsequently became best sellers and household words.[24] Valium (diazepam) is the most frequently prescribed drug in the United States, with more than 70 million prescriptions sold in 1976. According to NIDA reports, Valium is the number one abused drug in emergency room overdose episodes and is listed as the first or second most abused drug by nineteen of the twenty-three cities reporting to the federal Drug Abuse Warning Network (DAWN) reporting system.[25] Nevertheless, Valium is still pushed heavily in slick medical journal ads.[26]

Big advertising investments by drug manufacturers pay off by creating a need by physicians and their patients for psychoactive substances. The result is that by 1972, next to mining, the pharmaceutical manufacturing industry was the most profitable in America in terms of sales.[27] This high profitability results directly from government protection of the industry's oligopolistic practices and heavy promotional spending.

The inescapable conclusion is that drug advertising is associated with prescription drug misuse and is a contributing factor in the translation of social, political and economic problems into medical ones supposedly amenable to chemotherapeutic management.

THE NATIONAL DRUG ABUSE CONFERENCE

The yearly National Drug Abuse Conference has become the gathering place of treatment and rehabilitation interest groups and a sales convention where addiction industrialists hawk their latest wares. It is a huge social event where some in attendance abuse most every drug in the book, especially gallons of liquor at many free cocktail parties (one such drunken party at the Conrad Hilton in Chicago was billed to the National Institute of Mental Health!)

Included in the program notes of the 1974 National Drug Abuse Conference were "thank-yous" to these companies who provided conference "assistance"—mainly cash donations, hospitality suites and sales booths and decorations on the floor of the convention:

1. Eli Lilly and Company (a major manufacturer of bulk methadone)
2. Bristol Laboratories (another major manufacturer of methadone, whose product Methenex is laced with an antagonist)
3. Hoffman LaRoche, Inc. (manufacturers of Valium and Librium, the number one abused tranquilizers in America)
4. Brinkman Instruments, Inc. (manufacturer of urine-testing hardware for methadone maintenance and drug-free programs)
5. Drug Intervene Systems, Inc. (a urine-testing outfit)
6. Syva Company (another manufacturer of on-site urine testing equipment for treatment programs)

7. Ultrachem Corporation (a major lab performing urinalyses for addiction treatment programs)
8. Biochemical Procedures, Inc. (a urine-testing subsidiary of Bristol-Meyers)

It is ironic that major drug companies sponsor the National Drug Abuse Conference.

Computer firms with "client tracking systems" for sale also dominated the 1974 conference. Here is a promotional flyer issued by one firm to conferees:

> Welcome! Creative Socio-Medics would like to welcome you to the first National Drug Abuse Conference. . . . We have been successful in designing, installing and operating drug treatment program information systems. The following are examples of information systems we are currently providing to more than 300 addiction treatment programs across the country:
>
> 1. Central Intake/Referral
> 2. Central Pharmacy
> 3. Nursing
> 4. Counseling
> 5. Toxicology and Laboratory
> 6. Administration
> 7. Third-party billing (Medicaid)
> 8. Budget/Cost Analysis
> 9. Client I.D. Cards
> 10. Client Tracking

This firm's major competitor in the field offered this alcoholic inducement to potential drug program customers:

> You are cordially invited to visit with us in Suite 1000. Cocktails will be served between 4 p.m. and 8 p.m. We will be on hand to discuss our capabilities in computer technology for various substance abuse programs. We offer you the following benefits:
>
> 1. Continuous Client Tracking from Intake to Termination
> 2. Single Input Document
> 3. Easy-to-use Client Treatment Aid

4. Improved Communication Among Counselors
5. Enhanced communication between program components
6. Counselor and Client Accountability
7. Tailored Packages to Fit your Specific Needs

Both these computer firms wined and dined me in Chicago, San Francisco, San Jose, Sacramento, Los Angeles and San Bernardino. They wanted to land a large federally funded client tracking contract for a whole network of addiction treatment programs. Neither company was selected, however. Instead we developed an in-house system, and hand-tracked client movement at half the expense. Nevertheless, with the winding down of the space program, these computer soft- and hardware firms have made a significant entry into the drug abuse-industrial complex.

Various interest groups, some supported by government grants, have combined to maintain and expand addiction treatment programs. The following groups "sponsored" the 1975 National Drug Abuse Conference in New York City. They contributed substantial sums of money toward staging this annual gala event of the addiction treatment community:

1. National Institute on Drug Abuse (NIDA)
2. National Institute on Alcohol Abuse and Alcoholism (NIAAA)
3. The Drug Abuse Council, Inc.
4. The International Council on Alcohol and Addiction
5. The National Council on Alcoholism
6. Therapeutic Communities of America, Inc.
7. North American Association of Therapeutic Communities, Inc.
8. The Greater New York Coalition on Drug Abuse
9. P.A.C.T. (Provide Addicts Care Today)
10. The National Free Clinic Council, Inc.
11. The National Federation of Concerned Drug Abuse Workers
12. The National Association for the Prevention of Addiction to Narcotics
13. The National Association of State Drug Abuse Program Coordinators

14. The National Association of County Drug Abuse Coordinators
15. The National Coordinating Council on Drug Education
16. The National Addiction Services Guild

Nineteen similar groups sponsored the later 1977 National Drug Abuse Conference in San Francisco. On the surface, at least, these groups seem to hold widely divergent treatment viewpoints and ideologies. The effort to separate medicine from politics in this area, and the rivalries and jealousies among drug abuseologists have complicated the addiction issue. The treatment field is filled with zealots, each convinced he has the best, perhaps the only, program capable of reaching addicts. Their advocacy of one final "solution" or another to the heroin problem is suffused with emotion that turns differences of opinion into heated conflicts. Many such organizations, with great sincerity, extol detoxification and abstinence. Others, with equal fervor, trumpet the substitution of methadone or Darvon-N for heroin. Some say residential treatment is the only way to keep addicts "clean." Still others recommend narcotic antagonists, Jesus, hypnosis, transcendental meditation, psychotherapy, biofeedback, acupuncture, electro-sleep, aversive conditioning, nutritional therapy, or chanting to various mantras. It almost seems appropriate to turn to drugs to escape the clamorings and confusion that permeate the quest for the addiction treatment dollar. And here all these groups coalesce: Addicts are diseased and need the kind of treatment only these organizations presumably have the expertise to provide. To provide this "therapy," all they need is more and more taxpayers' money.

UNIONIZATION OF ADDICTION TREATMENT WORKERS

Increased pressure in addiction treatment programs and government funding agencies to drive out experientially trained paraprofessionals, mainly ex-addicts, to make room for degreed professionals has led to the unionization of drug treatment workers. The National Federation of Concerned Drug Abuse Workers is composed mainly of ex-addict East Coast black and Puerto Rican counselors. Their union, they say, is a response to increasing professionalization of the treatment field. They feel that although they have a "Ph.D in streets," they are being squeezed out, and that services in the future will be provided by drug abuse "experts" with degrees, but without know-how. "Credentialing" of treatment program staff workers by governments is their main concern. The union members want their experience as addicts counted when licenses to treat addicts are given. Whether or not those with raw experience will be successful is still questionable. If they are not, most of them will be out of jobs with little prospect for other work.

NONPROFIT CORPORATIONS IN ADDICTION TREATMENT: THE DRUG ABUSE HUSTLE

An important vehicle for delivery of addiction treatment services has been the private, nonprofit corporation set up to receive government treatment grants and fee-for-service contracts. Over half the treatment programs nationwide are nonprofit, and their road to funding is paved with "RFPs" (Requests for Proposals) from all levels of government. Marketing ability, not service delivery or evaluation skills, may account for a contract award in the request-for-proposal process.[28] Recently, the principal in one of the nation's largest consulting firms in the substance abuse area told me the grant award process was "90 percent politics." This service-delivery and evaluation research community consists of RFP readers, bidders and winners.

The nonprofit groups have flourished in addiction treatment for three major reasons. First, relative to government agencies themselves, these groups provided a vehicle for rapid and relatively inexpensive expansion of addiction treatment services and mobilization of resources during the Nixon war on heroin. Few of them are burdened either financially or operationally with the elaborate bureaucracies associated with government agencies. Their argument to funding sources is that they can do the treatment and rehabilitation job better, cheaper and faster than government itself. Second, extant nonprofit treatment providers had a natural involvement in their surrounding communities. New ones were often implemented with substantial input from local elites as well as "community advocates" on their boards of directors. Although addiction treatment programs are difficult to locate in communities because citizens fear addicts, the nonprofits were not viewed as invading foreigners (as government agencies so often are) imposing their will without community support and input. Third, in a capitalist society nonprofit corporations are surrounded by halos of probity. They are not burdened with the tarnished image of profit-making companies out to rip off governments and consumers nor do they resemble government programs wasting the taxpayers' money on "moon-shot" approaches that do not work. The image is of a sincere administrator of a nonprofit program in the poor part of the city spending his time in good works on behalf of sick addicts and the victimized community, not in calculating new and devious ways to beat the government out of more money.

In nonprofit corporations the pecuniary interest of the board and staff is uncoupled from the rises and falls in corporate output and income. In theory this allows nonprofits to concentrate on client needs and services without concern that this will affect staff incomes.[29]

Nonprofit treatment programs in the same communities cooperate extensively, bouncing clients back and forth by mutual referrals. Various territorial claims and each other's effectiveness are never openly questioned, unless the financial going gets rough and war breaks out between programs over who is going to get the remaining grant scraps. Some "networks" of nonprofit addiction treatment corporations have tumbled like houses of cards under these battles over who gets how much of what.

What cooperation there is among such programs is frequently incestuous, as when the director of one treatment program is a paid consultant to two others, or when the ranking member of a drug abuse task force or coalition that distributes government treatment dollars is the head of an agency destined to receive part of the money. The same individual may sit on the governing board of directors of several nonprofit addiction treatment agencies and have a financial interest in a profit-making firm doing business with the treatment programs. Potential conflicts of interest are passed off in the field as "pooling of talent."

FRAUD IN ADDICTION TREATMENT PROGRAMS

Mind-boggling fraud and illegal activities in and between addiction treatment programs are not uncommon. A person who finds out too much about these under-the-table dealings can be murdered. A number of homicides in Los Angeles have recently been attributed to shadowy deals in and between drug abuse treatment programs.

Fraudulent practices include:

1. Bribes and kickbacks
2. Rampant self-dealing
3. Double billings and padded billings to funding sources such as Medicaid
4. Charging funding sources for services never performed
5. Phony reports on numbers of clients in treatment
6. Unreasonable and uncustomary fees, salaries and fringe benefits for addiction treatment program staff
7. Using work hours for profit-making (or political) activities
8. Embezzlement and theft
9. Violent assault
10. Murder

Self-dealing is a common racket in the treatment "business." It is a business transaction in which the same person(s) appear(s) simultaneously on both sides of a money-making deal, on one hand as the staff of a nonprofit addiction program and on the other as a profit-making provider of services to that program. The arrangement usually involves siphoning off government grant and fee-for-service money into a subsidiary profit-making corporation.

For example, a typical operation might involve the following parties, all engaged in self-dealing and other criminal acts: (1) the director, deputy director and intake director of a huge addiction treatment program, (2) two small profit-making hospitals to which the treatment program sends its addicts for detoxification, (3) a profit-making consulting firm composed of two partners, one of whom is intake director at the drug program, and (4) the owner of the hospitals where the addicts are detoxified. The scheme works like this. The consulting firm makes a deal with the hospitals, which are going broke, to turn a quick profit by converting them into inpatient detoxification units for heroin addicts. All detoxification cases will be reimbursed through Medicaid at the rate of $120 a day per client. The consulting firm agrees to write the licensure protocols, for which the owner of the hospitals will pay a flat fee to the consultants. The fee is withheld until enough patients have been detoxified to pay it with Medicaid funds.

After the hospitals begin operations, the consulting firm signs a contract with them to provide ongoing "training and consultation" to the detox units at the rate of $3 a day per patient, paid from Medicaid reimbursements. The consulting firm's "take" from this arrangement eventually exceeds $60,000 a year. However, the consulting firm never provides the "training" services, an unfortunate development since the hospital nursing staff lacks even the most rudimentary knowledge of detoxification procedures. They do not know, for example, how to treat a narcotic overdose if it occurs on the ward. Thus, the lives of the patients are endangered. No matter. Money is the goal in this operation, not quality care.

This whole arrangement between the drug program, the hospitals and the consulting firm is characterized by conflicts of interest, fraud, kickbacks, bribes, self-dealing and misrepresentation of financial records. One member of the two-man consulting firm is in a direct conflict of interest. He earns substantial profits from the consulting firm and at the same time manages the drug program intake unit where he uses his position to funnel addicts into the hospitals for which he is a paid consultant. He uses his work hours at the federally funded drug program to feather his consulting firm's nest. The consulting firm of which he is a member, in turn, bribes *his* boss, the executive director of the drug program, with under-the-table payments of $500 a month (from Medicaid funds) and the deputy director of the same program with $100 a month to make sure that these administrators "keep their mouths shut" regarding their intake director's self-dealing and also to be certain that the program's detoxification cases are all channeled into the designated hospitals.

In addition to this arrangement, another treatment program director in another part of the city gets $100 a month (in Medicaid money) to make sure that all *his* detoxification cases are funneled through the same two hospitals. A virtual endless flow of clients is thus guarenteed through this series of bribes and kickbacks utilizing taxpayers' money. The drug program directors get paid off because they have the addicts. The administrator of the detoxification hospitals gets a kickback of $600 a month from the consulting firm, again Medicaid money, because he guarantees the availability of hospital beds for detoxification cases. The bribes paid by the consulting firm are covered in its financial ledgers by recording them as payments for "consultant services" rendered to the hospitals. Such "services," however, are never rendered. The real service is guaranteeing an interminable flow of sick junkies in order to line the pockets of all involved.

Finally, out of its take the consulting firm pays street people a "finder's" fee of $25 for every addict they bring to the drug program intake units for detoxification. Phony Medicaid cards are sold at some drug programs for about $25 apiece.

This whole operation could be run on an honest basis with the interests of clients at heart. It is not a fraudulent practice, for example, to use a portion of Medicaid detoxification reimbursement for legitimate training, evaluation and some consultation if such "expert" services are actually provided. But in this case greed got in the way—greed on the part of the consultants, the hospital administrator and owners and the drug program directors. They preferred to take the money and do nothing. As a result, the detoxification unit staffs were never properly trained, the consulting firm made money without rendering contracted services and the bribes and kickbacks remained in full swing to the drug program administrators and the "body snatchers."

The operation outlined here is only one of many suspect enterprises in the drug treatment industry. For example, the doctor leading the list of American physicians receiving more than $100,000 a year for treating welfare patients operated three methadone maintenance clinics in New York City.[30] In a similar vein an addiction treatment program in New York City receiving over $3.2 million a year from federal, state and city grants was recently charged with purchasing profit-making properties with federal funds, forging payroll checks, padding treatment enrollment lists, and maintaining a $200,000 "slush fund" of NIDA monies to cover unauthorized program expenditures.[31]

The drug abuse treatment hustle goes right to the top—to the National Institute on Drug Abuse, which supports a tight little network of "experts" in the medical approach to the heroin dilemma. Using taxpayers' money, the members of the NIDA fraternity take turns hiring one another to study, quantify, assist and evaluate heroin control policy. Perhaps for this reason, NIDA recently was investigated by the Inspector General of HEW for a whole series of possible abuses of grants and contracts.[32]

A typical NIDA research project involved showing pornographic movies to subjects stoned on marijuana. Unfortunately for those lining up for the experiment, Congress got wind of it and terminated the project. But similar imaginative studies have slipped through unnoticed: an $80,000 grant to measure how drugs and alcohol affect a person's ability to recognize smiles, scowls and other facial expressions; a $363,000 study to find out whether marijuana smoking makes a person susceptible to hypnosis. Researchers armed with NIDA grants roam the globe. One group examined the sociocultural aspects of marijuana use among the Zulus of South Africa. This expedition cost the taxpayers $174,000. Later a team of scientists was off to North Yemen, spending $275,000 to study a stimulant obtained by chewing leaves found only in that country.

A research rationale is not necessary to see the world on government travel vouchers. During 1977 NIDA's director, Robert DuPont, visited Bangkok, Geneva, Honolulu, London, Miami, Denver, Houston, Montreal, Nigeria, Paris, Puerto Rico and Rome. The official purpose was to deliver speeches at various drug conventions. A review of the talks indicates that they were all variations of the same basic speech.

When critics call NIDA's cozy circle of bureaucrats "the family," they are not being metaphorical. Consider the case of Lee Dogoloff, a NIDA official who later moved over to the White House as a drug advisor to President Carter. While Dogoloff, an ex-social worker, was at NIDA, his wife, Mary Lou, was paid about $17,000 by a Rochester, New York, firm called BRX to work on a NIDA-sponsored study of drug abuse treatment programs in rural areas. She also collected at least $7,200 on another NIDA contract from a Maryland consultant firm named Macro Systems, Inc., whose mission was to update drug treatment manuals used by NIDA program officials. Dogoloff himself hired his wife to accompany him to an official conference in Thailand. He paid for her plane ticket, but the government footed the bill for her salary and expenses. Her job was to "prepare seminar logistics" or, more plainly, to take notes.[33]

Dogoloff met his wife in the early 1970s when she worked as his assistant in Washington, D.C.'s, Narcotics Treatment Administration (NTA). The director of this program was Robert DuPont, later director of NIDA. Another official in the program was Richard Katon, who was close to both the Dogoloffs and DuPont. The four of them have been picking the fruit of the heroin addiction tree ever since. DuPont became the head of the White House Special Action Office of Drug Abuse Prevention (SAODAP), which evolved as NIDA in 1973. Then Lee Dogoloff was named a top official at NIDA. Richard Katon put aside a career as a medical doctor to form a private consulting firm which soon began winning lucrative NIDA contracts. Mary Lou Dogoloff, whose chief qualification as a drug abuse expert is a BA in English, joined Katon's firm.

Friendship can be almost as useful a credential as marriage when the drug abuse bureaucracy is looking for experts. For example, DuPont's friend Katon obtained a $78,000 contract to "develop NIDA statistical publications." He also was given an $800,000 contract for "Drug Abuse Management Information Technical Assistance." In 1977 Katon won the information contract again, but the cost jumped to $1 million.

This "old boy network" extends to the House Narcotics Committee, which is supposed to oversee NIDA. The committee's chief counsel, Joseph Nellis, said he did not have enough staff to check out allegations properly that NIDA was wasting taxpayers' money. Maybe his wife should have helped. In 1977 NIDA awarded a $150,000 contract to Muriel Nellis. For this she was supposed to assemble a "national coalition on women's issue in substance abuse." The fact is that most of these consulting contracts are not worth the requisition forms they are printed on. They are a form of white-collar welfare that has made government drug abuse consulting a boom industry.

Take, for example, the federal CODAP contract with Macro Systems, Inc. This million dollar plum is for compiling statistics on drug users, their problems and their treatment at NIDA-funded clinics. Unfortunately, the numbers frequently do not jibe with reality, and the jumbled picture they present is of no value to individual treatment programs. But the staff at every NIDA-supported clinic has to spend an inordinate amount of time filling out the complicated computerized CODAP forms. In fact, they must be trained to fill out the forms by still other paid consultants.

What do all these NIDA consulting contracts add to resolving the heroin problem? The millions spent do a great deal for the financial health of a small group of "experts" but nothing directly for the mental health of heroin addicts. In fact, one easily gets the impression that many NIDA officials and consultants have never seen a real addict. All they talk about is "data acquisition," "treatment modalities" and "targeting" federal drug abuse treatment dollars. The plain truth is that the average college student knows more about drug abuse on the streets than the NIDA professionals. This was graphically demonstrated when NIDA and the federal drug abuse bureaucracy failed for ten years to detect the rapid spread of a popular but extremely dangerous dissociative anesthetic, phencyclidine hydrochloride, or PCP. NIDA did not spot the upsurge in its use until the drug already was making headlines in forty states.

NIDA spends 60 percent of its treatment budget on heroin addicts, but devotes only 5 percent of its money to the more than 5 million Americans who abuse barbiturates, which are responsible for far more injuries and deaths than heroin. Heroin addiction obviously is the more politically attractive problem, since it is associated in the public mind with street crime. There is not much political mileage in taking on the drugs that much of middle-class America abuses. Moreover, these prescription medications are produced by large, influential corporations that would not welcome a federal assault on their products. But the teenager who swallows a handful of Valiums at a party, guzzles some tequila and takes a few barbiturates is the one who most often ends up with an overdose in a hospital emergency room.

What we have at NIDA, then, if one looks beyond the blatant conflicts of interest, is a growing band of academic experts, armed with the latest jargon, who are as hooked on federal dollars as their clients are on dangerous drugs.

ADDICTION COST ESTIMATE STUDIES

Most analysts of addiction treatment do not stress the kinds of economic benefits to providers that have been outlined here. The analysts focus instead on the social and economic "costs" of addiction to American society. I have tried to demonstrate that these very costs can be interpreted as benefits to agencies and their personnel.

A recent federal report put the "annual costs" of heroin addiction to the American people at $10 *billion*—a figure fourteen times the federal government expenditure in 1975 to combat air and water pollution, nearly eight times the federal health research budget, and almost four times the 1975 federal investment in elementary and secondary education. This $10 billion estimate does not include welfare, insurance and other public health costs related to illegal heroin abuse, nor the indirect costs heroin addiction supposedly inflicts on families and communities. The federal report cited the following costs:

1. $6.9 billion in property loss resulting from "drug-related crimes"
2. $1.5 billion in lost productivity costs (absenteeism, unemployment, loss of earnings)
3. $1.1 billion in direct program costs (federal, state, local and private treatment, rehabilitation and prevention, including drug traffic prevention)
4. $620 million for criminal justice system costs (police salaries, court and correctional system costs) in cases directly involving drug offenses
5. $200 million in health costs (hospital emergencies, inpatient and mental health hospital care for drug-related cases)[34]

Such huge estimates should be subjected to closer empirical scrutiny, since they suffer from major methodological problems.

UNANALYZED BENEFITS OF HEROINISM

The economic *benefits* of heroin abuse, such as those outlined above regarding profit makers in the drug abuse industrial complex, must be subtracted from cost-estimate studies. Admittedly, the purpose of such investigations usually is to measure costs. Intelligent public discourse and policy formulation must be based on some sort of cost-benefit analysis, however crude. But when one considers the impressive cost statistics, it is interesting to speculate on the adverse economic effects if heroin abuse were eliminated. Not only drug law enforcement and treatment organizations benefit economically from heroin abuse. Underworld beneficiaries also exist, including opium growers, laboratories converting morphine base to heroin, smugglers, distributors and street-level bagmen.

Illicit heroin use provides a kind of "shadow welfare system" in big American cities. Traffic in goods stolen by addicts represents a broad avenue through which merchandise flows down from the more affluent society into the indigent strata. The fence is the middleman, paying 10 to 20 percent on stolen goods. This secret domestic Marshall Plan is perhaps one of the more successful and less well-advertised anti-poverty, pro-business programs in the nation.

The nonaddicted disadvantaged population benefits because valuable and desirable stolen goods are available at vastly reduced prices: stereos, tape decks, kitchen appliances, color television sets, new clothes, auto parts, and so on. Even those who have property stolen by addicts from their homes, apartments and businesses sometimes benefit by lodging inflated claims against insurance companies who, in turn, benefit by raising the cost of premiums to cover their losses. Anti-theft insurance is booming.

The government benefits indirectly by the fact that the poor can acquire merchandise such as clothing and other household items which otherwise would have to be supplied through public assistance at taxpayers' expense. Benefits to manufacturing abound. Small appliance producers and their employees should realize, for example, that for every MixMaster "ripped off" by an addict, a replacement is usually purchased at retail price. Burglar alarm manufacturers and installers have never been so busy, and parallel private police systems have sprung up to guard against residential than public police in America. Large department stores and supermarkets, who budget for "shrinkage" due to shoplifting by addicts, manage to sidestep disaster by passing their losses along to customers who, in turn, demand raises at work to help defray the higher cost of living. One begins to see that heroin abuse plays a part in the inflationary spiral. Secondhand stores, pawnbrokers, swap meets and flea markets would undoubtedly feel the pinch if their supplies of goods stolen by addicts were suddenly reduced. The list and ramifications go on. The point is, these "benefits" are not addressed in heroin addiction "cost-estimate" studies.

For the present, the government should do the public a service by quietly interring the $10 billion heroin "cost" figure and honestly recognize the economic *benefits* heroinism produces for upper- and underworld people and organizations.

UNDERWORLD BENEFICIARIES OF HEROIN CRIMINALIZATION

The upper-world interests discussed above are just one element of the drug abuse industrial complex. Heroin directly provides a profit-making system with an expansive infrastructure of growers, couriers, distributors, salesmen, customers, cutmen, bagmen, bag followers, fences and informants. Dealing heroin is an important means of social mobility for individuals who, because of ethnic/racial background and lower-class position, are blocked from advancement in the more respectable "channels." This subeconomy in dope probably plays a role in thwarting potential and real dissent among the poor over the existing allocation of legal jobs and opportunities which the dominant society holds:

> Politics and the rackets have furnished an important means of social mobility for individuals who, because of ethnic background and low class position, are blocked from advancement in the "respectable" channels.[35]

Merton also felt that the culturally induced success goal exerts pressure on the disadvantaged to engage in criminal behavior as the only available means of getting ahead.

Economist Paul Bullock has argued that one critical reason for the existence of heroin subeconomies is that it has been profitable to important sectors of the regular economy:

> Society has deemed the preservation of the subeconomy [in heroin] preferable to the establishment of family income guarantees at a level above the poverty line, or the reform of existing employment structures to accommodate the needs of those excluded.[36]

In other words, the existence of the subeconomy in junk helps thwart dissent among the urban poor over the existing allocation of legal jobs and opportunities which the dominant society controls. Hustling dope:

> . . . contributes to the quasi-stable social existence in slum areas capable of exploding from the tremendous economic and social tension generated by poverty, uncertainty, hunger, disease, and insecurity. . . . Instead of sporadic or permanent explosions, crime, narcotics selling and gambling operate as social depressants built into the life of the ghetto.[37]

So much of the so-called "heroin problem" is the consequence of class and culture conflict over the distribution of opportunities in society and over approved forms of recreation and entertainment that to eliminate heroinism would require almost unimaginable social reform. In many ways the heroin subeconomy in America helps perserve the status quo.

NOTES

1. On the manifest and latent functions of public policy and organizations, see Robert K. Merton, *Social Theory and Social Structure*, 3rd ed. (New York: Free Press, 1957), p. 199.
2. Dwight D. Eisenhower, *Public Papers of the Presidents of the United States, Dwight D. Eisenhower, 1960-1961* (Washington, D.C.: U.S. Government Printing Office, 1961), p. 1037.
3. On the social service "pork barrel," see Walter Shapiro, "The Two Party Pork Barrel," *The Washington Monthly*, April 1975, pp. 24-30; and David A. Stockman, "The Social Pork Barrel," *The Public Interest* 15 (Spring 1975): 3-30.
4. Shapiro, "Two Party Pork Barrel," p. 25.
5. Michael R. Sonnenreich, "Discussion of the Final Report of the National Commission on Marijuana and Drug Abuse," *Villanova Law Review* 18 (May 1973): 818.
6. Commission to Investigate Allegations of Police Corruption and the City's Anti-Corruption Procedures, (Knapp Commission), *Report*, in *Police Corruption: A Sociological Perspective*, ed. Lawrence W. Sherman (New York: Anchor Books, 1974), pp. 30-31.

7. Ambrose quoted in "Ambrose Critical of Local Efforts," *Los Angeles Times* (March 30, 1972), Pt. II, p. 1.

8. Mitchell quoted in "Attorney General Sees Problem in Drug Law Enforcement," *Los Angeles Times*, (January 29, 1972), Pt. I, p. 7.

9. See "Bell Wants Panel to Pick FBI Chief; Plans Drug Agency End," *Long Beach Independent Press-Telegram*, (February 11, 1977), p. A-16.

10. This view of DEA is suggested by a respected economist, Thomas C. Schelling, "Economics and Criminal Enterprise," *The Public Interest* 7 (Spring 1967): 61-78.

11. Commission to Investigate Allegations of Police Corruption and the City's Anti–Corruption Procedures, (Knapp Commission), *Report*, in *Police Corruption*, ed. Sherman, p. 135.

12. Among the relevant cases here are *Angello* v. *United States* (1925); *Johnson* v. *United States* (1948); *Rochin* v. *California* (1952); *Jones* v. *United States* (1960); *Wong Sun* v. *United States* (1963); *Kerr* v. *California* (1963); and *Delaware* v. *Prouse* (1979).

13. See *Olmstead* v. *United States* (1928) (prohibition); and *Lee* v. *United States* (1952) (narcotics).

14. Thomas S. Szasz, *Ceremonial Chemistry: The Ritual Persecution of Drugs, Addicts, and Pushers* (New York: Doubleday, 1974), pp. 56, 108.

15. Harmon L. Zeigler and G. Wayne Peak, *Interest Groups in American Society* 2nd ed. (Englewood Cliffs, N.J.: Prentice-Hall, 1972), p. 164.

16. Philip Selznick, *TVA and the Grass Roots* (Berkeley, Calif.: University of California Press, 1949).

17. On the cooptation of minorities and the poor into social service bureaucracies, see Dale Rogers Marshall, *The Politics of Participation in Poverty: A Case Study of the Economic and Youth Opportunities Agency of Greater Los Angeles* (Berkeley, Calif.: University of California Press, 1971); and Paul B. Fischer, "The 'War on Poverty' and the 'Blackening' of Urban Bureaucracies," *Policies Studies Journal* 2 (March 1974): 179-86.

18. Peter Goldberg, "The Uses and Abuses of Urinalysis," in *Developments in the Field of Drug Abuse: Proceedings of the National Drug Abuse Conference—1974*, ed. Edward C. Senay, Vernon Shorty, and Harold Alksne (Cambridge, Mass.: Schenkman Publishing Co., 1974), p. 932.

19. Paul M. Blachly, Letter to the Editor, *Journal of the American Medical Association* 238 (July 4, 1977): 27.

20. David C. Lewis et al., "The Ethics of 'Ethical' Drug Promotion," in *Developments in the Field of Drug Abuse*, ed. Senay, Shorty, and Alksne, p. 968.

21. *Medical World News* (May 31, 1976), p. 9.

22. Ibid., p. 10.

23. On drugging in schools, see Edgard Z. Friedenberg, "Schools Out," *New York Review of Books* (November 23, 1975), pp. 30-35; and Peter Schrag and Diane Divoky, *The Myth of the Hyperactive Child and Other Means of Child Control* (New York: Pantheon Books, 1975).

24. John Pekkanen, *The American Connection* (New York: Follet Books, 1973), chapters 1-5.

25. Reported in: "Federal Agency Lists Most Widely Abused Drugs," *Journal of the American Medical Association* 236 (August 2, 1976): 432.

26. For example, *The Western Journal of Medicine*, which generally contains very little advertising, devotes its full back cover to Valium in *The Western Journal of Medicine* 133 (December 5, 1980).

27. Pekkanen, *The American Connection*, chapter 1.

28. Albert W. Biderman and Laure M. Sharp, *The Competitive Evaluation Research Industry* (Washington, D.C.: Bureau of Social Research, 1972).

29. Amitai Etzioni and P. Doty, "Profit in Not-for-Profit Corporations: The Example of Health Care," *Political Science Quarterly* 91 (Fall 1976): 433-40.

30. "State Names Doctors on Medi-Cal $100,000 List," *Los Angeles Times*(November 1, 1975), Pt. I, p. 20.

31. "Bronx Drug Program Under Investigation," *New York Times* (March 29, 1977), p. 1.

32. "HEW Investigation," *Science* 193 (June 1978): 200.

33. H. Kurtz, "The Drug Abuse Hustle," *The New Republic* (April 15, 1978), p. 10.

34. "Heroin Use in U.S. on Increase Again," *Los Angeles Times* (December 13, 1974), Pt. I, p. 1.

35. William F. Whyte, "Social Organization in the Slums," *American Sociological Review* 8 (February 1943): 8, 34-39.

36. Paul Bullock, "Youth in the Labor Market: Employment Patterns and Career Aspirations in Watts and East Los Angeles" (Los Angeles: Institute of Industrial Relations, University of California, Los Angeles, mimeographed), p. 241.

37. Stanley Friedlander and Robert Shick, *Unemployment in the Urban Core: An Analysis of Thirty Cities with Policy Recommendations* (New York: Praeger Publishers, 1971), pp. 188-89.

10

Conclusions and Future Prospects

The facts presented here support several tentative conclusions: (1) the federal government's treatment response to heroin addiction is political and shaped by questionable scientific evidence; (2) rehabilitation of addicts has not generally worked; and (3) the criminalization of heroin since 1914 has led to a powerful upper- and underworld interest group structure that resists alteration of basic prohibition policy.

Neither repression nor rehabilitation have constituted an effective response to heroin addiction in America. Governments at all levels have poured money and resources into drug law enforcement, treatment services, and prevention/education programs. Hundreds of thousands of people have been arrested on heroin charges. Hundreds of thousands more have entered addiction treatment programs, voluntarily or against their will through court-ordered diversion. What are the results?

Law enforcement efforts to control heroin abuse by interrupting supply lines of the drug have not provided a solution to heroin addiction. This nation has just emerged from a ten-year "war on heroin" by the criminal justice system. We have little or nothing to show for these efforts except a gargantuan law enforcement structure that is now dependent on the inexorable generation of more and more illicit addicts. The tail is wagging the dog. Unabated availability of heroin, in spite of massive worldwide, national and subnational efforts to suppress its production and distribution signals a failure of law enforcement efforts, but more, of the underlying prohibition policy that perpetuates these attempts.

How many heroin addicts have been cured by addiction treatment programs? The evidence indicates that once a person becomes a bona fide heroin addict, it is often for life. No treatment of *any* kind results in sustained narcotic abstinence in more than 10 to 30 percent of cases. The major addiction treatment strategies—methadone maintenance, simple detoxification, aftercare counseling and residential therapy—have been highly visible programmatic assaults on a national problem, but have failed to reduce substantially demand for heroin or other drugs.

There are few old heroin addicts. Three choices are generally available to the habitue: clean up, die, or go to prison. For those who do manage to get out of the heroin culture, factors like love, opportunity and brains account more for abstinence than the interventions of treatment programs.

The United States still has more heroin addicts than any other nation, and the drug abuse problem goes way beyond heroin. We arrest more juveniles on marijuana charges than does the rest of the world. Americans drink more alcohol, smoke more cigarettes and pop more pills than anybody else. We have identified the drug abuser in our society, and he seems to be nearly everybody. As Pogo remarked: "We have met the enemy and he is us."

Perhaps it is time to concede that we are a nation of confirmed mood-molders and will remain so for the foreseeable future. Drug abuse cannot be stamped out by legislative fiat. The supply of illegal drugs cannot be interrupted by the most massive law enforcement efforts, and treatment and rehabilitation programs have not made the slightest dent in drug abuse. Setting unrealistic goals invites failure.

THE LEGISLATION OF BEHAVIOR

Can we really legislate behavior? Or could it be that people's craving for an altered state of consciousness is uncontrollable by means of public policymaking and therapy? Some anthropologists suggest that people have an inherent and primitive drive to "get loaded"—to alter their normal consciousness for recreational, religious or medical purposes.[1] Are we driven by an innate, inborn desire to get out of our heads?

When I was eight years old a fad among children on my block was "going out"—you hyperventilate twenty times, blow as hard as you can on your thumb, then pass out (acapnia to doctors). A group of fairly "healthy" middle-class kids, naive to drug use of any kind, thought this was great fun. We had simply discovered a nonchemical way of getting "stoned." Or why, for example, do children like merry-go-rounds so much? Ask a child stumbling off one and he is apt to reply, "It's fun, it makes me dizzy, tee-hee-hee." What is it that drives us at age three to "bend our heads" like this?

If there is any truth to the axiom that people are drug-taking animals, we should not expect demand for chemicals or devices that alter consciousness to diminish in the future. On the contrary, a large segment of the population will continue to seek release from ordinary reality through drugs or other mind-altering techniques. The heroin addiction problem and other kings of substance abuse therefore will remain insoluble through crisis policy, subject to incremental approximate solutions at best, mainly in rhetoric emanating from trusted sources—government and scientists. It is in light of these considerations and conclusions that the following scenario unfolds.

LOOKING BACKWARD FROM 2080: DECLINE OF HEROIN AND THE RISE OF NEW HIGHS

Looking backward from the year 2080, the record will show that in the long run, addiction treatment and drug law enforcement did not have a very profound impact on the heroin problem. But other, more powerful factors led to its amelioration.

Heroin never was decriminalized, so addicts could not legally acquire doses sufficient for their needs. By 1980, even England, considered liberal in its heroin maintenance policy of the 1960s, had gone largely to oral maintenance of addicts with 1-alpha-acetylmethadol, better known as "LAAM," a drug that is similar to methadone but gives the user a three-day "high." Because of the powerful upper- and underworld interests allied against heroin decriminalization, it simply never came about, though liberals continued to press for it well into the 1980s.

Heroin addiction, however, began to "peter out" after 1990. A major reason was that the birthrate leveled off, which was completely unrelated to addiction treatment or police efforts to suppress heroin. Better contraception, the impact of "family planning" and medical advances to keep old persons alive longer led to an older society by the turn of the century. Intravenous heroin use is confined mainly to younger persons. The "at-risk" population of potential heroin users dwindled as persons between the ages of fourteen and twenty-one became an ever-shrinking percentage of the population. In 1978 persons aged sixty-five and over constituted 10.5 percent of the nation's population—up from 9.2 percent in 1960. The "graying of America" continued, and by the year 2035 more than 20 percent of the population were aged sixty-five and over. Increasing rates of substance abuse among the elderly continued to be an issue into the early twenty-first century, but heroin was not the preferred drug.

Under these demographic changes, the incidence and prevalence of heroin addiction started a gradual decline in 1985 and continued to drop until 1990, when a slight up-turn in addiction was noted. The short-lived, minor resurgence of heroin use was due largely to the fact that the second generation from the post-World War II baby boom began to enter the fourteen-to-twenty-one "at-risk" age range around 1990.

As the population became steadily older, the abuse of alcohol also decreased. Youth are much heavier drinkers than middle-aged and elderly persons, and as the percentage of young persons declined, so did drinking.

Because of an older population, and parallel to the leveling off and decline in heroin addiction, street crimes and the nation's prison population also began to decrease. As people got older, the crime rates and prison populations fell. Some prisons, hastily built to house criminals during the "panic" years before 1980, found themselves underpopulated. Young people are statistically much more likely to commit serious crimes than middle-aged or elderly people. By A.D. 2080 problems of the aging and the aged dominated public discussion and domestic policy concern. The "youth culture"—the milieu of impious, hubristic youth with all their emergent crises—faded into the mists of yesterday.

It was not simply an older society that led to the ultimate disappearance of heroin into a prolonged limbo, a twilight realm of lesser concern or spasmodic recurrences of interest. Heroin addiction also receded because (1) peer pressures exerted a decline in use, (2) credible "hip" drug abuse experts were present, (3) the system producing and distributing heroin collapsed, (4) nonaddictive depressant drugs 5,000 times as potent as heroin became available, and (5) electronic remote control brain stimulation devices finally supplanted mind-altering chemicals altogether.

Peer pressure is a factor disposing young people toward or away from heroin use.[2] These pressures seemed more amenable to experimentation with a variety of chemical substances between 1960 and 1980—war years, times of increasing scarcity, a period marked by insecurity over domestic and international politics and economics. By 1985, however, heroin use was "uncool" among most youth. They increasingly viewed it as unhealthy, counterrevolutionary, anti-erotic, too expensive, or destructive of one's self-image. As these newer predisposing attitudes and values developed, heroin use declined. Other, more esoteric drugs and devices, however, would ultimately supplant heroin use among the at-risk age group. These other mind-altering methods would eventually create as many social dropouts as heroin had a century before.

The heroin abuse problem began to ebb with the advent of young, well-trained, credible experts in substance abuse who shared common characteristics with the at-risk age group. These informed experts established the reputation among potential heroin users as "hip people telling it straight" about the effects of heroin use under prohibitionist policy—adulterated dope, high prices, crime necessary to support the habit and, finally, police bullets, prison or death. These effects of illicit narcotic use were accepted by young people, who are the most susceptible to heroinism.

Another factor contributing to the ultimate decline of heroin addiction was the collapse of the heroin market under the pressure of rapid expansion, greedy profit taking and the development of new, more exotic psychoactive drugs and devices. The heroin production and distribution system expanded rapidly during the halcyon days of the 1960s, 1970s, and early 1980s. Many people in many parts of the world were attracted into the heroin trade as production and distribution personnel. So many production and distribution strata eventually developed—each stratum greedily diluting the product and raising its price as high as possible—that by 1990 the whole market degenerated and collapsed. The goose that laid the golden egg was gone. By the twenty-first century, laboratory analyses of street heroin revealed it to be a low quality, expensive substance, less than .05 percent pure. These factors played a part in decreasing the use of heroin by the most susceptible group.

Since the latter half of the twentieth century medicine had sought a nonaddictive drug with the pain-relieving powers of heroin. By 1990 psychopharmacological breakthroughs with the endogenous substances enkephalin and the endorphins led to development of a number of nonaddictive, powerful pain relievers. These substances had few toxic side effects, were orally effective, and weight for weight were 5,000 times more potent than heroin. No longer was addiction a concern of doctors treating patients in pain. Analgesia could be induced without risking addiction. But, as often happens with discoveries of this kind, by the year 1995 these drugs were diverted to illicit use. In 1997 clandestine laboratories in Los Angeles and Houston manufacturing these analgesics were raided.

Sometimes the use of a specific drug can increase dramatically because it becomes fashionable, like a musical group or a clothing style. Thus alcohol and nicotine were "in" during the 1920s and 1930s. Marijuana use accelerated in the 1940s and 1950s. LSD was popular in the early 1960s. Amphetamines were popular by the late 1960s. Heroin became the drug of choice for many in the mid-to-late 1960s and the early 1970s. The culture of the street, of musical styles, of weekend parties, and places for youth gatherings reinforce these chemical fashions; people do not want to have an inappropriate "high" at the wrong time in the wrong place. By 1990, heroin continued to be supplanted by other trendy drugs. There was a noticeable outbreak in 1995 of nonaddictive analgesic abuse. Users enjoyed all the pleasure heroin affords, but without risk of addiction.

Chemicals are crude substances with which to pollute the human body, as anyone who has had a hangover will attest. As America moved into the twenty-first century, the nation journeyed beyond drugs entirely into the era of electronic brain stimulation. In the 1950s and 1960s José Delgado, a Spanish physiological psychologist in the tradition of William Penfield, pioneered brain implants in animals.[3] These devices emitted small electrical charges identical with the effects of various drugs, either stimulants or depressants. By the year 2025 a few "Relaxa-Chairs" were already available to the public. These models were equipped with electrodes which attached to the scalp. One arm of the chair had a set of three buttons—green for "go fast," stimulant-type effects, yellow for "simple relaxation," and red for inducing somnolent effects similar to those produced by heroin a century before. By 2075 the bulkier chair models were replaced with compact wrist units about the size of a watch, with the three buttons. In that year Congress held hearings on whether or not to outlaw these devices, making them available only in government-licensed "recreation parlors." State health and police officials began conducting door-busting raids to seize the devices. In California a wayward band of "electricity fiends" was arrested in 2077 and charged with illegal possession of the electrical wrist units and Ray-O-Vac dry cell battery packs.

The president was moved to declare an all-out war on electronic brain stimulation, and she vowed to enlist the full resources of the nation to combat these insidious devices. Historians and public policy experts were divided on the prognosis of success for this new, most massive effort in history to alter human behavior and turn people away from "juice."

NOTES

1. For a fascinating account of the ancient drug cult in Iraq around 10,000 years ago, see John M. Allegro, *The Sacred Mushroom and the Cross* (Garden City, N.Y.: Doubleday and Co., 1970). Professor Allegro was removed from the British commission studying the Dead Sea Scrolls for implying that Jesus Christ was a mushroom freak and leader of a fanatic, rebellious, drug-using cult of *amanita muscaria* (fly agyric) eaters who ultimately became "Christians." Also, on people's inborn drive to alter their normal state of consciousness, see Andrew Weil, *The Natural Mind: A New Way of Looking at Drugs and the Higher Consciousness* (New York: Houghton Mifflin Co., 1972).

2. See Isadore Chein et al., *The Road to H: Narcotics, Delinquency, and Social Policy* (New York: Basic Books, 1964); and Barry S. Brown, Mark H. Greene and N. J. Turner, "The Spread of Addiction—The Role of the 'Average Addict,'" *American Journal of Drug and Alcohol Abuse* 3 (October 1976): 521-28.

3. José M. Delgado, *Physical Control of the Mind: Toward a Psychocivilized Society* (New York: Harper & Row, 1969). Also, on the mind-altering possibilities of electronic brain stimulation, see Yoshio Hosobuchi, John E. Adams and Rita Linchitz, "Pain Relief by Electrical Stimulation of the Central Gray Matter in Humans and Its Reversal by Naloxone," *Science* 197 (July 8, 1977): 183-186; and Elliot S. Valenstein, "Science-Fiction Fantasy and the Brain," *Psychology Today*, July 1978, pp. 29-39.

Bibliographic Essay

REVIEW OF POLICYMAKING AND POLICY IMPACT LITERATURE

A thoroughgoing review of the literature on heroinism reveals barely one or two investigations by political scientists of government-supported addiction control programs. Studies by sociologists, economists, criminologists, medical researchers and others abound, but many unexplored issues of heroin policy remain to be categorized and investigated according to current approaches in political science. In fact, political science has neglected heroin addiction and drug abuse in general.

PUBLIC POLICY APPROACHES TO ADDICTION TREATMENT STRATEGIES

In recent years public policy (roughly, whatever governments choose to do or not to do, and what difference it makes) has been treated analytically both as a *dependent* variable and, less often, as an *independent* variable. Two broad schools of policy research have distinguished themselves primarily on the basis of which strategy is employed: the "policymaking" school and the "policy impact" school.

The Policymaking School and Treatment Policy Formulation

Emmete S. Redford admonished each political scientist in "Reflections on a Discipline," *The American Political Science Review* 55: 761-72 to ". . . grapple with a policy problem." In that vein, many political scientists view public policy as *the* major dependent variable to explain in political life. In their view, the task of professional political science is to find and explain the independent and intervening variables that account for policy differences. A number of researchers have tried to describe policy and explain how it is made at both national and subnational levels. Three aggressive attempts are Richard Dawson and James Robinson, "Inter-Party Competition, Economic Variables, and Welfare Policies in the American States," *Journal of Politics* 25: 266-79; Lewis Froman, Jr., *People and Politics: An Analysis of the American Political System* (Englewood Cliffs, N.J.: Prentice-Hall, 1962); and Richard Hofferbert, *The Study of Public Policy* (Indianapolis, Ind.: Bobbs-Merrill, 1974).

Indeed, most policy research since World War II has sought to explain the *processes* of policy formulation—how public choices are made—rather than policy impacts or outcomes. These "process" studies have sought to understand and explain why governments choose some policies over others. Policymaking is viewed as a process of choosing.

Robert A. Dahl suggests that a policy decision is a set of actions related to and including the choice of one alternative over another. This policymaking approach taken in his article, "The Analysis of Influence in Local Communities," in *Social Science and Community Action*, edited by Charles Adrian (East Lansing, Mich.: Michigan State University Press, 1960), takes the decision and the events surrounding it as the basic and stable unit of analysis fundamental to all political life.

Among the leading proponents of the policymaking school is Harold D. Lasswell. In *The Decision Process: Seven Categories of Functional Analysis* (College Park, Md.: University of Maryland, Bureau of Governmental Research, 1956), he laid a foundation for analyzing the policymaking process. To him, decisionmaking consists of a series of phases, including intelligence, recommending, prescribing, invoking, policy application and finally, policy appraisal. Note that Lasswell's steps in the act of decisionmaking deal mostly with policymaking rather than policy evaluation. He pointed out that most political science publications deal with ". . . the assessment of . . . specific factors that influence the outcome of official acts." (p. 25)

Richard C. Snyder's "A Decision-Making Approach to the Study of Politics," in *Approaches to the Study of Politics*, edited by Roland Young (Evanston, Ill.: Northwestern University Press, 1958), like Lasswell, posits the *process* by which government decisions are made. Snyder broadly classifies this process as one involving a sequence of: (1) predecisional activities, (2) choice, and (3) implementation. Similarly, Austin Ranney's book *Political Science and Public Policy* (Chicago: Markham Publishing

Company, 1968) focuses on policy as the dependent variable to be explained by political science. Ranney's definition of the policymaking process in *Political Science and Public Policy* does not speak to the question of policy impact; it ends with ". . . an implementation of intent." (p. 7)

Continuing with the policymaking approach, Charles O. Jones's book, *An Introduction to the Study of Public Policy* (Belmont, Calif.: Wadsworth Publishing Company, 1970) takes the processes of public policymaking as the independent variables and policy itself as the dependent variable to be explained. Although Thomas Dye urges ". . . an evaluation of the impact of public policy on society . . ." in his work *Understanding Public Policy*, 3rd ed. (Englewood Cliffs, N.J.: Prentice-Hall, 1978) he, too, concentrates primarily on the analytic schemata used to make sense of the policymaking process.

Richard Hofferbert's *The Study of Public Policy* (Indianapolis, Ind.: Bobbs-Merrill, 1974) is another invitation to a full-course banquet of public policy contents and impacts where only stale process appetizers are served. Hofferbert writes, "To focus upon policy as the subject of study is to focus on the product side of the political equation." (p. 7) He says, ". . . we are primarily interested in what comes out of the process." (p. 7) It turns out that his real interest is in what comes out (policy) as effect, not cause.

The title of James E. Anderson's book accurately reflects its content: *Public Policy-Making* (New York: Praeger Publishers, 1975). This is another book about policymaking, not a book about the study of policy impacts or policy evaluation. Like Dye, Anderson is aware of the opportunity to analyze public policy as cause of changes in the environment. He acknowledges that ". . . systematic evaluation of policy . . . has clearly become a more widespread and potentially significant part of the policy process." (p. 153) However, Anderson is all but mesmerized by the ". . . number of barriers or obstacles that may create problems for the evaluation of policy." (p. 138) These barriers persuade him that "It is, of course, often impossible to measure quantitatively the impact of public policies, especially social policies, with any real precision." (p. 138)

Ira Sharkansky's and Donald Van Meter's *Policy and Politics in American Governments* (New York: McGraw-Hill Book Company, 1975) is yet another public policy analysis text with a process "fix." Although the authors adopt the Eastonian systems framework of inputs, conversion, outputs and outcomes (David Easton, "An Approach to the Analysis of

Political Systems," *World Politics* 9: 383-400; and Easton's *A Framework for Political Analysis*, Englewood Cliffs, N.J.: Prentice-Hall, 1965), Sharkansky and Van Meter fail to encourage analysis of policy outputs as independent variables.

Perhaps political scientists, chasing the holy grail of "value-free" research, are simply afraid to analyze public policy as cause for fear of falling into advocacy of one policy over another. The opportunity to investigate public policy as an independent variable is outweighed by the risk they perceive in "espousal," however informed. Continued preoccupation with the policymaking process is the resultant "fallback" position in most of the policy analysis literature.

Unfortunately many policy researchers are ivory-tower residents and lack the real-world experience necessary to tell when government policies and programs are achieving their overt goals, much less their covert ones. How many political scientists, for example, are black and in a position to analyze government-sponsored programs to aid blacks from the vantage point of a consumer? Or how many are ex-convicts who go on to analyze correctional programs and policies? How many were street heroin addicts who subsequently research policy and progams in this arena? Given, we cannot experience everything, but most policy researchers do not have the "Ph.D. in streets" necessary to acquire a more accurate view from the bottom.

POLICYMAKING APPROACH OF THIS BOOK

In accordance with current academic conventions, Part I of this book, "Formulating Heroin Control Policy," focuses on recent addiction control policy formulation at the federal level, emphasizing the interplay among key congressional and executive figures, scientific elites, "opinion leaders," executive branch agencies, and the rapid spread of heroin in the 1960s. This approach takes addiction treatment policy as the *dependent* variable. The goal is to locate systematically the generalizable and predictable factors that influence the decision-making process in the area of drug law enforcement, heroin addiction treatment and the rehabilitation of addicts. The question is: How do policymakers decide when they choose alternative addiction control strategies? Do they rely on professional and technological advice more than political and ideological suasion? Further, if they do utilize recommendations of scientists, what is the quality of scientific research in the area of addiction treatment program efficacy?

The Policy Impact School and Treatment Program Evaluation

Does political science stand to gain from the study of public policy as cause of changes in the environment? Focusing solely on the policymaking process is undeniably important; the decisional process itself directly impacts program results. Nevertheless, this narrow focus on policy as the dependent variable neglects the wider interests and forces that might exercise a crucial, more lasting influence. The emphasis on input factors closely related to the official making of decisions often leads scholars to underplay or ignore completely policy impact. Analysis of the actual effects of policies and of their repercussions on future policy options is too often left to news media pundits.

As scholars, political scientists should therefore concern themselves more with the quality of information that supports policy decisions. In planning for policy it is better to argue from reliable data than from mere conjecture. Planning would want to take into account the likely outcomes of policy decisions—What has actually happened out there in the real world when certain programs have been implemented? Were the desired results achieved? If not, why?

Politics, most certainly, does not end with the enunciation and implementation of official policies and programs (Easton's conversion and outputs). Policies have impacts, sometimes intended, sometimes unintended; they hit real people in the real world. Therefore, Part II of this book, "Heroin Addiction Treatment and Its Outcome," examines the impact of addiction treatment policies and programs. How much difference is there between the goals of addiction treatment policy and its actual impact on heroin addicts and other features of the environment, such as crime reduction?

Robert Lineberry and Ira Sharkansky in *Urban Politics and Public Policy* (New York: Harper and Row, 1971) recognize the importance of impact evaluation: "There may be no question for the policy-makers that is more important than policy impact" Professor Easton's *A Framework for Political Analysis* draws a distinction between "outputs" (roughly, what governments do) and the "outcomes" of these outputs (roughly, what consequences follow from the outputs—pp. 351–52). Sharkansky's *Policy Analysis in Political Science* (Chicago: Markham Publishing Company, 1970) also distinguishes between public policy, policy outputs and policy impacts (p. 63).

Thus, as Lineberry and Sharkansky note in *Urban Politics and Public Policy*, any public policy can be analyzed as an *independent* variable in terms of its impact on the community and on subcommunity units (pp. 10-11). The policy impact school studies the *effects* that government actions have upon the populations they are designed to impact. Some of these effects are encompassed by the terms "outputs," "outcomes," "spillover effects," "impacts" or "feedbacks" of policy.

Feedback from evaluative research on policy and programs is relatively new, but gaining in importance. See, for example, Donald Campbell, "Reforms as Experiments," *The American Psychologist* 24: 409-29; Carol Weiss, *Evaluation Research: Methods of Assessing Program Effectiveness* (Englewood Cliffs, N.J.: Prentice-Hall, 1972); Donald Campbell, "The Social Scientist as Methodological Servant of the Experimenting Society," *Policy Studies Journal* 2: 72-78; Daniel Glaser, *Routinizing Evaluation: Getting Feedback on Effectiveness of Crime and Delinquency Programs* (Rockville, Md.: National Institute of Mental Health, Center for Studies of Crime and Delinquency, U.S. Department of HEW, U.S. Government Printing Office, 1973); and Carol Weiss, "Policy Research in the University: Practical Aid or Academic Exercise?" *Policy Studies Journal* 4: 224-28.

Suffice it to say that more and more government decisionmakers at all levels are coming to depend on evaluative research reports when choosing among competing courses of action to combat social ills. The United States Congress, for example, is currently being guided in heroin control policymaking by a General Accounting Office evaluation report entitled "Action Needed to Improve Management and Effectiveness of Drug Abuse Treatment" (Washington, D.C.: Comptroller General of the United States, U.S. Government Printing Office, April 1980).

Until policy impacts are studied with the same zeal and skill that policy processes have attracted, political science may contribute little to the evaluation of exisitng policies or the consideration of possible alternatives. In this newer tradition of policy impact analysis, Part II of this book investigates the impacts of various narcotic addiction treatment modalities implemented under federal funding. This research is necessary to ascertain whether or not heroin addiction treatment policies and programs have achieved their desired goals or have been responsible for trends that make the realization of formal goals possible.

Based on such evaluation, policymakers might decide to discontinue treatment policies and programs that have had little impact. The purpose of the evaluative research undertaken in Part II is to measure the comparative effects of addiction treatment policies and programs against the goals they set out to accomplish as a means of contributing to subsequent decisionmaking about the programs and improving future programming. Presumably, the most prominent objective of any heroin addiction treatment program is somehow to change its clients so as to eliminate the reason they came to the agency in the first place. Whether such changes are achieved is the question addressed in Part II: Are addiction treatment programs helping addicts become abstinent? Turning to the extant literature, this question becomes very difficult to answer.

POORLY CONCEIVED RESEARCH

The overall quality of scientific research on addiction treatment impact is poor. Serious methodological mistakes beset most studies, making it difficult to obtain objective and reliable data on the relationship of treatment to outcome. Most studies are not clear, but obscure and vague. They abound with unsystematic, unverified and unspecified judgments on program efficacy. On close review this literature reveals many impact investigations that are narcissistic; they are palpably self-serving measures of policy/program "success" intended to defuse criticism and harness government funding. Even the most respected researchers in this field fail to address the weaknesses of their research designs. A good example is Avram Goldstein, Ralph Hansteen and William Horns, "Control of Methadone Dosage by Patients," *Journal of the American Medical Association* 234: 734, who rigged their research design to try and prove that methadone maintenance clients actually prefer lower dosages to higher ones.

SPECIFIC PROBLEMS IN THE RESEARCH

The difficulties in devising controlled evaluations on addict populations are easy to imagine. Street "hypes" are highly mobile, sometimes deceptive, nonconforming and often an uncooperative group upon whom to conduct research. Nobody even knows how many addicts there are. L. G. Richards and E. E. Carroll, in "Illicit Drug Use and Addiction in the United States," *Public Health Reports* 85: 1035-41, estimated 65,000 American heroin addicts in 1965. David E. Smith and David J. Bentel, in *Drug Abuse Information Project: Fourth Annual Report to the Legislature* (Sacramento,

Calif.: Drug Abuse Information Project, 1970) estimated 500,000 heroin addicts by 1970 (p. 5). The estimate of heroin addicts apparently dropped to 450,000 in 1978, according to the General Accounting Office's "Action Needed to Improve Management and Effectiveness of Drug Abuse Treatment" (Washington, D.C.: Comptroller General of the United States, U.S. Government Printing Office, April 1980, p. 2). This same report estimated there were 550,000 addicts only two years later in 1980. Given the difficulties of even counting addicts, the best the literature can offer as to incidence and prevalence are informed "guestimates."

Beyond the difficulty in counting addicts, treatment programs themselves discourage good research. Given the nature of treatment populations, programs have their biggest job in handling the mechanics of client intake, treatment and retention; few programs are geared for long-term scientific evaluations, says Stanley Einstein in his "Methadone Treatment: Views of Program Directors," in the *Fifth National Conference on Methadone Maintenance: Proceedings, 1973,* edited by the National Association for the Prevention of Addiction to Narcotics (New York: National Association for the Prevention of Addiction to Narcotics, 1973), pp. 718-22. In a word, program directors could not care less about research. The costs for this type of research are often prohibitive within the usual clinic budget. Further, appropriate staffing and good evaluative research are almost never available within purely clinical treatment teams. One result is that most evaluative research reports on addiction treatment display the following methodological weaknesses.

NONEXPERIMENTAL RESEARCH DESIGNS

Most studies do not construct rigorous experimental research designs to determine treatment program efficacy. A classic example is Carl Chambers and James Inciardi, "Three Years After the Split," in *Developments in the Field of Drug Abuse: Proceedings of the National Drug Abuse Conference—1974,* edited by Edward Senay, Vernon Shorty, and Harold Alksne (Cambridge, Mass.: Schenkman Publishing Company, 1974). Such studies employ nonexperimental or quasi-experimental methodologies with no matched controls or reference groups for comparison. The result is that typical outcome studies conveniently "find" program impact or positive treatment effects without critically attempting to exclude competing research hypotheses.

The possibilities for other explanatory variables in the area of client outcome are so numerous and the number of potentially relevant factors so large that exhaustive explanation of outcome is really impossible. In the end, it may be scientifically impossible to isolate the specific program, client and situational variables that "cause" success or failure during and after program exposure. Maybe the best explanation yet is that some addicts simply "grow up"; they get sick and tired of being sick and tired. See, for example, Charles Winick, "Maturing Out of Narcotic Addiction," *United Nations Bulletin on Narcotics* 14: 1-7; and M. Snow, "Maturing Out of Narcotic Addiction in New York City," *International Journal of the Addictions* 8: 921-38.

This problem is handled in most evaluation studies by confining explanations of client outcome to factors judged by the *investigators* to be most significant, including the impact of treatment itself on client behavior or standard sociodemographic classifications of clients according to sex, age, education and race/ethnic group. Such is the case with hundreds of studies. Typical among them are Thomas Henchy, Byron Erickson and Jesse Paez, "The Relationship Between Age and/or Negative Experiences and Success on a Methadone Maintenance Program," *International Journal of the Addictions* 9: 221-27; Vincent P. Dole and Marie E. Nyswander, "A Medical Treatment for Diacetylmorphine ('Heroin') Addiction," *Journal of the American Medical Association* 193: 646-50; and William Aron and Douglas Daily, "Short- and Long-Term Therapeutic Communities: A Follow-Up and Cost Effectiveness Comparison," *International Journal of the Addictions* 9: 619-36.

While other factors—like love—may be related to treatment outcome, they are often difficult to measure and are therefore frequently omitted from research designs. These factors include developmental history, lifestyle, drug and alcohol abuse history, criminality, work record, family relations, physical health and psychiatric history. Little is offered in most studies on these competing independent variables that influence client behavior. In other words, an extremely complex event like positive or negative treatment outcome is explained by selecting what are considered to be the most significant variables; other causal factors are neglected or ignored.

Most published studies also fail to take into account "system effects." For example, in studies that do employ an experimental research design, do the "treated" groups perform better along selected behavioral criteria because of the enthusiasm of staff and the attention lavished upon them (Hawthorne Effect)? Almost all the work of Vincent P. Dole and Marie E. Nyswander on their methadone maintenance experiments would seem to be open to this criticism. Further, many clients really "shape up" when the "feds" drop around for an on-site program evaluation. Or do some treated groups perform better because staff look the other way when they fail? Have police and other elements of the criminal justice system tended to look the other way if narcotics law violators are enrolled in a treatment program like methadone maintenance? For these possibilities, consider Wayne R. LaFave, *Arrest: The Decision to Take a Suspect into Custody* (Boston: Little, Brown and Company, 1964); James Q. Wilson, *Varieties of Police Behavior: The Management of Law and Order in Eight Communities* (New York: Atheneum, 1971), chapter 4; Donald E. Newman, *Conviction: The Determination of Guilt or Innocence Without Trial* (Boston: Little, Brown and Company, 1966), pp. 60-79; Frank Miller, *Prosecution: The Decision to Charge a Suspect With a Crime* (Boston: Little, Brown and Company, 1969), pp. 11-27; David W. Neubauer, *Criminal Justice in Middle America* (Morristown, N.J.: General Learning Press, 1974), pp. 117-18; and G. Hayim, "Changes in the Behavior of Addicts: A One-Year Follow-Up Study of Methadone Treatment" (mimeographed, 1972).

PROBLEMS IN DATA INTERPRETATION/ANALYSIS

The literature is weak in the area of data interpretation and analysis. It is questionable, for example, whether the data presented in most studies are valid. We know, for instance, that client self-reported follow-up information and urinalysis data are notoriously unreliable. For example, Emile J. Pin, John M. Martin, and John F. Walsh interviewed program dropouts without corroborative performance data in their paper, "A Follow-Up Study of 300 Ex-Clients of a Drug-Free Narcotic Treatment Program in New York City," *American Journal of Drug and Alcohol Abuse* 3: 403-7. So too with George De Leon, Sherry Holland, and Mitchell Rosenthal in "Phoenix House: Criminal Activities of Dropouts," *Journal of the American Medical Association* 222: 636. On the serious pitfalls of the reliability of urinalysis data, see Virginia Lewis et al., "Nalline and Urine Tests in Narcotics Detection: A Critical Overview," *International Journal of the Addictions* 8: 169; and David Sohn, "Analysis for Drugs of Abuse: The Validity of Reported Results in Relation to Performance Testing," *International Journal of the Addictions* 8: 72. Finally, on the general unreliability of client self-reported data, see Thomas J. Cox and Bill Longwell, "Reliability of Interview Data Concerning Current Heroin Use from Heroin Addicts on Methadone," *International Journal of the Addictions* 9: 161-65.

Further, intake or "baseline" information drawn from addicts entering treatment cannot really be trusted. For example, a client's self-reported degree of heroin addiction is often unreliable, with frequent underplaying or exaggerating of its extent and duration. Nor do most investigations adequately explain different types of validity, how they are measured, the reliability of measures as a psychometric property and their methods of computing and interpreting reliability coefficients. The methodologies of most studies, therefore, are obscure.

CONCEPTUAL VARIABLES AND OPERATIONALIZATIONS

Further, conceptual variables are not often clearly linked to operationalizations. For example, measures of "success" and client "failure" in follow-up studies do not all measure the same thing; operational definitions of success and failure differ somewhat from study to study, making it difficult to compare research reports in order to verify conclusions. Frances Gearing, for example, in "Successes and Failures in Methadone Maintenance Treatment of Heroin Addiction in New York City," U.S. Public Health Service Publication #2172 (Washington, D.C.: U.S. Government Printing Office, 1971) looked at alcohol and barbiturate use among discharged methadone maintenance patients but failed to examine heroin use, the reason they entered treatment in the first place. Success criteria in client follow-up studies of residential programs vary. Drug use, alcohol use, criminality, social functioning of some kind and health are areas in which client status on follow-up is consistently examined. Closer scrutiny, however, reveals that while the categories are similar, the definitions of these outcome measures vary wildly. Some studies examine use of licit and illicit drugs, demanding abstinence from both as the criterion of success. Others look only at illicit drug use after discharge. Compare, for example, DeLeon et al., "Phoenix House"; Chambers and Inciardi, "Three Years After the Split"; and Walter Collier and Yasser Hijazi, "A Follow-Up Study of Former Residents of a Therapeutic Community," *International Journal of the Addictions* 9: 805-26. All of this makes outcome studies difficult to verify. A scientific conclusion is verified when it has been checked or tested by other investigators (replication) and when they all arrive at the same conclusion. The curative powers of addiction treatment modalities are difficult to verify in this manner, since their operationalizations differ so widely.

Further, in the impact literature types of outcome data presented vary widely. Actual measures used include drug abuse, illegal activities, employment, program retention, psychophysiological functioning, mortality and morbidity rates, personality and social functioning. Some studies like Dole and Nyswander's "A Medical Treatment for Addiction" use only during-treatment data; others like Collier and Hijazi, "A Follow-Up Study of Former Residents of a Therapeutic Community," rely solely on posttreatment outcome along certain selected variables. Additionally, periods of follow-up vary from study to study, ranging from just a few months to several years. George Vaillant quite correctly recommends follow-up after *five years* in "A 12-Year Follow-Up of New York Narcotic Addicts: III. Some Social and Psychiatric Characteristics," *Archives of General Psychiatry* 15: 599-609. Moreover, a number of studies compare incomparable periods of time; they juxtapose baseline addiction histories of from two to twenty years with data derived from only a few months or a few years of treatment.

RESEARCH POPULATION SELECTION FACTORS

Most studies give improper attention to research population selection factors, such as limiting analysis to clients retained in treatment while excluding all program dropouts from the study group. Collier and Hijazi, in "A Follow-Up Study of Former Residents of a Therapeutic Community," make this mistake. So do Pin et al. in "A Follow-Up Study of 300 Ex-Clients of a Drug-Free Narcotic Treatment Program in New York City"; and Chambers and Inciardi, in "Three Years After the Split." Virtually all of Dole and Nyswander's reported research findings eliminate dropouts from their study groups, thus neatly "cleansing" research samples.

Thus, study data usually are reported *only* for subjects who have remained in treatment for variable periods and not for the entire cohort ever admitted to the program. Since it is usually those very subjects with more severe personal or social problems (including continuing drug and/or severe alcohol abuse, arrest and incarceration) who leave or are kicked out of treatment programs, study samples usually "shrink" and consist increasingly of clients who are able to comply with program rules by refraining from "unacceptable" behavior. Eventually, most study samples reported in the literature consist solely of "successful" clients with the "unsuccessful" ones having been terminated and eliminated from the study group.

This kind of rigged sample selection process works to overestimate the positive effects of most narcotic addiction treatment programs. Generalizations from such reports are totally unreliable and, by the way, are policy plagues. Additionally, there is the problem (technique?) of preferentially loading study populations with older, whiter or socioeconomically better-off clients. Dole and Nyswander did this consistently. Their study samples never did reflect the characteristics of addicts listed in the New York City Narcotics Registry. This slants research results and renders them inapplicable to the total population of heroin addicts who have had treatment.

CAUGHT POPULATIONS OF ADDICTS

Finally, almost every study of heroin addiction is open to all the dangers of generalizing from "caught" populations of addicts in treatment to the whole universe of heroin addicts, including untreated, unarrested ones. The result is that pictures presented in the scientific (and popular) literature of "average addicts" are not necessarily representative of *all* addicts, especially those addicted to physician-prescribed narcotics. Thus, most study groups are confined to analyses of addicts snagged for one reason or another in criminal justice and treatment "nets." Significantly, these addicts are usually socioeconomically disadvantaged. This is why their "wheels fall off" and they either "get busted" or have to enter treatment. Drug experts rarely see heroin and other opiate addicts who are unarrested or untreated like the Hollywood producer's wife, Century City attorney or top-notch musician.

THEORETICAL FRUGALITY

Perhaps most important, there is a theoretical thinness or frugality to most outcome studies. True, in human behavior there are no general empirical laws or universal generalizations. But theories of addiction treatment are usually collections of vague and loosely formulated generalizations and speculative hypotheses dressed up to *look like* theory. As such, these "theories" are not reliable, lack much explanatory power and hold little predictability. In other words, conceptual schemata are pawned off as real theories, useful perhaps as heuristic devices, but of little value in explaining or predicting. The result is that "theories" of addiction and its treatment are identified with everything from typologies, analytical schemata, confirmed experimental hypotheses and speculative hypotheses to the more traditional, normative ethical injunctions like "heroin is bad."

STUDIES OF LITTLE HELP

What, then, is the overall quality of impact research in this field—research on which policy choices must be based? It varies, of course, but most studies have not been well presented. Their purposes, methods, results, and other data are not clear, cogent or easily assimilated. The majority of them are so poorly designed that they are virtually useless in terms of accurately determining the impact of various forms of treatment on client outcome.

DEFINING THE HEROIN PROBLEM

What *is* the exact conceptual realm and logical class of the so-called "heroin problem"? The phrase itself is deceptively simple. What this country actually has is a multiplicity of heroin-related problems and a surfeit of policies and programs—often conflicting and self-defeating—to deal with them. When we talk about the "heroin problem," we are referring to an exceedingly complex and often confusing set of interrelated issues affecting society as a whole and individuals in lonely isolation. The "heroin problem" embraces everything from the personality characteristics and social-political-economic conditions that may underlie heroin dependence to the psychological and physiological effects of opiates themselves on different people. It includes both the economic costs and benefits produced by heroinism. It refers, perhaps most poignantly, to the price paid by addicts under a harsh prohibitionist policy—economic hardship, crime, jail, shattered family relationships, failing health and death.

THE HEROIN ADDICTION SYSTEM

Future research in the whole area of addiction and addiction control would do well to keep in mind the following network of people, activities, organizations and values, which together constitute a kind of "heroin addiction system." Though not a system in any servo-mechanical or biological sense of the term, it does demonstrate some patterned interrelationships and interdependencies. Each element within this heroin addiction system appears to serve the survival, adjustment or maintenance of others: others:

1. The active *heroin addict population* in the U.S.
2. *Heroin suppliers*, including producers and distributors.
3. The history, goals and outcomes of international, national and subnational *narcotic law enforcement* policies, laws, rules, regulations and programs aimed at reducing the supply of heroin through surveillance, arrest, jail, prison, civil commitment, fines, probation, parole and/or court-ordered diversion.
4. The history, goals, and relative outcomes of national and subnational *heroin addiction treatment, rehabilitation and prevention/education* policies, laws, rules, regulations and programs aimed at reforming

heroin addicts through abstinence or chemically supported treatment and at preventing addiction by educating and giving information to nonusers.

5. The attitudes, beliefs, opinions, values, norms, economic interests, research, training and backgrounds which affect the reciprocal relationships between addicts, suppliers, law enforcement and treatment/rehabilitation/prevention organizations and personnel.
6. Reappraisal of ongoing heroin abuse control policies in light of programmatic consequences and recommended changes in narcotic law enforcement and treatment/rehabilitation/prevention policies, laws, rules, regulations and programs.

This whole system helps define and generate propositions regarding the exact conceptual realm and logical class of heroin addiction, government response to it and what difference government efforts make. Although each group throughout the multiple layers of this system sees the causes, consequences and control of addiction somewhat differently, the interrelated, interdependent thread of people, activities, beliefs, laws and organizations intersect at various points. This conceptual schema includes all identifiable structures (values, norms, roles and statuses) functioning to fulfill: (1) the needs of addicts, and (2) those whose formal mission it is to control addiction either through law enforcement or treatment. We would want to know, for example, what would happen to heroin suppliers without addicts. Or, if heroin faded from the scene, what would be the impact on police narcotic details and other elements of the criminal justice system which are geared to focus mainly on heroin? If heroin disappeared tomorrow, what would be the impact on addiction treatment programs and personnel?

Index

ABOUT THE AUTHOR

DAVID J. BELLIS, formerly on the faculties of the University of Southern California and California State University, Long Beach, is a consultant to various drug treatment programs, and is a city councilman in Signal Hill, California.